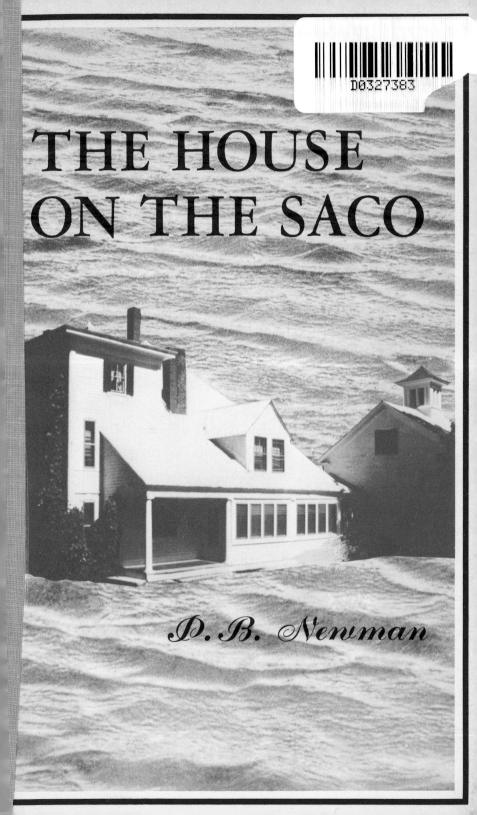

THE HOUSE ON THE SACO

D.B. Newman

The House on the Saco

Books by P. B. Newman

The Cheetah and the Fountain

Dust of the Sun

The Ladder of Love

Paula

The House on the Saco

The
House on the Saco

POEMS BY

P. B. Newman

1977

WILLIAM L. BAUHAN, Publisher

DUBLIN, NEW HAMPSHIRE

Library of Congress Cataloguing in Publication Data
Newman, Paul Baker
The House on the Saco
I. Title.
PS3564.E92H6   811'.5'4   75-11956
ISBN 0-87233-038-9

Some of the poems in this volume first appeared in *Arizona Quarterly, Back Door, Crucible, Eleven Charlotte Poets, Literary Review, New Orleans Review, Red Clay Reader, St. Andrews Review, Shenandoah, South Carolina Review, Southern Poetry Review, Southwest Review, University Review,* and the *Virginia Quarterly Review.*

THIS BOOK WAS SET IN LINOTYPE BASKERVILLE
AND PRINTED BY THE SEAVEY PRINTERS, INCORPORATED
PORTLAND, MAINE, U.S.A.

For

ANNE

Contents

One

One

Georgetown Jetties

I. *South Carolina*

Dark seaweed on the rock,
low swells come cruising in and break.
Something unspeakably fresh and silent
reminds me of the beach at Puerto Rico.
Relaxed in the pleasure of concentration,
the images remembering themselves
the way Maine existed once, in my mind,
clear as its own streams in winter.
Sometimes you see them like that,
trickling beneath the ice, the tails
of delicate green moss, a few bubbles
frozen above the trout that hang there
motionless in the current.

II. *Chicago*

It was sunny and filled with green leaves
in the summertime, and in the spring
we used to walk in Jackson Park
with Miss Louise and the raked gravel
         on the walks was shadowy
as water with the leaves' reflections
restless as the ripples beneath the bridge
where rain had dripped rust and green
against the concrete grit.

III. *A synthesis*

Well, let's say we put the South against that
and then Maine, and hold them there

like crystals in a tube and then dissolve
them in the clear air of thought.
What do we have? The appetite
you feel when clouds come blowing from some peak
white and distant in the dry blue air,
    clear water sweeping green fronds of algae,
a lonely stretch of sound lying motionless and blown
beneath the wind to ever-changing shape.

At Withers' Swash

"On his tour south, President George Washington spent the night of April 27, 1791 near here at the home of Jeremiah Vereen, revolutionary patriot, where he was 'entertained (& very kindly) without being able to make compensation.' The next morning Mr. Vereen piloted the President, en route to Georgetown, across Withers' swash on the strand now called Myrtle Beach." *

You can see the two of them on horseback,
riding leisurely to the swash:
G. Washington and J. Vereen.

Eighteenth century sunlight on the leaves
flickered in the calm hope of discipline
and the tall spear-shaped grass bent back

and sprang beneath their horses' bellies.
The wind blew up the smell of myrtle,
and the strong salt odor of the flats,

earthy and serene, was in their grasp
as what was most essential in themselves
and in each other. Washington

went on to Georgetown on the sandy road
winding past Long Bay, through the yuccas
and the flies stinging, and that eighteenth

century freedom rippled on ahead of him
like the sunlight scintillating on the
stiff but pliant stalks of marsh grass,

or the smell of beach wort in the wind
that tastes of lemon when you bite it,
and he waved farewell to J. Vereen.

*Highway sign on Route 17, South Carolina. Withers' Swash is
now the site of the South's largest roller coaster.

Indian Creek

Everything is wet.
The dry ticks on the undersides of branches
fall as though by accident into our socks,
    some principle of order
like dry rock
in the midst of the trillium
the wet needles
    of the balsams and the pines.
Springs gurgle.
The ruts of the road have cut
through the red earth to the stone
where wheels crush the Bermuda grass
and tear it from the muck.
We climb to the sound of drips.
Our boots squish
to the music of water.
We could believe in Thales,
    were it not for ticks
who incline us toward Heraclitus,
dry among the forget-me-nots
and the violets,
        or even in Zeno
hot as fine blades of sunlight
in the spring goldenrod or barbed
blackberry
with its creamy flowers
sprinkled with the nutmeg of their stamens.
The rhododendrons like blue flames
among the mountain laurel

turn the world into a fight of wet and dry,
ticks, passionate
    water burning in the sunlight into
flame azaleas and white dogwood in the boggy hollows.

Nineteen

The old house with its chimneys and shuttered windows
its cool air and musty crevices
its fanlights and French doors
is translucent as her mind,
where all things are symbols
ordering rituals, rituals, rituals:
it is all so set. Like white paint.
Why don't they ever let it peel?
Like getting up for breakfast. And always
the same glasses for the orange juice.
And always sunlight on the old table
shadowed by the pines at the east window,
the green cones growing at the top, the brown cones
lower down, in June, the window open
and its thin panes a little violet-colored
in their lattices of dry wood. But still
the pines that barely move in the first sea-breeze
are only dusty clouds of silence
that hang above her sometimes, depressing and frightening.
It is in that mood she sees
how everything, the cut-glass bowls,
the wax oranges, the carpets worn by feet long dead,
by ghosts now,
    the chandeliers, the curving
stairs, are really stuffy—incredibly
pompous and self-assured—as though the first spark
of any black arsonist's match
wouldn't send them crackling to kingdom come.

In January

The sand still has the rain-marks. Wind
blowing light and cool from the north hasn't
smoothed them out yet, although it's dried
the surface. My heels scuff through to
the moist sand underneath. I stand and feel
the ocean pouring through the wind
that makes a sound as constant as the beach,
the trees awake and sieving it
through thousands of long needles
the thick soft brooms swaying and yielding
on their brittle stems. I sit down.
The grassblades make quick movements
in the sun that blinds me in the south,
low above the ocean, and dry fuzzy seeds
stick out of the grassblades at the joints
and the pine needles are scattered on the sand.
Sitting here I am sheltered from the wind.
The sun comes down hot against my eyelids
and I feel it and see it too, both black and orange,
as it stings a little against my face
the wind blowing cool behind my ears
and I lie down and look up at the sun
and the white thin clouds and the pine needles
deep green against the blue and only the sound
of the wind in the needles like the sea
over against the real sound coming distant
and hard to tell it from the other
and the wind swinging over in big gusts,
now and then, rushing on out to sea
and I wish that I was out there
using the beam reach and the slow smooth

swells coming in from Spain and Africa
and breaking on the beach—the wind seizing
at their crests and throwing them up like hair
blown back behind heads shaken
and diving downward—using all that
to Murrell's Inlet, then to Pawley's Island,
to Cape Romain, to Georgia and the Keys.

The Wire at Bird Island

It scalped him and broke his neck.
He was travelling toward the wire
too fast to see it, probably downwind.
He has the feet of a grebe,
the toes unwebbed,
each bladed on both sides
with collapsible fins.

His feet are fine,
wild, natural developments,
highly suited either to swim
or walk on mud. He's a marsh
bird, not a great flier. The kind
that flaps ahead of you
when you're in a boat, scarcely
getting off the water, but puttering
like a motor with his feet
and slapping the water with his wings.

His neck is thin and broken
and just above his beak
the skin is shaved off from his skull.
He must have hit the wire head on.
You can imagine the great slamming blow
much greater than surprise
and the bird relaxing like a shot
had hit him into the wonderful
new world of technology.

Memories of an Early Marriage

I.

Your body brown from the sun
is open to the sunlight as a peach
filled with the light and glowing its own color.
Your hair spreads softly on the pillow,
where you drowsily lie talking, wondering
a little on some question I can answer
only when I hold the sunlight warm
and clear as you are in my eyes.
I would like to be rewarded like the sun's light
that finds rebirth in you—itself again—
becoming flesh that glows like wisdom
in a face turned warm and smiling toward it.
Into your body goes the light, awakening
the life that lies there, hoping to be given birth.
Give forth light, then, and let the giving be
return for what it gave you, sun and life.

II.

My dear, there is this lovely openness
in your outraged and silent hurt, that says
you do not need to blind me with your courage,
always reticent and warm, like sun
behind palms placed firmly on my eyes and held
until I speak those words that show I know you
more than all others who have so invoked
the silent struggle that brings recognition.

Just Now

I.

Waves are grey in the hazy air
where clouds are little more
than strands of evening.
The beach is a mirror
giving back our actions.

"The bush honeysuckle
that I brought in two
or three times this spring
is called wild azalea," she says.

II.

Out of the time's vast
circling like a sea-hawk's wings,
the whole of time suspended
on a soft rushing, outspread,
thoughtful, in its great dihedral,
a single moment flutters to the earth:
a feather from a bird's dark wings.
The silently encircling light
rises from the foam-slides
air and beach still soaked with spray
and the great roar of blue and sky rejoices
with a boy like a pinpoint in the silently
defining mirror of beach sea and cloud,
reflections flowing like the colors
laid on smooth and soaking wet.

Epistle to the Romans

Those who beat upwind complain of chop and gusts,
they want serene and confident resistance,
the others ride the contemporary thunder,
quantums of sun and rain wash free again
those calms that breed the soul's continuity.

Bleach and crumble, fragile bones, though aeons
of anonymity exist, instants
individualize, the rest is merely time.

Two

Maine

Routine of silence. Plunge hysterical,
smoke flushing from the cracks in wind gusts
thrust kindling in and clang it shut
come memory above that soft great rush
not of silence. Outside, snow thickening,
the ice left where it thawed, flakes coming down,
blown noiseless on the panes, like moths, the barns
white anyway and hidden, camouflaged,
like houses hardly see their cupolas.
Church steeples gone. And see it through the pines,
two lines along the intervale that vanish
before they meet the town in the swirl,
darkness into whiteness blurring gone.
The stove-pipe roaring up into the snow
you can hear it now the hard dry grains
that rustling through the pine tree leaves
slide down in clearings where the needles
give and pack. The heel-crunch where you step
comes vertical and clean or snowshoes pluff.
Then the bright sharp sunlight. Off the mountains
swirls of snow blowing from cloud shadows.
Fleck or two comes down, tumbling in the light
before the long white trails come closing in.

The House on the Saco*

The smoke of lives and births
blows into my head like flash
and silence of a shotgun mouth
stunned into the crisp pines
wind scarcely blowing in the morning
wetness on the ground to hold the scent.

I feel the rain splashing in my breath
wet and smoky like my blood with birches
burning in the heat-splashed chimney,
death and birth in the dark rooms
the pacing and the screams behind me.
The narrow uneven stairs I climbed

rising in my mind again to stand
the unlatched window open in the rain,
the square room to my right three stairs up,
its floor covered with dead flies.
I open the door where a phoebe nests
above a pillar, close beneath the roof.

The old ungainly clumsy house
its sheets of tarred iron clinched
with lead washers and big nails
driven into the wet metal sliding
with water into the thick rafters
dry in the steady rain and hammering.

*My father's house on the Saco River in Fryeburg, Maine is thirty
miles by river and three miles by road from the family camp on
Lovewell's Pond.

The smoke rising through the trees
birches pines strong-smelling in the fall
the cool lingering above the river
mist above the clear smooth water rippling
where the noses of the chubs the back fins
of the yellow perch break through to your blood.

You can smell them in the darkness
the deep holes circling at the river banks
steep with the falling trees
the darkness of the water in your blood
leisurely flowing there over dark boulders
where the black bass hide holding the current

swallowing the water through their gills.
And the thin membranes of their mouths
breathe the water through their blood
opening and closing in the blackness
their slime like soot hiding and merging
with the darkness of their fins.

And the black flies gather on your skin
stinging and silent as the memory
of the house upriver joined
by the outflung coiling to the camp
the thirty miles of Saco that you
cruised sleeping on the beaches

and the bodies of the mosquitoes
fighting silence in the dark clear air
and stars above the sandbars where you fished
the burning driftwood blowing silvery
in the dying wind or drumming of the rain
cold on the river as you slept

beneath the overturned canoe.
Dark in the blood turning the three miles
on foot the high-wheeled dolly
crunching on the gravel with the duckboat
guns the smell of oil and silence
in the blast sudden of concussion

and the ducks falling soft spattered feathers
on their breasts their long necks limp.
And the dust struggling with the dolly
blowing in the high leisure of the pines
the elms the great trees silent in their speaking
never to be understood but rougher

less intangible, when once you left
the village with your father and his brothers.
The high trees speaking cool languorous
behind you contradictions to the
harsh mysteries of the blood
the harsh speaking of a deeper hotter blood.

Caroline Gibson Newman
Fifty

I married twenty-eight. Plus twenty-two
makes four. Gibsons marry old. They're old
they carry too much time in them. How can you
make a healthy child when everything's old in you?
He was a sweet baby kicking around in you.
Couldn't. I was too old. What has an old,
a flat-breasted woman got business doing
having a child? Most menopause by now.
But Ben. He was young. And I risk taking
didn't chance think. It was. But who? It was I
who chance the think risk taking was who suffered.
Who else? Another soul but Rudy. He. He thought
chance think. Yes, but I the soul who now the body
swelled nine months old bones must stretch. I had him.
I gave him birth I screaming in the bed here
split they cut you stretch too much. I gave.
I gave. But what do I have? Rudy. Nine months.
Who knows? Old women's children are better off dead.
I could have saved myself that. That doesn't
isn't. Rudy could have. Souls. Souls
you create there tearing in the darkness breath
that cuts you panting who says the old don't lust?
Lust for the risk and torment breath rising to the hard
Gibsons nasty sweet Gibsons heirs of Boston.
I wish we were. The money to Ben but father.
Father a sweeter man than Ben? But father
I must from father. A spinster from Ben saved me.
Even though a curse we were. Each other cursed.
Ben saved me. Curse we were then Rudy. No.
Rudy blessed. My hatred on myself I chanced.

31

I Rudy gave. Then why the child old lust
breeding in its selfish bitter condemnation?
Why hate? Why screaming arguments I sharp
flashing as an axe my cold certainty
of family money education? I religious
harsh the screaming. That. Because. That.
I split broke myself flesh brittle as a bread-crust.
Broke. I gave willing. Willing the child.
Willing what my flesh broke willing. Gave.
But Rudy. Red flesh sliding hardly head shaped
when he squeezed the torture of it his too
birth my body old his bones squeezed out of shape
he died. Flesh flesh flesh flesh. Bitter he was a soul
flesh gave. I. No other. Mine the guilt.
My other sons. Four. One in college now.
An engineer. The others things I gave them.
Paul books. George his butterflies. Arthur
I'll send to West Point. Father will get him in.
My other sons. All passionate successful
cut thread? Ever? Will it? Fire like a razor
thrust burning up you will it Rudy? Draw.
Draw heavy burning will you steel you have
to thrust guts bear down the head shape squeeze.
Thrust through burning like a razor scream it helps.
Burn for the grinding. Burn for the harsh high thing
you burned for grinding harsh you knew you wanted
one last not old not old knew high hating
this last time hoping give the flesh once scream.

The Covered Bridge

I. *Fryeburg, Maine*

Beyond the New England transcendental
blue of the mountains past Chatham
past the river past the boundaries of seeing
the green of the fields the elm trees
cold of the snow hills blue shadowed in the sun
the forests between you when you stand
on top of Pine Hill and see Lovewell's Pond
quiet and certain in the distance
shadowed by a cloud and rippling slightly
in a long dark gust the three miles deepening.

II. *Sunday: Caroline Gibson Newman's house.*

And my grandmother prim and bundled
in her robes her father visiting—he
built it—with his paints the two of them
the small horse trotting leisurely to Chatham
across the bridge creaking and thundering
pausing to let another sleigh and joking
their breath visible in the shadows
and the sunny afternoon he talking
watercolors blue shadows and she of Paris
he alert blue-eyed bearded hands trembling
with his haste the reins shaking as he mused
the Civil War his military and how to catch
the pale shadows on the rippled surface
smiling at her small intense white face.
And she fuming narrowminded
and righteous in the arguments later

blowing like sunlight through a darkened room
the power of her flesh to scream made only sons.
His money. Her father's money. And Paris
she conceived in 1887 home for birth.
Like sunlight the dark board-planked the boring
walls long curtains marble-topped commode
old bleak dark but not so quiet then
epesiotomy like raw sunlight.

III. The oak.

They planted the oak in 1888.
His birth year. Near the corner of the barn where
the horses wouldn't step, turning to get the buggy in.
She got pregnant in April. Hoping to have a girl,
the city foggy in the evenings,
quiet snapping of the fire in the grate
but brilliant in the sunlit mornings
the servant girl Eloise smiling as she went out
and Ben working on his paints, the charcoal softly
brushing on the canvas pulled drum-tight
she loved to see him stretch it
his mouth full of tacks the precise hammer-blows
and nothing more comical somehow than his haste.
Although it frightened her. The smells of the city
he was just a journeyman printer's son
from Bath no match without his talent
really. That amused her. Frightening
was being so amused and not, not hastening
her first child tugged but pausing slow and watching
smelling Paris hearing Ben's hands charcoal
sketching on that canvas her and Max
and playing while you held that time the clopping
of horses in the cool air off the Seine was not.

IV. Maine. Her second son Paul.

What if he were Cotton-Mather-like
without religion? Would that be possible?
The thought amuses her. She plays with the tones
the moods running through her, sunlight on an old
trickle of water in the moss and granite,
dead leaves, more human or less human? More
tolerant certainly. Or would he be?
Some intricate thought chills her. A fly
caught in the sunlight between the window
and the screen is in her thoughts musing
or is it only something buzzing in the distance?
He had never cared for Swedenborg.
That seems disloyal. Put it that he doesn't yet.

V. Entries in her dairy.

My father was a colonel in the Union Army.
Augustus Abel Gibson. He painted in watercolors.
Water and fire make the rainbow,
a candle dipping in a fountain
joining the earth to air, the feminine and masculine,
to make the Great Androgyne.

VI. Her third son Arthur.

Trotting the field he remembered seeing
not so much what happened as what he was
the game beginning silk shirts and whipcords colors
of his regiment the better because he thought
of nothing. Sucking in his breath he felt
the air against his teeth and realized
he was smiling. Everything was better
sucked in like nothing against his teeth.

He swung close skirmish shock and lightness
of his breathing the moment that he fell
confusing ground and sky that he was rising
toward a heaven like green water
where he would splash into a liquid
like you breathe in dreams before the black.

VII.   Her diary: ten years later.

Arthur gone. Max killed, a heart attack.
George my fourth son sickly Rudy dead.
My second son. Paul. He is the oak you planted.

VIII.   The present.

Crossing the bridge its tunnel hollow
in my mind. The steep bank below the Westons'
edged with granite. The road falls turning sharply
at the cool shaded smelling of tar and horses
through the windows' splashing of sunlight.
And as I watch my father and his brothers
pushing the dolly rumbling beneath the duckboats
I cross the river its fallen trees swaying and drowning.
The blood open in their lungs and breathing
they hauled the duckboat like a caisson
three miles to the Lovewell's Pond road
turning into the dim moss and resinous
air breathing among the cedars and the pines,
ferns open in the still green stinging
of the droplets touching against their faces
and their necks prickling with the spiderwebs
while they looked into faint sounds that might
be lynx or deer or argued suddenly with a partridge's
explosion the gunsmoke standing blue and still
above their barrels. And they rolled

the duckboat toward the coolness
not yet visible through the rotting
birches the tangle of the vines the mouldering leaves,
into the air dripping and strong with pines,
until they reached the water's edge
undid the stiff knots and slid
the boat off easily beached it and made camp.
I cross the bridge thick planks arched and
clinched the corners bolted nails toed in.
An old man now. Fear in the blood flows softly
rain small drops blow dripping on the white
clapboards overlapping shutters closed,
still summers there, in the white house above the river.

Virginia Murray Newman
Sixty-Six

The whole story is really me, Mama. I'm it.
Everyone else comes back to it. Nothing
nobody else can not avoid not crazy
Mama seeing that just nothing. Not.
Help me with my foot. Maybe there is. Maybe
grey trimmed with yellow thread she sewed
it for him I suppose called Julia Jude he
the gold he officers always mocked.
Mama your Mama's name was Julia not
Judith? You cut his head off.

I married a New England yankee Mama.
Won't somebody help me with my foot?
We rubbed the poison ivy on our faces.
He was so white I was like an Indian,
thick-skinned, coarse-haired. I made him crazy.
I was so black and moles I pulled the hairs out
not fat I used to squeeze my waist white dresses
my hair long and pinned up falling almost to my waist.

Grandpa Baker fought at Pea Ridge Mama.
A line of stones and dirt the Arkansas Missouri.
Brothers killed each other. South Missouri
that was yankee. We were north at Warrensburg
but southern. But honor is southern
man and woman say that touch not
crinkly hairs that kinky as a nigger's head.
That's my hurting. I'm not southern anymore.
I'm not warm and black-haired in a white
not feeling there my blackness laughing nigger

half the other saving feeling that my grace.
Grandpa fought he cut the bullet out it's not
the family curse. But Grandpa cut.

I'll pull the tubes out. Don't they know
that six months' dying is too long? Mama
I'm not crazy Cally went but I'm
but Mama after me there's no one.
No one to help her. I ruined
his life once. Ruined her to do it.
Mama I killed a yankee Mama him
his blue-eyed fair-skinned child foreskin
to get him Mama these are awful thoughts
killed cock-robin. It was awful Mama.
Or did he ruin her to get me? Ruined
me through her to get me him?
I did it because I'm I I had to southern.
There's not much time left.
They fought the Civil War to keep the blackness down
not to free it. All that talk to free the slaves
was just to keep the blackness under their control.
That's why we lost we're part slave nigger.
Now there's nothing but the blackness.

Schizophrenia

In that clear and emotionless mirror
where the world, reflected, flawless, grows
to ideal shape and size, smaller but more
perfect than its counterpart, I bent firmly
my attention, until my own reflection
intervened. My head ached, my eyes grew dizzy,
and going to my room I took my mirror
for a window. There staring in I sinned
still further. The dark wall disappeared,
I stepped within, my pupil was my world,
that hollow ball where my reflection seemed
to crawl like an ant on a washed marble.

Caroline Murray Newman
Forty-Eight

All shattered, broken. Tenderness. Don't start the shrieking.
It's everybody that thinks. Today I must not.
He broke me into twenty pieces, everything counted.
Pieces of me speak like this. One piece that shrieks
says piece you're a fool to think piece anything
can make you more than pieces shrieking or thinking.
Take your choice. You can't because you're not.
You had a mother. She was southern. Your father
was a poor baby. He was from the North. He still
is. How can that be possible? A father is not
but he is in mother's isness, can't he, thinking?
That's why I say she makes, he thinks. He is
if she is making. He makes only if she lets.
That's why I say my father poor baby even
twenty pieces later. Well, I broke me. I
my father let poor baby even though I broke.
I. He is eighty. Years or pieces, does it let?
He knows. He knows everything but how to stop me.
Pieces that shriek or think. Pieces that live. A
tenderness. God. Don't think. I must not. Only in pieces.
All right. Anyway, that way it thinks, not me.
That he is eighty. Anyway I think he is forty.
I think that he is white houses. Old white houses.
Sweet wood old New England houses. Sweet.
Dry, musty. Cold keeps them. White. High weathervanes
on little spires thin windows make you freeze.
I chill. I stink. I know that, still. Forgiveness.
Is there any father forgive me? Hallowed be thy.
Snot. I wipe my will be done thy isness butt.
Grandpa tells me I'm another piece. Disintegrate.

I care. Care, he said, that worried him, paint snow
blue in the shadows. He was always seeing shadows.
Another piece. It was blue as heaven on the day.
On the day he said Cally has talent.

I could go right outside my head and light there
singing in that elm tree if I wanted to. I mustn't cry now.
Mrs. Harper hates that. She's a switch. Goes click.
She had a short tail. We left her in the woods
when winter came we couldn't take her to Chicago
it was too old for her too grey and grim.
I wonder if I have a soul? I am a soul.
That's what I always wanted. I hate my body.
Your brain is part of your body. It's attached
to it with nerves. I always wanted to pull the nerves out,
one by one. My brother was always so tense. And always
talking about bourgeois hypocrites.
That's what I hated in myself, I guess.
Not that I really hated others for it,
or even me. I hated because I am.
If I wasn't I wouldn't hate. That's why I'm not.
My brother was so determined. Sad, really. Trying
was his way to save me. Trying wouldn't,
of course. The Buddhists say you don't. Try,
not trying. I should be good at that.

After awhile my mother didn't come to see me anymore.
But it didn't matter, because I'm not me.
When I first came here, she came to see me.
When I first was she is. She sees me then.
My father still comes. He sees I. When I asks
he says she will come. Now she's resting.
I burned myself out for Daddy. I'll start to giggle,
if I say that one. Mustn't. Mustn't say it.
My mother loved me though she didn't show it.

My father loved he loved he loved he loved he.
The two together twitched. They socketed.
Maudlin. Magdalen. Isn't that at Oxford,
where they say you can see the little deer,
their tails shaking in the sunlight? That's where
you lean over from a bridge and throw the fish breadcrumbs
the little figures on them stained black and brown
and sunlight standing underneath you gaze
and hear the bells plunging and singing
they must play such lovely tunes.
Pluck. Nerves out. Twitch. Got that one.

Ashore my father working at the rock. The camp.
At Lovewell's Pond. He. Wouldn't let us go beyond that.
We were so much more mature in some ways.
But he wouldn't. Like when he beat me. Nothing.
Except the timing. That was well. Scream sass
too nice he always spat. He must have liked that.
Like to kill it. Really it's a scream.
Scream, scream, that's what I do too much.
Or giggle. Mrs. Harper hates that. Screaming's
easier. Just click, it makes you vomit,
but you can't. Or try to. Foam. Ashore
the old man, rock. Afloat, on Lovewell's Pond,
we two, like lovers, drifters anyway.
Baldface, Chocorua and Kearsarge in the distance,
loons, the loons crying as it darkened. Crying.
God comes to see me. He's anything that's little.
It's the little things that make you or break you.
They teach you everything, but they make it too it.
It doesn't mean it. And so you have to crack.

Forgiveness

His hands once so quick and strong
to prize a pinch-bar or snap a thong
that did not measure to his haste
or harsh idea that nothing should waste
his time by rot or weakness, now hang
weakly from the wrists as he totters along.
He holds them like some priceless evidence
of rocks he's dug, work to make you wince,
out of the Lovewell's Pond road
with crowbar and pick and carried or rolled
downhill to a jetty in the sand
that in twenty years would inch his land
three feet further into the lake.
But no matter how pitiful and weak
they are now, in ominous contrast
to their swiftness in the past
to cuff, seize or beat in furious
rage the first of us
who blundered on his moods
of horror at the endless roads
that rolled away his life like stone,
who can deny at eighty-one
he's had it, no matter what he's done?

The Saco

I walk across the river the water yellow
above the sandbars, clear black in the channels.
It is a new bridge, the road straightened
and the covered bridge taken down.
I can see the granite pilings in the river.
I used to watch the Fryeburg boys
    jump there into the clear black water.
I walk along the river, through the fields of seedling pines.
There is the fragrance of honey locusts, and the smooth
clear water of the river, high within its banks.
My father spends his summers in the house above the river.
I pick some of the flowers,
                    thick bunches with their leaves,
thick strands of strongly scented flowers,
and drop them in the river.
They drift in the black water smoothly
following the current among the swirls and eddies.

Three

Elegy For a Young Prof

A hell of a lot of good your roots did you, Mel.
You drove your Rambler at eighty miles an hour
into the concrete
          dividing wall between your town and Kansas.
Exploitation and injustice are in the nature of things.
You said that yourself, referring to man and woman.
You had a devilish, generous smile for barbs like that
that must have stung
          you more than you could satisfy
by those amusing comments on the world. God knows
you would have laughed to hear
          such priestly explanations
as this poem. Just take it as hypothetical.
Ibid the following questions by Cardinal Newman:
One instant of peaceful silence before the crash
did you feel a sense of gladness like a man
at getting his yearly reprieve from cancer,
the X-rays clear and his chest-
          cough no worse?
I mean,
    did you feel at ease at last
with all your faults—faults like a curse
that no accomplishment could ever cure—
did innocence come back and dazed gladness,
the gladness of a man who's died so many times
  in agony
      he cannot believe he's still alive,
yet suddenly feels gay, knowing he's found himself?

Dunes and Cedars

My mind is like
light. It takes on
the color of what it reflects
upon.

If I don't break my teeth out on
the strong
French bread, I will
explain it.

My mind is like light
above an expanse of nothing
like a dune above the ocean
or a cedar.
It isn't anything
particularly
          a receptacle
creating what it holds
like earth in a pot

like water in a beach pool
rippling clear grey
because the sand is grey
and hiding a few crabs and minnows
because
the crabs and minnows
are really crabs and minnows.

And I splash my feet there
and the wind tastes salt
                against my lips.

But if there were no salt water
where I had ever washed my feet
my mind would be a chalk
pit where little creatures of the sea's
accumulated bones
catch rain and hold its pools.

Rhynchops

Water like clear
        grey light pools the wash
of the breakers,
permitting minnows
        a breathing space
before the tide's suction
draws them down the stairwells
leveling
        and steepening
in places where the inshore
current has been hastened
        or slowed by the wind.
The skimmers judge
        the distance between
them and the water's surface
and
        at the same time
the water's depth
computing
                the angle that will bring
them through the air-currents
        and into
high-winged flight their lower
jaw scooping the two inches
        of liquid constantly thinning
as the waves slide out,
finding easily the vector of all
the resistances
        and sliding powerfully
against it

easily gliding the great orange jaw
jerking only
occasionally against a crab shell
    or a piece of whelk
and swallowing the minnows
as they go weaving easily
and freely.

On the Coast

The beach in November
sends a spume like oil
against the windows
greasy with film
    like an atomizer
like a great aerosol can
hissing and breathing
in the dark air without wind.

The elements of chaos
attack
by inner sympathy, feeling
    the power in the molecules
not alien to themselves,
they let themselves
pure bits of anti-form
among the particles.

The beach in November
is
night with its stars creating
new worlds
new destructions into order.

Returning to the beach in the mornings
is different each morning
the long sheet of glass
molding itself through varying forces
of pressure and inertia
    into bottle-curves and breaking
with a smell of salt.

The tide
is out. The sun informs me
that it is the sun.
If I was a child I would sit on the cool edge
and wonder
        at the water so cool and grey
in the pools formed by the coastal currents
and rustling the debris,
the skins of parchment worms, thin shells
in ripples over the sandbars
        smooth sheets of colorless
water drifting over
the low humps of sand and stirring
grains of brown gravel
in the shallow pools and spreading
in fine ripples, circular
across the transparent water that,
beyond a certain angle, becomes a mirror.

I can see that the sun reflects
from everything that lets it.
Everything, that is,
that lets the eye
gather its rays into a point.
The water, for instance,
doesn't do this within a certain angle.

The cool hard sand of the beach
has something like green algae
on it, that flows in patterns
where the surf has washed back and forth.
And here too the sun reflects,
a dot, a point, on the wet sand.

I could argue with the sun.
It has an effect of emptiness.
The cool damp air of early winter
or early spring, it hardly matters which,
is blue and misty,

not very satisfying.
One wants it harsh and positive,
sensual, not gradually
becoming not negative. There isn't enough pressure
to make the concentration
        of its rays
perceptible to the scientific skin.

Probably this sense
that survival
is gained at too small expense, given
by the swallows flying through the dead sea oats,
means simply
that survival provides too wide a point
of view, in which
one sees too many suns reflected.

One sees the sand grains, after all,
by the light of the sun.

It isn't stress that bothers me
so much as the lack of variety
of stress. A new stress
is a shock. For example,
scientific insight was a shock
to the middle ages.

The smell of rain on the sand and on the pavement
    cools
            the hot sand and asphalt giving it
that smell of heat.

What does it mean to worship?
To submit
to powers other than those the mind,
thoughtfully considering, can call its own.
To feel the shocks
other than those the intellect
    can order.

The smell of rain
produces that potential.

The Unremorseful

Suffering
> is a matter of definition.
White oleanders do not suffer
and yet you might say they do
as children suffer for a mushroom
or an oyster, enjoying a sauce of tears.
The worshippers of the great bronze bull
> at Rhodes, probably
did not consider that their victims
suffered, honored as they were
at being sacrifices—whose howls
emerged appropriately as roars
> from the bull's throat.
Did they know, did anyone know
how much the pleasure that they felt
> was a relief from suffering
in whose honor the great bull roared?
For so,
> the suffering of the victims did not exist
little as it was.
And they could enjoy the creepy feelings
> of children eating oysters
or mushrooms, without
the blurring and unclear
> emotions of remorse,
until they thought of the victims
inside the smoking bull, and smiled.

Her Answer

I.

My mother's dying mind hung motionless
above itself and questioned all
that it had ever failed to solve
and knew itself a mass of failures,
coming at last to that belief
it never would acknowledge but to itself,
having no more to hide in honest death.

II.

Gone in the deep flood of time,
almost a demand for death, her love
existing like a bubble in a whirlwind,
and I, awakened and aware of her demands,
remembering at moments how she lives still,
buried there in time but still alive,
a memory that has its feelings, sanctified
by its imperishable love for what has happened,
for what it holds with such intensity
that nothing more can ever happen; such
a happiness wills itself in spite of fate.

The Crucifiction

The Buddhist act of silence sometimes halts
the decay of all things into thought
or, subtly, how explain the agony of God
who wills himself again, back into being,
through acts more painful than the crucifixion?
Seeking in my defeat the meaning
I am ignorant of most pretenses
that others use, but have the naked soul
to deal with, like a pool that listens,
hushed and still, and open to the wind.
There movements of the insects seem
loud knockings, and the frightened race
of thought their feet on its meniscus.
I have seen the world end. Things happen.
There is a real. The fear of death is nothing,
after all, to the terror of rebirth.

Marsh Birds

In the silently encircling
moving yet somehow motionless
intensity, earth air and sea afloat
on being's perfectly austere stillness,
I can see a heron casually at work.

Once I thought that death
was like some clear and dreaming infinite
where perception freed goes turning
like a gull on slowly up-borne
reasoning, as a cloud forming
on a rising summer's day
grows upward into spaces
always more open to its light-filled
endlessly expanding gentleness.

And then, watching a diving tern,
I thought that death was like a darkness,
silently aware, a form of light around
the edge of things that trembled
as the soul lay, silently rejoicing
to be free at last of self.

Chain

The velvety petals of a rose,
the smoke-black spores of fungi,
those smells of resin in a chunk
of yellow pine or oak, the musty smell
of closets and of rooms you've left
clean and well-kept, cold all winter long—
not dusty—filled with half-forgotten things
that spring to mind at just that smell,
the feeling of light snow that drifts and teases
down across your cheeks, the air as still
as thoughts it seems to want
and softly struggles to arouse,
as catching on the hairs it clings there
till it melts, the sound of nothingness
that lingers in the air above the snow,
a rustling silence, calm above the drifting,
and the smell of sunlight in the air
when snow stops and you stand
poised above it like that sound
when clouds go on and leave you
in the clear, your thoughts above that
sound of nothingness—and seeking
what must make it—and the buried things
that tremble on the instant
letting you wait, aware of them:
the red sunlight through a mist
of salt grains half condensed
from water like a frost, glowing
beneath the cool and darkening sky
that seems to draw that color
into swift contracting cold,
stained rose almost to the zenith,
yet barely, where it's dark clear blue.

Washington and the Apes

Touring the San Francisco Zoo
I watch the movements of animals, their lack of plan.
It is important to do things new.

Washington might have felt so
watching a gorilla family roll
like barrels in the dusty hold

of a Barbados rum ship he had sailed.
Cracking nuts and joking by the hour
he must have felt no particular desire

to call himself the great white ape
rolling like a hogshead with his kind
across the playful continent,

or to substitute Jamaica grog
for his particular wine. But made it do
at the officers' table in seventy-nine.

I love these images.
Washington at his table. The gorillas
in their zoo, wild wolves behind him.

Man is an aimless animal.
That gave him a plan. To stay between
the British and the mountains,

his flanks extended by the forest,
his communications open to the rivers,
his rear protected by the animals.

Washington, Diseased

If I could only settle my intestines,
put my kidneys and my gall to order
I could show those British Army snots

what it means to be a Virginia gentleman.
The bloody flux I got fighting their wars
was enough shit, without theirs

even if I killed the French ambassadors,
setting Europe on its end for seven years.
When you come right down to it, that's no more

than I've sat bloodying for my sins
another pot. At Fort Necessity I learned
the man who wins must have patience

with causes. And what the cause is
of this disease, which also makes me cough
and wheeze, I know not, although my brother

Lawrence died of phthisis.
Once, in the mountains, I watched the mist
blowing up a cliff and forming droplets

on the mullein and on my hat.
Now while the French and British fight it out
I'll look for better devils in myself.

Perhaps they'll destroy each other
and I'll be well again on my own account.
If not, the Virginia earth will heal me

and I will rest the better for their help.
Sometimes it seems a century since this fight
I started in the wilderness first began

and mist and Indians both skulked
up from the rivers. I've seen
the Appalachian range a hundred miles

of smoking valleys, and the dark hills
rising from the mist like whales
until they faded into greyness. The rod

I've kissed was made of oak. But if I live
I'll take a mattock to the root, whether French
or British, in this century of God.

NOTE: In 1754 Washington fired on a group of French carrying ambassadorial credentials, triggering the Seven Years War. The French retaliated by attacking Washington at a place he had fortified, called Fort Necessity; and he was forced to withdraw. In November, 1757, he came down with the bloody flux, an illness which brought him close to death. In March, 1758 he recovered (he was then twenty-six). One of the great disappointments of his life was the refusal of the British to offer him a commission in their regular army.

Washington's Cure

To resist the appeal of dissolution
and to create a more perfect union
with ourselves, we must first resist

the British. They will yield
as soon as they perceive
we're resolute. We must insist

on bodily strength. Impress the head
or it will impress you
in all sorts of piracies,

gang actions and military coups.
They see us as a sort of raw
material. They're manufacturers

and they will make of us
any number of things. Wanters
of sick goods, drinkers of strange flowers

and teas, visualizers without power
whose heaven is a drug, Chinese
escapists clutching their opium,

Dionysian fools who do not realize
the main joy of the body,
to make it horse and head

at one with the rider. The best cure
I know for bad nerves is a horse.
I go everywhere at a gallop.

I like to waken a horse's lust
to the memory of his past,
his freedom to break loose

from every trust except your own
and let him try to show you who's boss
until he's yours, muscle and bone.

Washington in New York

He had always hated
the great gilded lead
statue of George the Third

pulled down and smashed
on July 4, seventeen seventy-six,
yet he had his doubts also

of the ones who did the job.
Who would pull them down
when they became the rider

upon the heads
of all intelligent
and sensitive men?

And what would happen then,
when one of them became
the kingpin and straw boss?

Who would rescue those
unstable patriots
when they were saddle

for an ass as fat
as that lead bottom
they had just unsat?

NOTE: The statue was located on the Battery at New York City.

Washington on Fleas

My victories outlast.
Single defeats like lice
give them their pattern.

In the meantime I
will bleed into a thousand tongues.
I will answer industrious

fleas. I will scratch
and crack my fingers
bloody while they suck, and yet

the British guns will rust,
before I sacrifice a single life
because I could not stand the itch.

Crossing to Georgetown

Nothing but Winyah Bay to get across
and then the young girls
to dance with, all the swells

of Georgetown would be there
rough as Winyah Bay was
with the wind against the current.

Back in England they wouldn't think it much.
They had the English Channel
and all the dukes and earls

of Europe to contend with,
their figures and their curls,
their sentimental parts,

artillery and ball to kill the girls
in battle, dropping by the thousands
on a bright sunny day, the waves breaking

like a sea of beating hearts. Here
we have thickets, jungles of bamboo
and rice. Why stay at home? When home

was an English lawn carved out of a cypress swamp?
Fear of the northern weather
couldn't make an Englishman of a southerner.

In the whirls of a minuet
he loved their powdered faces,
they had their chance to dance with a general,

but he'd be damned if the music
of fiddles and clarinets
would make him forget the greater chance,

the jungle to the west. And yet
crossing the current in a chop
was nothing to dancing a gavotte.

NOTE: Washington's journey of 1791 took him along the King's Highway through such coastal cities as Georgetown and Savannah. The purpose of the journey was to build support for the ratification of the Constitution.

Washington, Osprey and Owl

At Hopsewee he will spend the night
and he will pause above the river
somehow brown and silver

with the waves lapping up the current
and the oak and gum trailing in the wind
from the ocean their leaves and moss,

and the crisp beauty of the eighteenth
century in the imprint of each leaf
notched into the light above its greener side

and the holly will prick the salt haze
both with its berries and its leaves
and the palmetto trail its white hairs

along its hard green edges.
Osprey will dive, dangling their claws
into the water after fish.

And owls will breast-stroke leisurely
the darkness of the Carolina night,
the darkness above the river.

Constitutional Journey: 1791

Up from the mud among the fiddlers
they follow the corduroy road.
The calamus leaves are tipping

in the wind from the sea, and the marsh
grass makes a slow rustling
in the long gusts that riffle up

against the current. They are following
a long road across the rice-fields
with the horse snorting at the logs

half-buried in mud, and the black-
birds singing in the cat-tails
and the dragonflies as swift as fish

that see you and are gone with one swish
of their tails. He must remember to praise
those who were for the Constitution.

It takes a particular man to raise
rice in all this mud and choose right.
The sun and the clouds are fighting for the river,

as they approach the South Santee,
turning brown and silver as the light
hits it direct or filters through a cloud.

Washington on Wigs

Wild iris, jack-in-the-pulpit, thistle
in the burned savannahs out of Georgetown
(named for the wrong George), his horse

that galloped on the beaches, now
sedately ambles, in the state
where they shellacked Tarleton,

hoofs breaking the crisp stubble.
Among the silver-grey marshes
with quail and fiddlers in the road

they go a little faster. The flies
sting like guerrillas.
It's enough to make him buy a British wig.

But as events proved
it's not much good for that.
The deer flies dig into your scalp

hat or not. These insects make a point.
The best British worsted on your thighs
is not much good for flies.

The mountaineers who came down from Tennessee
had learned their lesson in the bush
whacking the god-forsaken bugs.

They stung the Hessians with good American
juice, stored up in their blood
for a hundred years.

What chance did the British have?
They were up against men
who had turned into mosquitoes
by slapping them.

Farther Along
on the Constitutional Journey

South of Georgetown it was all good weather.
The King's Highway
rode through high stands of pine

with monarch butterflies
clustering to tease him around the orchis
and the yellow jessamine.

His horse made good going on the moss and fern
growing at the edges of white sand
rutted by the carriage wheels.

He preferred to ride in saddle.
It was all good eighteenth century
ground, a space to go ahead

among the ordered rows, so high
they cut off the sun and splashed their needles,
a smooth carpet all around, for deer

to walk on. Like the brick columns
of St. James Church, a Parthenon
of little pieces, Carolina earth

packed in with white mortar. He would win
the bet with McMurghtry if they got
to Charleston in three days. But he

would rather lose some things. It was enough
to send the monarch packing, whether you meant
King George the Butt or George the One.

Why king it over men? Dead
to the joy it took to trot like stallions
feeling the surf in the sea wind?

NOTE: Washington was always a gambler.

Mount Vernon

Fireflies stir the quick water
of his mind like plankton
dying on the sand

in flashes, surviving
in the skin of drying
salt. They remind

him of hooves denting the hard strand
and disappearing in the swirling water
the beach made smooth again

of prints, but sparkling in the dark
where plankton come to life,
briefly, at their pressure.

It will be years
until they find a man
harder than he is

but as welcome
to the ocean—welcoming
the dark water of the air.

Questions for Washington

George, our father
who art in heaven, how much
did your example affect my father

and through him me?
Did his obedience and cold whim
come from your strong will

occasionally irascible?
When your teeth had ached enough
to make you rough on Hamilton

he took his time, and quit as aide
when you rode him for it. He was
no horse, he said, for your gold spurs.

And brilliant men have kicked at life
ever since, rough-ridden by you.
You drove your own body like a horse

in a breakneck steeplechase.
You whipped your nag at a pace
my father would have liked.

He worked as hard as you.
We were as ungrateful
as the Continental Congress.

European Monographs in Social Psychology
Speech and reasoning in everyday life

European Monographs in Social Psychology

Executive Editors:
J. RICHARD EISER and KLAUS R. SCHERER
Sponsored by the European Association of Experimental Social Psychology

This series, first published by Academic Press (who will continue to distribute the numbered volumes), appeared under the joint imprint of Cambridge University Press and the Maison des Sciences de l'Homme in 1985 as an amalgamation of the Academic Press series and the European Studies in Social Psychology, published by Cambridge and the Maison in collaboration with the Laboratoire Européen de Psychologie Sociale of the Maison.

The original aims of the two series still very much apply today: to provide a forum for the best European research in different fields of social psychology and to foster the interchange of ideas between different developments and different traditions. The Executive Editors also expect that it will have an important role to play as a European forum for international work.

Speech and reasoning in everyday life

Uli Windisch

Département de Sociologie, Faculté des Sciences Economiques et Sociales, University of Geneva

Translated by Ian Patterson

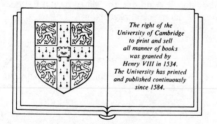

The right of the
University of Cambridge
to print and sell
all manner of books
was granted by
Henry VIII in 1534.
The University has printed
and published continuously
since 1584.

Cambridge University Press
Cambridge   New York   Port Chester
Melbourne   Sydney

Editions de la Maison des Sciences de l'Homme
Paris

Published by the Press Syndicate of the University of Cambridge
The Pitt Building, Trumpington Street, Cambridge CB2 1RP
40 West 20th Street, New York, NY 10011, USA
10 Stamford Road, Oakleigh, Melbourne 3166, Australia
and Editions de la Maison des Sciences de l'Homme
54 Boulevard Raspail, 75270 Paris Cedex 06

Originally published in French as *Le raisonnement et le parler quotidiens*
by Editions l'Age d'Homme 1985
and © 1985, Editions l'Age d'Homme, Lausanne
First published in English by Editions de la Maison des Sciences de l'Homme and
Cambridge University Press 1990 as *Speech and reasoning in everyday life*
English translation © Maison des Sciences de l'Homme and Cambridge University
Press 1990

Chapters 1, 2 and 6 were written by U. Windisch; chapter 3 by U. Windisch,
B. Plancherel and J.-M. Jaeggi; chapter 4 by U. Windisch and G. de Rham; and
chapter 5 by U. Windisch and F. Gretillat.

The author wishes to thank the Fonds National Suisse de la Recherche Scientifique
for their financial support in the research for this book.

Printed in Great Britain at the University Press, Cambridge

British Library cataloguing in publication data
Windisch, Uli
Speech and reasoning in everyday life. – (European monographs in social
psychology)
1. Language. Discourse. Analysis – Sociological perspectives
I. Title II. Series III. Le Raisonnement et le parler quotidiens. *English*
302.2'24

Library of Congress cataloguing in publication data
Windisch, Uli.
[Raisonnement et le parler quotidiens. English]
Speech and reasoning in everyday life/Uli Windisch: translated by Ian Patterson.
    p.   cm. – (European monographs in social psychology)
Translation of: Le raisonnement et le parler quotidiens.
Bibliography.
Includes index.
ISBN 0-521-35438-2
1. Languages – Philosophy. 2. Psycholinguistics. 3. Sociolinguistics. I. Title. II.
Series.
P106.W59613   1990
306.4'–dc20   89–17252   CIP

ISBN 0 521 35438 2
ISBN 2 7351 0332 3 (France only)

SE

Spoken language such as we all use all the time seems to me not to be purely intellectual at all, but deeply affective and subjective in its methods of expression and action.

Charles Bally, *Le Langage et la vie*

Let us expressly rectify what I believed correct in 1910: there is not a primitive mentality distinguishable from the other by *two* characteristics which are peculiar to it (mystical and prelogical). There is a mystical mentality which is more marked and more easily observable among 'primitive' peoples' own societies, but it is present in every human mind.

L. Lévy-Bruhl, *Notebooks*, trans. P. Rivière

How does it come about that people capable of behaving logically so often act illogically?

E. E. Evans-Pritchard, *Theories of Primitive Religion*

v

Contents

Contents

Foreword by Michael Billig

There are a number of reasons why an English language translation of Uli Windisch's *Le Raisonnement et le parler quotidiens* is so timely. At the most obvious level, Windisch's work provides further information about the language of contemporary racism and nationalism. In recent years there have been a number of studies examining the subtle and not so subtle discourses of prejudice. Investigators have listened to the way that white British people talk about West Indians, the French about North Africans, the Dutch about Surinamese, and, of course, about the ways that white North Americans still talk around their continuing American Dilemma. Most of these studies seem to ignore Switzerland. It is as if scholars assume that this traditional haven of European peace, neutrality and cuckoo-clocks could not possibly be a site of social prejudice. In overlooking the geographical entity of Switzerland, researchers overlook the work of Windisch.

Over the years, Windisch has collected a vast corpus of discourse of Swiss racism, having gathered his material from a variety of written and spoken sources. The results have been published in a series of books which provide a remarkable documentation of contemporary social insecurities. It is doubly unfortunate that this material has been overlooked by researchers from other countries. Not only is Windisch's data source fascinating in its own right, but he has sought to organise his material in a theoretical way, which, despite its independent genesis, parallels a number of important developments in critical social science.

The central theoretical concept in *Le Raisonnement et le parler quotidiens* is that of 'sociocognitive' structure. This very concept contains its own critical discourses. Windisch criticises those psychological approaches which ignore the social dimensions of human knowledge and which treat thinking purely as a matter of individual psychology. Similarly he rejects sociological or semiotic approaches which ignore the thinking subject. In this respect, his notion of 'sociocognitive' structure resembles that of 'social representation'. However, Windisch's treatment is much more firmly located within the analysis of language and discourse structures than is the work of most social representation theorists. In this respect, there is the potential for a future *rapprochement* with some of the new developments in the work of those critical

discourse theorists, who are moving towards an analysis of ideology from a background in ethnomethodology and pragmatics.

One striking factor to emerge from Windisch's analysis is the complexity of racist thinking, even when such thinking itself grossly simplifies the social world. The voices to emerge from his text do not attribute causes to social events in the antiseptic manner described by attribution theories in social psychology. Causal explanations are not innocent, but are often argumentative. As speakers give the 'causes' for the behaviour of 'foreigners', so they are blaming, excusing, describing and, above all, drawing upon myths about time and history. Windisch has devoted much effort to analysing the underlying patterns of the various discursive moves and their underlying 'logics'. With care, he has categorised the patterns of sociocognitive structures under different analytic headings and then examined the interrelations between the headings.

The discursive act is seldom a simple one, and the categorisations in some ways represent the beginning, rather than the end, of the analytic enterprise. The same form of words uttered at different times and in different contexts may have very different meanings. The rhetorical and argumentative functions of different discursive strategies need to be examined. One important issue is the ability of one and the same speaker to switch from one sociocognitive structure to its seeming opposite: at one time the speaker might adopt a 'material' (or sociological/economic) explanation of social events and at another time a more personal one, concentrating upon the actions of 'deviants'. Sometimes a speaker may draw upon the myth of linear historical progress and at other times that same speaker may articulate the notion of a decisive rupture with a mythic past. In *Le Raisonnement et le parler quotidiens*, Uli Windisch himself brings up these issues of variability and contradiction, and no doubt will address them again in his future work.

As such, Windisch has come by a different and independent route to a position which discourse and rhetorical theorists within social psychology would recognise. Like them, Windisch seeks to examine social thinking through the complex patternings and functions of discourse. Yet, he has worked at his long-term project in comparative intellectual isolation. It is to be hoped that the publication of the English edition of *Le Raisonnement et le parler quotidiens* will mark the end of this isolation, as monolingual English-reading scholars become aware of Uli Windisch's significant contributions to analysing the discourses of contemporary ideology.

Department of Social Sciences
University of Loughborough

Part I

I   General introduction

The research in which we are currently engaged is designed to provide a better understanding of the nature and operation of social thought, and of language as used in everyday life.

This particular book has two aims: to deepen and extend the theoretical and conceptual tools developed in our earlier book, *Pensée sociale, langage en usage et logiques autres*,[1] and to provide empirical controls over these theoretical and conceptual foundations. The reason for the wide range of empirical data in this book is that we wanted every theoretical proposition to have an empirical basis. Three detailed concrete investigations enabled us to situate and define the nature and working of everyday thought and speech: these were

(1)   sociocentrism (the extent to which cognitive organisation is centred or decentred),

(2)   causality (how the ordinary person explains the social reality that confronts him or her every day), and,

(3)   perception of time.

These three themes were selected because there is a general recognition of them as revealing indicators of the practical operation of social thought and language.

Underlying our research are a number of central points which are here advanced as postulates.

Eleven postulates

First postulate: By the expression 'thought and language *in use*', we mean the analysis of social thought and language as they are actually used by everybody in the most direct circumstances of day-to-day living. Talking about thought and language in use thus contrasts these terms both with abstract, scientific and learned thought, and with language as a general, universal, theoretical system. This approach also means that thought and language have to be studied as activities in process, i.e. ceaselessly being constructed, deconstructed and reconstructed. Thought is thus seen as something used, active, and not as an abstraction.

3

This approach can therefore be formulated as the question: how does the man in the street think and speak in response to the daily reality of his world?

Second postulate: In a sociological perspective such as ours *social* thought necessarily involves a *multiplicity* of forms of thought.

We know that patterns of thought and categorisation systems vary from one society or culture to another. Indeed this is the main subject of transcultural psychiatry, cognitive anthropology and scientific ethnology. The fundamental categories of human understanding – conceptions of time, space, causality and so on – may be totally different in different cultures.

What we are hoping to demonstrate is the way in which patterns and categories of thought – ways of knowing – can vary substantially within our own society according to *social group*.

Revealing *social variation* is one of sociology's basic concerns. Sociology shows us that nothing is general or universal: all social phenomena, whatever they may be, vary from one social group to another.

Third postulate: Different ways of knowing stem from *incommensurability*.

The demonstration that different groups in society perceive social reality differently is only a first step. There is also another sociological fact, which is that these various ways of knowing are not merely different. It is not that different social groups see the same reality is divergent ways, they do not see the same reality, even though they use the same words to talk about the 'same' thing. Their ways of knowing are incompatible and incommensurable. To give two examples:

(a)   A xenophobic individual (or group) does not perceive the same reality when they talk about foreigners as a non-xenophobic person does, even though they are both talking about the same foreigners, and both employ the word 'foreigner'.

(b)   An anti-feminist and a feminist do not perceive the same reality when they employ the word 'woman'.

In both instances, the ways of knowing, the patterns of knowledge, are incommensurable, not merely different.

Fourth postulate: Incommensurability is accompanied by *conflict*.

If individuals (and therefore the social groups of which they are a part) have incommensurable ways of knowing and yet nonetheless succeed in 'communicating' with each other, it is not enough to explain their interaction by saying that they are communicating or exchanging information on the basis of a system of mutual comprehension.

Their 'exchange of information' is more like conflict or confrontation. If there is interaction it will be conflictual interaction, and the conflict, the mutual incomprehension, will be what motivates the interaction.

At a more general level, interaction and conflict are not superadded to

social reality, but are constitutive of it. 'Society', in fact, is made by and through conflict; and 'interactions' are *constitutive conflictual interactions*.

Societies are not constituted by juxtaposing definable social groups which exist independently of one another; they are not defined by their participants but by the *relations* between the participants, which are a function of the nature of the relations between social groups. But more than these relations it is the *tensions* arising from them which provide the motive force of the social dynamic.

The same is true of social thought. The different ways of knowing social reality which operate in a given society at a given moment have more to do with a system of mutal inter-incomprehension than with one of mutual inter-comprehension.

Of course conflict and war do not account for everything. We have emphasised the conflictual aspect because, all too often, sociologists make a formal acknowledgement of its role at the outset of their work, after which it rapidly becomes a mere abstraction.

Fifth postulate: *Each mode of thought contains all the others*, which are often so far transformed and absorbed by it that one of the most difficult problems is to determine the intrinsic specificity of a mode of thought, and that of the part each plays in all the others.

Just as no purely individual person exists, uninfluenced and unaffected by society, so there is no completely idiosyncratic social group or social thought. Only the process of scientific analysis and its heuristic potential can justify such conceptual divisions and delimitations. Yet these divisions are not entirely arbitrary. The subjects of social-scientific investigations are always constructs, not objective reality, but, paradoxically, it is the very process of construction that enables us to make progress in understanding, analysing and explaining social reality.

Sixth postulate: Alternative logics.

There are other pitfalls too which have to be avoided in studying everyday social thought. It cannot be understood by the same criteria as we use for learned thought, as that would entail analysing it in terms of its 'lack' rather than in relation to specific criteria of its own, and we would end up revealing its 'lack' of rationality, and its 'weaknessess' and 'omissions' in comparison with 'correct' (i.e. scientific) thought. By rejecting that approach we are acknowledging that everyday social thought has *its own logic* which still needs to be specifically defined. In a way, this is reminiscent of the old argument about rational thought and the savage mind, logical and pre-logical thinking, but this time with the terms transposed to our own society.

There is no such thing as less or more logical thought: every system of thought has its own logic and its own form of coherence. But these other forms of coherence, these *alternative logics*, are not widely recognised; their

nature and the particular ways in which they function need to be better known.

At bottom, our work is concerned to take up the challenge posed by this paradoxical situation, in which the most commonplace, and thus most widespread, forms of social thought are either almost unrecognised or else misunderstood.

Because everyday thought functions in a different manner from learned thought, we are once again in an area of incommensurability, for two reasons:

(1)   there is an incommensurability between learned and everyday thought, and

(2)   there is an incommensurability within everyday social thought itself, between the ways of knowing current among the different social groups.

Seventh postulate: The attempt to grasp social phenomena at the level of everyday, practical reality means laying the emphasis on the *dynamic, processual, constructivist* and *interactive* aspects, all of which are diametrically opposed to a static, reified, compartmentalised approach to social reality.

Eighth postulate: The viewpoints of the *actors themselves*.

Our proposed approach thus supposes that the researcher try to discover the viewpoints of the *actors themselves*, which means employing empirical data which are as '*natural*' as possible, produced, that is, in real situations from everyday life.

The material needs to be as 'raw' as possible, and situations where individuals are asked to produce data *for the researcher* need to be avoided. Without wanting to deny the inevitable influence of the researcher's presence, or that of his own way of knowing reality, we must use all the epistemological and methodological means at our disposal to minimise it. Data produced independently of the presence of a researcher, in a normal, everyday context, come closest to this ideal, so it is not a coincidence that part of our empirical material is derived from spontaneously written letters to various daily papers which open their letters columns to anybody with a point of view to express.

Ninth postulate: Thought AND language; content AND form.

We want to look *simultaneously* at what the man in the street is thinking and how he says it, both at the content and the linguistic form through which a given content is conveyed. *How* does he think and say what he thinks and says?

The attention paid to linguistic form, to discursive materiality, explains the gradual integration into a sociological approach of elements learned from sociolinguistics and discourse analysis.

Tenth postulate: The ideas of *ordinary* people.

There is a tendency in political and social discourse analysis to look particularly at the discourse of people in authority, leaders or 'specialists', rather than at what the man in the street, the people who make up the *base* of the population, have to say.[2]

We have deliberately chosen to look as closely as possible at the ways of thinking and speaking current at the base precisely because there is so little awareness of it in the social sciences.

General comment

The various groups and sub-groups of a society are designated by widely differing terms: 'base', 'specialists', 'the silent majority', etc., and it is important to emphasise how relative and arbitrary some of these terms are. The phrase 'the silent majority' is a good example of this, as what it in fact designates are ways of speaking which are excluded from the official arena of authorised and legitimated ways of speaking.

The reason these ways of thinking and speaking are 'silent' is because they do not possess the same authority as the specialists who are authorised to think, and thus to think for other people.

The fact that a specialist, an actor who is authorised to think and speak, may on occasion represent a group which has not been authorised to express its opinion with more success than they could have done it for themselves does not mean that he embodies the intrinsic specificity of that way of thinking or speaking. He re-presents it, that is, he changes it, reformulates it and translates it into the terms of the way of thinking and speaking current in the official, authorised, legitimated arena. This is why it is necessary to look for social thought and everyday language in the places where they are actually produced, rather than in their manifold reformulations.

In fact, the expressive and communicative potential of a given society is far broader than that of the official, authorised and legitimate area of expression. A whole multiplicity of ways of knowing, speaking and feeling social reality are, explicitly or implicitly, involved.

Specialists are by definition a minority, and therefore only to deal with the specialists' way(s) of thinking and speaking is to ignore the nature of the cognitive and linguistic functioning of the majority of the population.[3] The reason for trying to find the most general and the most natural cognitive and linguistic situations, and the statements that they give rise to, is not nostalgia for some notional authenticity or original purity (nothing in the social realm is natural or original) but an attempt to comprehend the operation of society *as a whole*.

The dominant, authorised or correct way of thinking and speaking can never be representative of the operation of society as a whole, despite the fact that its impact far outweighs its numerically minoritarian nature as it serves

as an authoritative point of reference even for people outside that minority. A minoritarian but dominant form – whether of thought, speech, behaviour, dress or whatever – gains its legitimacy and is used as a reference point precisely because the whole of society, or at least the great majority of society, adopts and interiorises the minority form.

A model becomes dominant when all groups adopt it as their authority, even those who, despite long, costly and fruitless attempts, do not manage to conform to it, and when these latter groups are, in addition, ashamed of their own ways of thinking and speaking, which of course still continue to exist. The ultimate point is reached when all the people in the 'non-legitimated' groups fall silent, and no longer dare to think or speak, or even to express their opinions (which of course they still have), because they think of themselves as 'incompetent' and voluntarily delegate that right to people whom the dominant, legitimated model leads them to regard as more competent (as in 'Personally I don't know, you'll have to ask somebody who knows more about it').

These asymmetrical social situations can create easily identifiable *tensions* at the psychological level. Where ways of speaking are concerned, this takes the form of what, in sociolinguistics, is known as overcorrection. Confronted with somebody from the legitimated social group, a person from a non-legitimated background will, almost automatically, try to adapt his speech to the other's: this is the effect of legitimacy and authority. And in addition to this, he will feel uncomfortable because he is not speaking his own language. He will make 'mistakes', he will speak out of turn, or keep quiet when he should say something. He will not be able to find the right words or he will express himself awkwardly, because he is talking, trying to talk, or being forced to talk in a language which is not his. He will thus end up expressing himself in a language which is neither the legitimated one, nor his own. Whatever he does, thinks or says, he will eventually be regarded as not belonging to the group that controls the legitimated model and is able to impose it on other groups. The power of a legitimated model lies in the fact that it is self-imposed. If it is unable to impose itself on other groups it lacks the characteristics of a legitimated model.

Legitimation has to come from within, otherwise we have a contested dominant model which will be in conflict with other models claiming different sorts of legitimation. But this is not to say that the legitimate model is therefore static and reified. It is constantly being recreated and actualised just by being used. A legitimated model of behaviour which was no longer being used in everyday life would cease to be legitimated. No social behaviour is self-generating, and the mere fact of its continuation implies continual use, which may require considerable energy, the energy and activity needed to orient everyday social life in one direction, the legitimated direction. Ordinary social activity is fundamentally dynamic, and

does not develop randomly, its constant activity is constantly being directed.

There is another element which bears out this fundamentally dynamic aspect of social activity. One might think that, after a while, the non-legitimated groups would manage to use the legitimated model 'correctly'. But that model is evolving and changing all the time. It is not enough to imitate it, you have to master it, capture its essence, and be able to manipulate it, adapt it and introduce innovations. You need to be at ease with its dangers and, if need be, actually create dangerous situations to demonstrate how easily you can surmount them. You have be so much at home with it that the practice of it becomes a kind of game for those who can use it, and an endlessly renewed obstacle to the rest. The owners and creators of legitimated models of behaviour always have at least a head start over those for whom mastering them represents a constant tension. Using the legitimate model strengthens both its legitimacy and the illegitimacy of other models. Although they are not so crude or visible as political and economic power, cognitive and linguistic practices are much more effective in reinforcing, extending and intensifying the relations of domination, which are just as much relations of separation, exclusion and segregation, and of legitimation and non-legitimation.[4]

The above account should not be taken to imply a purely reproductive, mechanical idea of society. It is only one of the dimensions of the whole social reality, even though some sociologists see in it the essence of all society, or at least its principal component.

Eleventh postulate: Society: neither simple reproduction, nor pure production.

The notion of a society composed of unilateral relations of domination is no more than a notion, or indeed a myth. *Practical* analysis of the thought and language in everyday use allows a less caricatured and mechanical view of society to emerge, a more dynamic and complex view. Simplification is a product of the work of social scientists rather than a true reflection of how society works.

If we look at the language of the social sciences we will see that this simplification process is implicit from the outset. One of the most glaring examples of it is the frequency with which social phenomena are described as 'irrational'. Every time a social phenomenon resists being reduced to some catch-all conceptual schema (so catch-all, in fact, that they never manage to throw any new light on anything), it seems very easily (or possibly very lazily) to be described in terms of irrationality. This sort of designation, clearly unverified, shows nothing more than that the phenomenon in question cannot be understood by the kind of rationality underlying this sort of analysis. It is much easier (and less risky) to dress up a phenomenon one does not understand as 'irrational' than to seek out the several different rationalities it is governed by. Every time we describe the workings of ordinary

social thinking (as opposed to learned thinking) using adjectives such as 'irrational', 'illogical', 'deviant', 'incorrect' and so on, we are guilty of this kind of over-simplification and falsification.

What we hope to show is that the ways of knowing and reasoning current among ordinary people are neither 'irrational', nor 'illogical', nor 'incorrect', just dominated or non-legitimated. Ordinary people are not condemned to live their whole lives thinking badly or incorrectly, victims of domination, anxiety, tension, trauma and overcorrection.

To begin with, these forms of thought and language, with their specific and idiosyncratic qualities, do have an existence of their own, even though they are not so frequently encountered as the authorised, legitimated ways of thinking. The fact that they are less visible is directly related to their status as forms of thought which are excluded, rejected or unrecognised. They have less market value, less prestige, and bring fewer rewards than those ways of thinking which the legitimate authorities regard as worthy of being thought, but (so far as we are still able to see them) they do exist.

And, of course, legitimated thought is not expected to be completely homogeneous. Nothing is single, static and harmonised, even the authorised way of thinking. The latter is in fact the product of a continuous struggle between the different ways of thinking regarded as valid enough to compete for being THE way of thinking. The groups that are authorised to think are also in conflict. THE way of thinking will be the one which succeeds in imposing itself both on the groups that are, and on the ones that are not, authorised to speak and think in the official arena.

This conflict, it is true, forces the non-legitimated ways of thinking deeper into silence. But the unspoken is not non-existent. The unthought and the unspoken are in fact spoken and thought, only not in the arena where the authorised ways of thinking, and of thinking for other people, are established.

There is more than one kind of silence. It may be a sign of exclusion, or of resignation, or of suppressed rebellion. The last of these is merely the unspoken waiting for the right moment to speak, a moment which is bound sooner or later to come.[5] If the moment is slow in coming it may sometimes be created by force. The unspoken is suddenly said, but not through the channels normally used for the legitimate circulation of authorised ways of thinking. The wider the gap between legitimated and other ways of thinking, the better chance (or the greater the danger, depending on how you see it) there is of the latter bursting into utterance with crude – sometimes even violent – force. Those previously without the authority to express their thoughts, seize that authority for themselves and give them loud, unofficial but very public voice.

Conflict which is normally limited to those ways of thought which command a degree of value in the authorised ways of thought market then spreads to all ways of thinking and rapidly becomes open and inclusive, a

general symbolic war, at least as long as the symbolic confrontation does not spill over into action, or thinking and speaking turn into doing. Such instances are not merely theoretical: they occur in all societies, albeit at infrequent intervals.

Indeed, it is precisely this sort of situation that has provided us with our empirical material, a social and political situation in which ways of thinking about and imagining society which are not *officially* legitimated are *publicly* expressed. This is the situation which has developed in Switzerland since the 1960s in response to the significant proportion of immigrants in the workforce, a proportion which many of the population see as too large, and even as a threat. This section of the population does not share the official or specialist way of thinking about the phenomenon of immigration, in which the problem is seen as being competently and authoritatively dealt with. Discontent remained latent and unspoken, beneath the surface, for some years and then suddenly erupted into public consciousness. An underground, non-legitimated way of thinking about and imagining social and political reality suddenly found itself in confrontation with the authorised, official way of thinking about it. The unspoken began to be said.

This confrontation did not remain at the symbolic, verbal level, but extended to proposals for action, through the opportunities for changing the law that the Swiss political system provides in the form of *initiatives populaires*.[6]

This constitutional process enables groups with an unofficial, unauthorised way of seeing reality not only to reveal it openly but also to make the rest of the population, including the authorised groups, explain the way in which *they* understand social reality.[7]

Ten general comments

Although we regard the opinions expressed in connection with these attempts to limit the foreign population as *indicative* of the nature and operation of the ordinary social thought and everyday language of the middle and working classes, the present study is not concerned with the nature of xenophobia itself.[8]

The ten comments that follow are an attempt to allay objections which might be raised by readers unfamiliar with our earlier work.

(1) We are not in any way claiming that the middle and working classes are generally xenophobic. In fact, our empirical data show it to be an aberration: out of the 500 letters we made use of, most of which came from what we have termed the 'base' of the population, about half were in favour of these attempts and half opposed, and of the half that were in favour only one of the three groups was strictly speaking xenophobic.

(2) We do not postulate the existence of a single, generic man in the street.

Nor is there any single way of knowing and speaking among the working and middle classes; there are as many as there are groups and sub-groups in the base of the population.

(3) The contrast between learned thought and social thought is always less marked in practice. We do not find pure learned thought – rational, logical, deductive, based exclusively on logical reasoning and processes like abstraction, generalisation and conceptualisation – on the one hand, and unadulterated social thought, in which those elements do not figure, in which they are 'missing', on the other. There is always some degree of interpenetration, it is just a question of how much. Any given way of thinking will be somewhere on a line between the two poles.

Scientific thought, we know, is not exempt from social, ideological and even affective influences,[9] although of course everyday thought and language are far more extensively subject to them. Conversely the most ordinary thought can, and does, contain – in varying degrees – elements which belong more to the scientific mode of thought. With social thought, as with many other social phenomena, we are dealing not with dichotomies but with variable combinations within a continuum. Elucidating the actual nature of these different combinations enables us to develop a *typology* of ways of thinking and speaking.

There have been very few studies primarily concerned to analyse everyday thought as such, and even those which do have tended almost automatically to set it in contrast to the rational thought of science. There are effectively no examples at all of the reverse approach, the analysis of learned thought as differing from everyday social thought.[10] This is not coincidental: it is partly because we still do not know enough about the nature and workings of everyday thought, but more centrally because learned thought is still THE way of knowing, the only one with any real validity, and the one in relation to which 'the rest' (all other ways of thinking) are – negatively – located.

(4) Analysing thought and language in use, *in action*, means adopting an actionalist and constructivist epistemology. Hence the use of concepts like work, elaboration and activity, or more precisely cognitive and linguistic work, and logico-discursive activity. A form of thought or of language can be elaborated or worked to a greater or a lesser extent. These concepts avoid the reification of social phenomena, and enable us to analyse them as processes or activities.

(5) We all know that the social sciences have to be satisfied with identifying *probabilities*, *tendencies* and *dominant factors* rather than real laws. But even identifying those consistent features successfully is a considerable achievement. One of our aims is to identify some of the consistencies to be found among different social groups' ways of knowing and speaking.

(6) We are not interested in trying to establish a hierarchy of values

between learned and ordinary thought. All we want to do is to establish their *respective specificities*, and to follow the traces until they gradually reveal their deep structure, the particular principles and mechanisms by which they operate.

(7) These developments have other epistemological implications which we can now underline. The postulate of the multiplicity of forms of thought and language is not based on philosophical a prioris, but on *concrete observation and analysis* of ordinary language and thought. Such an approach is bound to emphasise the purely speculative nature of abstract, generalised reflection about Language and Thought in the singular.

(8) Our approach is equally far removed from idealism and from pure structuralism. Thought and language are neither pure, free creations nor pre-existing universal structures. Even as disposition, as abilities or competences present in every individual, this cognitive and linguistic ability is not in any sense identical in all individuals and social groups, at least when it is seen in its practical form.

(9) It is not our intention to advocate a return to a day-to-day empiricism or to call a temporary halt to theory. We are trying to elaborate a theorisation which approximates more closely to the actual nature and workings of thought and language in use, but without becoming involved in theoretical speculation. Our theory develops by constantly bringing to the reader's attention the concrete material on which it is founded, in the form of extracts from interviews. We want empiricism and theory to go side by side. The theorisation will be gradual, becoming increasingly inclusive and cumulative; we want to weave more, and more complex, links between thought and language in use.

(10) Eventually we will come to a general and systematic comparison with other researchers' results. But this does not mean that we will not occasionally refer to other work which can help us to situate our own results more effectively.

We can, however, say that it is as impossible to extrapolate general, universal laws from *relations* between thought and language as it is from the study of thought and language in use. Chomsky, for example, has tackled the problem of the relation between thought and language, but always in general, abstract, 'ideal' terms, using *ad hoc* examples[11] or intuitive judgements, not by empirical analysis of concrete forms of language and thought, or of whole discourses produced in real situations.

The ordinary, everyday speaker or thinker is not a universal, abstract, 'ideal thinker' or 'ideal speaker', he is a real social actor, with a particular location in space and time who acts in different ways depending on a whole range of factors and determinants which have to be identified and defined through extensive concrete analysis.

2 Theoretical and methodological foundations

An improved understanding of the workings of ordinary social thought and language in use can also cast new and important light on one of the classic problems of social science, the extraordinary effectiveness of some political discourses. Why is it that some discourses rapidly acquire a large audience while others never succeed in involving more than a few individuals?

As it relates to our work, the problem takes the following form: how is it that the discourse of xenophobic movements, which in the sixties was restricted to a few individuals, comes to be accepted – even if only in a limited way – by nearly half the population?

The central concept in our approach to social thought is that of *sociocognitive structure*. A sociocognitive structure is defined by the cognitive and social elements in a given way of knowing. The term *socio*cognitive emphasises the fact that a way of knowing, social thought, is not composed purely of cognitive elements, but of both cognitive and social elements. In the realm of social thought, unlike formal thought, the social and the cognitive are *indissociable*. Let us now define the concept of sociocognitive structure by setting it in relation to some other, at first sight similar, concepts.

Sociocognitive structures, mentalities, habitus and ideology

In our earlier work we demonstrated the need to move on from traditional content analysis – which proceeds by identifying *topics* – to an approach which sets out to locate elements that operate at a more fundamental and determinant level than topics, namely *configurations* or *sociocognitive structures*. A discourse such as the one used by the adherents of xenophobic movements can of course be defined by the topics, or leitmotivs, which most often recur in it. Thus we can say that such a discourse is nationalist, conservative, traditionalist, nostalgic, corporatist, and so on. But further analysis reveals a deeper reality underlying the discourse and its topics, *a way of knowing, perceiving and feeling* the whole of social reality. A way of knowing is thus the overall sociocognitive disposition through which a social group perceives and feels social reality as a whole.

A precisely identified and defined sociocognitive structure will therefore

have a certain predictive capacity; once we can successfully locate the deepest criteria underlying the way of knowing and perceiving social reality shared by a group of individuals, we are in a position to predict – as probabilities, of course, not absolute certainties – the ways in which this group will perceive and feel other phenomena.

Sociocognitive structures are characterised by a fairly specific set of *sociocognitive mechanisms*. They are not completely specific because some mechanisms may turn up in several different structures. In such cases, though, they occur in different combinations. A mechanism may play a central determining role in the working of one sociocognitive structure, and a secondary role in another. Sociocognitive structures are defined by the regularities, or one dominant tendency, in the mechanisms of their operation. Thus in our work on xenophobia we were able to distinguish six sociocognitive structures, three among the supporters of the movements, and three among their opponents.

It might be objected that empirical material such as readers' letters has too many limitations for sociocognitive structures to be satisfactorily identified. This is why we followed up the original empirical source material with more than one in-depth interview (each lasting from two to eight hours, or 20 to 80 typed pages) with some 50 of the most representative letter-writers.[1] It is this latter material which provides the empirical basis for the analyses in the present book.

We are not looking for statistical representativeness, but for cognitive structures that are shared by a sufficiently large number of people to justify them being termed collective, social or *socio*cognitive. A way of knowing which was shared by no more than a few individuals would not constitute a *socio*cognitive structure because of its idiosyncrasy.

Let us begin by distinguishing the concept of sociocognitive structure from both *mentalities* (increasingly used by historians interested in subjective experience), and *habitus*, as used by sociologists like Pierre Bourdieu.

When users of the term *mentalities* are asked to explain its exact meaning they explicitly compare it with the traditional term *Weltanschauung*, or world-view, but although it has helped to cast light on important issues, it is too general a term for us. And from the sociological point of view we would have considerable reservations about using a term which tries to define the attitude of *the whole population* of a country or a region. There are too many determinant variations between the social groups that make up those populations for sociologists to be convinced by such a high level of unsociological generality.

Sociologists are quite happy to accept that attitudes to death (ways of knowing it and feeling about it) vary from one historical period to another, but they are also bound to ask how this general attitude varies between different groups within the same society.

The concept of *habitus* seems adequate to describe the system of long-term dispositions which is at the root of the multiple forms of behaviour and practice of any given social group. However, it lacks sufficient flexibility to be able to account for the ways behaviour varies in relation to *situation, time, context*, etc. A sociocognitive structure is not something changeable, either, else we would not call it a structure. It is both structured and flexible. The behaviour and practices which develop in situations of passion or social tension (as in politics and its typical confrontations) cannot be reduced to a system of stable, lasting dispositions, or a *habitus*. Social and political practices of this sort necessarily include an element of instability, uncertainty and unpredictability, as well as being influenced by affectivity (affective logic), and symbolic and mythic elements. By incorporating these other elements (which the notion of habitus does not do), the concept of sociocognitive structure becomes flexible and complex enough to enable us to account for both the constancy and the variability of the social, cognitive and linguistic practices through which ordinary people deal with the changes and chances of every-day life.

In comparison with the notion of *ideology*, sociocognitive structures consti-tute a more profound level of reality. Sociocognitive mechanisms have a more fundamentally determining effect on behaviour and practice than the topics dealt with by an ideology. Social thought, which is a sociocognitive structure, is to ideology what deep structure is to surface structure. Defining the content of a political ideology is not enough to give us access to the essential mechanisms determining social action, i.e. social, cognitive and linguistic practice.

A political ideology is characterised by the fact that it invests and motivates certain sociocognitive mechanisms, but only certain ones, those which can be oriented and *made parasitic* on the political aims it is pursuing. This is the reason why a political ideology can mobilise several, even mutually antagon-istic, social groups. All they have to do is invest and motivate the mechanisms shared by the different social groups, and not invoke or use those which set them apart. Some sociocognitive mechanisms will necessarily be common to all, or almost all, the groups in a society, because for all their differences and conflicts these groups will inevitably be subject to some common influences.

A political ideology always effects a *work of transformation* (ideologisation) on the different sociocognitive structures, which involves assimilation and accommodation, parasitism and adjustment, and this work is never random, but always directed towards the ideology's political ends.

From this it can be seen that sociologists and political scientists are more likely to be concerned with effective political discourses than ineffective ones. Yet the latter are legion; we only have to think of all the minority, sectarian, small group political discourses which *never develop beyond that stage*. This is

because their way of knowing social reality (their sociocognitive structure) is so specific that it never finds a point of anchorage, never shares any common ground with the other ways of knowing in operation in that society. These discourses do effect a work of *assimilation*, but this side may be so important (so that they reduce, or obsessionally attempt to reduce, all other ways of knowing to their own) that they neglect all *accommodation*[2] to these other ways of knowing. But for a discourse to be effective, it needs accommodation as much as assimilation.

Thought AND language

The importance of the linguistic level has come increasingly to govern our research.

Traditional content analysis is also based on language, and also involves the analysis of texts and discourses, but language is only regarded as a *means* of gaining access to content and meaning. It studies the signified, not the signifier, paying no attention to the specifically linguistic nature of a discourse, to discursive materiality. Content is more meaningful than *form*, and what is said is more important than *how* it is said. It investigates variations in the content of certain forms of thought without pausing to consider that different forms of thought are expressed in different *discursive forms*.

Sociolinguistics and discourse analysis have shown that analysis of linguistic forms can provide information which content analysis alone cannot begin to reveal. This also means asking different questions of texts. Instead of asking what the text is saying, we ask questions such as the following:

> How is what is said being said?
> How does a discourse function discursively?
> Why does it function in this way rather than another?

This does not mean abandoning content, and only concerning ourselves with form. Our approach tries to take both thought and language into account. More specifically, we want to extend our understanding of: (a) the *relations* and interactions between thought and language in use; and (b) the *variations* of these relations according to social groups and ways of knowing.

This approach means that we have serious reservations about arguments which are too unilateral or too general.

Overestimates and underestimates of the role of thought or language
(a) There is first of all a line of argument which *overestimates the determining power of language*. This is generally regarded as taking its most developed form in von Humboldt,[3] who said 'we only think what our language allows us to think'. Language thus becomes an epistemological prison-house. This posi-

tion was later most notably adopted by Sapir and Whorf, and has become known as the 'Sapir–Whorf hypothesis'. However, it ignores some of Whorf's outstandingly interesting research, the conclusions of which are much more subtle than this argument allows, and which its frequently stereotyped form tends to obscure.[4]

(b) There is also another trend, uniting quite disparate disciplines and researchers, which by contrast underestimates the role played by language. This applies to a number of the social sciences in which language is regarded as no more than a means, or a tool, for analysing other phenomena which are considered to be more important, such as ideologies, collective representations, and so on. Language here is treated as if it had no specific nature, properties or functions of its own, and no independent dynamism.

(c) Among the arguments which *overestimate the determining power of cognition, or thought* are those of two authors who paradoxically enough hold radically opposed views on other issues, Chomsky and Piaget.[5] Piaget's fundamental interest is in the development of mental structures. He is not concerned with linguistic reality as such. In his view it is action, and the interaction between patterns of thought and concrete actions, which are the motive force of cognitive development. Yet this thoroughly actionist and constructivist position, for all its importance, is not applied to language itself, which remains a useful means of analysing thought, or a simple tool to help the development of the intellectual faculties.

It may seem surprising to criticise Chomsky,[6] the analyst of language, for overestimating the role of thought. But our criticism is not levelled at his innatism (which we reject), in which he is diametrically opposed to Piaget, but at the fact that even while he is analysing language he regards it as 'fundamentally a system for expressing thought' or as a 'mirror of the mind', and sees its organising principles as stemming from 'the mental characteristics of the species'. Statements such as these grant language no determining power at all: the independent dynamisms of language and the action of language upon thought are therefore underestimated, as they are in Piaget.

At a more general level, the abstract and universal nature of Chomsky's postulates excludes empirical analysis of the variable relations of interaction between thought and language in use.

(d) *Underestimating the determining power of thought*, on the other hand, is pervasive in recent microsociolinguistic trends in the 'ethnography of communication' and 'speech acts'. The great merit of these studies is that they analyse language in use in concrete situations, thereby emphasising the pragmatic, active, productive side of language, the side that acts rather than merely being acted upon. But language is almost always studied without reference to cognitive activity, the role of which – however important or insignificant – scarcely figures at all in consequence.

None of these four lines of argument will therefore enable us to analyse the concrete relations of interaction between thought and language in use, and the way these vary according to social group.

What conception of language? Language as practice

Like other social phenomena, and like society itself, language in use is not a 'thing', static and reified; it is action and the result of action, a process in ceaseless activity, in short, *a practice*. Put more generally, the notions of 'society', 'thought' and 'language' can be replaced by *social practice, cognitive practice* and *linguistic practice*. And these different practices are interconnected. Thus a linguistic practice is also a social practice, dependent, that is, on society and the social context in which it is produced, and liable to vary in accordance with the social allegiance of the speaking subject. By using such terms as language in use, everyday linguistic practice, and social practice, we can cut out any tendency towards universalising generalisation.

Everyday linguistic production will vary again depending on the social identity of the speaking subject, and on several other factors, such as time, place, situation, the issue involved, and the intended purpose of the words said.

These primary characteristics of all linguistic practice can be summed up in a formula which will govern all our concrete analyses.

The guide-formula

An individual is not simply free to do or think or say *anything, anyhow*, to *anyone*, at *any time, anywhere*, for *any purpose and to any effect.*

Sociology and language

There are one or two more things that need to be said about our approach to language itself. Our intention should be clear: despite the fact that language is occupying more and more of our attention, we are not, and do not claim to be, linguists. It is as sociologists, with a sociological problematic, that we are interested in language. However, this does not prevent us from using aspects of debates currently under way in disciplines concerned with language, and reformulating them in terms of our own aims and preoccupations. One example of this is the opposition between a *linguistics of language* and a *linguistics of discourse*, which we have taken up because it helps us to define the place occupied by language in use.

The linguistics of language is interested in language as a general, abstract, universal system, and as an immanent system in itself, i.e. as an autonomous

entity. The linguistics of discourse, on the other hand, is concerned with the real, concrete discourses which circulate in practical social reality. It tries not to separate linguistic from extralinguistic, i.e. social, elements which, in any concrete discourse, are inevitably linked.

We shall now look at some of the ways in which notions developed by the linguistics of discourse can enhance our approach to language in use.

The idea of the subject, the idea of the social, and the idea of language

The idea, or the conception, of language cannot be dissociated from the idea of other social phenomena, particularly that of the subject, the speaking subject, because the whole notion of language in use entails an actual person who speaks. There can be no discourse without a speaking subject.

So far we have not had much to say, at least explicitly, about the actual individuals who speak, the speaking subjects. But the actionist, constructivist point of view is primarily concerned with them. Anybody who speaks, any speaking subject, is first and foremost an actor.

The subject as social actor

Any discussion of ideas or conceptions of the subject must begin with a definition of the 'individual', the actual person who speaks or thinks or acts in any other way. He is both a subject who acts – an actor subject – and a member of a social group, determined and socialised by the group he belongs to. This dual perspective needs to be emphasised: at the same time as acting on society, the actor subject is himself being 'acted' by it. Hence the term *social actor subject*.[7] This conception of the subject contrasts strongly with two other, antithetical, ideas current in the social sciences, that of the *cultural dope* (the individual shaped and determined by society, with no autonomy or margin of action of his own), and that of the *Cartesian ego* (the free, autonomous individual, not socially determined, omnipotent, and in a state of social weightlessness).[8]

The idea of the individual as a cultural dope belongs to those sociologising approaches in which individuals are seen as moulded and fashioned by a 'one-way' relationship with society, which steamrollers them into shape. If the subject is conceived as a Cartesian ego, on the other hand, it becomes very difficult to allow for any influence of society, and especially of their own social group, on individuals. It is a view which treats society as composed of people who are simultaneously individual and universal, all relatively identical and interchangeable. The Cartesian ego is an actor, but a socially unidentified constantly shifting actor; the idea of a society made up of people like that is really more like a heap of sand composed of myriads of practically identical, interchangeable individuals. It is a unanimous, single-class society, with no social groups or inter-group conflicts.

But, of course, individuals are neither completely individual, undetermined, and free to do whatever they like, nor totally shaped by 'society'. They are social actor subjects, *both* socially determined and acting on the social that determines them. This is equally the case whether the social actor subject is acting (in the ordinary sense of the word), thinking (thought) or speaking (language).

Our conception of language is thus directly linked to this more general idea of the subject and the social, and is therefore at some remove from the conception current in the linguistics of language. It excludes, for example, the idea of a universal 'linguistic competence' which is identical in all individuals, and the similar notion of 'cognitive competence'.

In practical social reality, all individuals are not equal before language or thought. A term like linguistic competence becomes unworkable. At best, one could only speak of the linguistic or cognitive competence of one particular social group. The term we use is 'sociocognitive structure'.

Similarly, we shall be dealing with social, linguistic and cognitive practice, the practice of specific groups, in which the three elements are indissociably linked. The word *practice* refers by definition to practical realities, and *indissociability* points to another fundamental aspect, the impossibility of analysing language without simultaneously analysing the thought and the other social practices of a given group.

The notion of discourse

In discourse linguistics, the term discourse acts as an umbrella for a large number of approaches. We shall be using it very simply, to refer to our *corpus*, the written transcripts of 50 or so in-depth interviews, amounting to about 2,000 typewritten pages. This corpus is subdivided into two further discourses: the texts of interviews with supporters of the xenophobic movements, and the texts of interviews with their opponents. Discourse analysis must be *comparative*.

Our use of the term discourse is also designed to show that an analysis of *words*, or even of *sentences*, is not adequate. In this sense, discourse analysis is sometimes contrasted with lexicology. The unit of reference needs to be broader, in this case either the *paragraph* or whole sections of the *discourse* uttered by representative members of a given group. Thus the quotations from interviews which provide concrete illustration of our analyses are whole paragraphs, sometimes even several paragraphs or whole pages.

As well as the term 'discourse', or 'discursive practice', we also talk about *discursive style*. This can only be collective, and so if we are to use the term we need to have an extensive and profound knowledge of the form and operation of the discourse of *a group as a whole*. A sociological approach to language is not concerned with individual styles.

This brings us up against a paradox in discourse linguistics, the opposition between *discrete* and *continuous*. A discursive style is necessarily continuous, and cannot be identified on the basis of discrete elements, simple word-counts, or partial elements taken out of context. Nonetheless if we want to define a (continuous) style empirically, we have to start with discrete units, such as key-words, and particular expressions or turns of phrase. This is the apparent paradox. These discrete elements, however, are not treated as single, isolated units. They only take on meaning as elements characteristic of a larger totality, namely a whole discourse, or style. For example, a discourse that is regularly punctuated by words like 'perhaps', 'probably', 'possibly' and 'I don't know' obviously corresponds to a hesitant, uncertain style. The words are discrete units, of course, but they are also more than that, because they constitute one of the dominant features of the discourse. Their sum is greater than their parts. They acquire a structural character and role, and they help to define a discursive style.

These points echo the criticisms usually levelled at lexicologists for doing no more than *count* particular words, terms or expressions. Discourse analysis also picks out and uses certain words, terms and expressions, not in order to count them but to return them to their context or to the discourse as a whole. It is only by returning them to their context that they yield their meaning.

This brings us to the difference between *sense* and *meaning*, the definitions of which tend to vary considerably from one approach, or even one author, to the next. But whatever definition is chosen, it is important to keep it constant. The *sense* of a word is its dictionary definition, a general, fairly universal, sense which has been authoritatively defined. However, we know that a single word may take on very different senses in language in use, depending on the situation, the context, the time it is uttered, the type of discourse of which it is a part, and so on. Once this sense has been identified, we call it *meaning*. Meaning cannot be unique and universally applicable, but neither is it purely circumstantial or shifting. A discourse is primarily a totality, a structure. Discourse implies discursive structure, with discursive rules and constraints. Meaning is always governed by the rules and constraints of such a structure.

Linguistic code, communication and the extralinguistic
The criticisms levelled at different notions of the linguistics of language by discourse linguistics enable us to be more specific about language in use, and to extend the notion of discourse.

The notion of linguistic code
Being a practical discourse, language in use does not obey a purely linguistic code. The different social realities encompassed by language in use show that it can never be purely linguistic, nor follow a strictly linguistic code. We

therefore say that the linguistic code is overdetermined by other codes, like social ones. This requires us to explain what is meant by 'social', a term which is often imprecisely invoked. We have preferred to replace it with the concepts *social groups*, *conflicts* and *social actor subjects*.

The notion of communication

Linguistic exchanges between social actor subjects who belong to conflicting social groups do not follow the pattern of exchange represented by an ideal conversation between two totally free, totally aware individuals who transmit transparent information to each other and immediately achieve complete mutual understanding. A pattern like that implies a conscious desire to communicate, the notion of choice (a free and independent subject), perfect mutual understanding, and the fact that nothing is exchanged except ideas. Language here becomes a simple instrument enabling a purely intellectual exchange to take place.

But there is more to speaking than just exchanging ideas. Language is also action, and action on another person, or other people. It can be used to dominate or to exclude, or on the other side of the coin, to argue or rebel. As well as immediate, harmonious, general mutual understanding, there are also instances of mutual *incomprehension*, disagreements, (linguistic) conflicts, which follow dynamics of their own, which fall outside the traditional pattern of communication. Not all exchanges are conducted on an equal footing, and language has *other social functions* than strict communication.

So rather than talking about communication, we prefer to use the concepts of linguistic *practices*, linguistic *action* or linguistic *work*, linguistic *conflicts* and conflictual linguistic *interactions*.[9]

All social phenomena reflect both conflict and consensus. Social scientists will tend to lay their emphasis on one or other of these, but if that choice is not made explicit, there is a danger that what is merely one side of the case will be taken for the whole state of affairs.[10]

The extralinguistic

There is general agreement in discourse linguistics on the need to take *extralinguistic* features into account if we are to reach an adequate understanding of language in use, and to look for these extralinguistic factors within the linguistic ones. This latter point is fundamental if we are to avoid, as we must, merely juxtaposing the linguistic with the extralinguistic.

The difficulties inherent in this can be reduced to some extent by the term *indissociability*. Verbal behaviour is actually never purely verbal, it is always verbal, cognitive and social at the same time. Linguistic practice is indissociable from cognitive and social practice. A linguistic practice *is* a social practice.

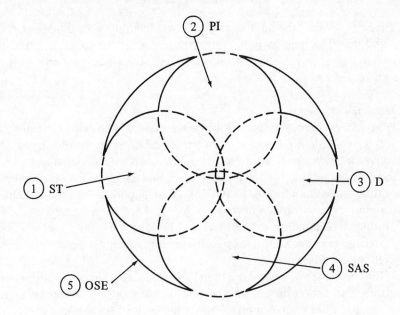

Key   1. ST = social thought
       2. PI = political ideology
       3. D = discourse
       4. SAS = social actor subject
       5. OSE = overall social environment

Figure 2.1 Diagram of relations between levels of reality

At a more general level, a *relational* approach shows that it is impossible to construct a true theory of social action on the basis of these levels of reality alone. The kind of analysis of social and political actions that sociology currently provides is not adequate to the construction of such a theory, nor is an analysis of linguistic or cognitive practices on their own. We need to turn away from defining types of actions or sectorial practices, and concentrate on the search for *articulations* between the different types of actions and practices, particularly social, linguistic and cognitive ones.[11] The ultimate aim would be a general theory of everyday human activities (rather than a supplementary general and abstract model), a theory which would enable us fully to understand practical social realities.

Figure 2.1 demonstrates both the different levels of reality and the way they relate to each other.

The unbroken lines represent the autonomous, independent, irreducible aspect of each level of reality (the specific nature and functioning of each level).

The dotted lines represent the heteronomous, dependent aspect, the per-

meability of each level to other levels (bonds of dependency, indissociability).

None of these levels is an autonomous entity, and the second category can only be conceived and defined by their *relations* with other levels of reality.

Each level of reality is the product of two sets of components. Levels are defined on one hand by their particular nature and laws of operation (the unbroken lines), and on the other they are determined by all the other levels (the dotted lines). Each level is both autonomous and heteronomous, independent and dependent, impermeable and porous. And at the same time as being structured by the other levels, and contributing to their structuration, each level possesses its own particular properties and autonomous dynamics.

The autonomy and heteronomy (or the impermeability and porousness) of a level are not inflexible, definitive attributes. The balance between the autonomy and heteronomy of a level, and its share in the structuration of other levels, are variable; they vary in accordance with the social group, the type of issue, the context, the moment and the situation in which a given practice develops. There is not an infinite degree of variation and instability, as some micro-social analyses sometimes seem to imply, but nor do we find the rigid structures and strict determinism postulated by some forms of sociologism.

We therefore need to look simultaneously at:

(1)   the nature and operation *specific* to each of these different levels of reality;

(2)   the indissociability of the different levels (the impossibility, for example, of analysing a linguistic practice without also analysing the accompanying cognitive and social practices); and

(3)   the *variations* in the relations of dependence among the different levels, according to social group, context, moment, situation, issue and final aim.

Summary information about the different levels of reality

The overall social environment (OSE)

This is a very general term used to designate the whole set of economic, social, political, cultural, historical, imaginary and mythic characteristics of the overall society in which the discursive practice under analysis has been produced. The four levels of reality inside the large circle are broadly determined and shaped by the overall society (OSE) in which they come into being, even though at a more limited level these four levels are mutually determinant of each other and all have their own specific nature and properties. There is no need for us to draw up a great map of all the society's characteristics, but later it will sometimes be necessary, in order to interpret some particular results, to relate them to some of the characteristic features of the overall social environment.

We have deliberately avoided any attempt to map all the characteristics of the overall society, because our approach to 'society' is through the mediation of the social groups it comprises and which constitute it, and more specifically through the linguistic and cognitive practices developed by these social groups.

We are looking for a classification in terms of linguistic and cognitive practices rather than of the normal weighty sociological variables such as occupation, age, sex, education, etc. Our contention is that such an approach is likely to produce a subtler and more exact typology of social groups, and also to throw new light on the nature of social groups and the way they function, as well as on social functioning in general.

The social actor subject

Although we are trying to identify collective cognitive and linguistic practices, characteristic of groups of individuals, we nonetheless have to start from the basis of what these individuals say, from the opinions held by this or that particular social actor subject. The way of knowing or speaking which characterises a group (which will be a sociocognitive or sociodiscursive structure) can only be apprehended through the medium of the concrete individuals who constitute it. The members of a group do not think or speak collectively out loud. A group only exists by virtue of all the single, concrete actors who constitute it and bring it into existence by their actions and their practice. A *collective* way of thinking or speaking is created by social actor subjects who remain singular but have a number of shared characteristics.

So from the repeated, and increasingly extensive, analysis of the words and the discourse (in the form of the in-depth interviews) of a large number of individuals, certain ways of knowing and speaking gradually take shape which are common to groups of individuals. If there are enough individuals, and if they manifest this way of thinking and speaking in connection with a range of different topics and problems, we can legitimately conclude that we are dealing with a collective, rather than merely an individual, phenomenon. A way of knowing and speaking has a coherence and structure of its own; it obeys regularities and rules of functioning which it must be possible to identify and define. What we therefore find are *socio*cognitive and *socio*discursive structures and practices with a certain consistency and constancy.

All the social actor subjects who are grouped within one sociocognitive or sociodiscursive structure (or practice) do not, however, create it or put it into practice in the same way, which is why we sometimes quote extensively from one subject. In such instances, the subject is not quoted because of his individuality but because he illustrates and represents certain important characteristics of a way of knowing or speaking more effectively than others would. All qualitative in-depth approaches make the same point: the most

social can be revealed through the most individual. Some subjects, for instance, whatever their social background, are better than others at expressing themselves, and are better representatives of the way of thinking and speaking that characterises the group they belong to.

The other benefit that stems from using the concept of the social actor subject rather than that of the individual is that it allows the active and dynamic side to emerge, because we can state immediately that these activities and practices do not have the same nature or the same importance in all social groups. The cognitive and linguistic *work* varies considerably according to the social groups to which the social actor subjects belong.

In our brief comments on the two levels of reality represented by the overall social environment and the social actor subject, we have also alluded to the three other levels – the ideo-logic, social thought and discourse. It is thus unnecessary to dwell on them at any great length. All we need to do is define them by relating them to a few of the other key concepts in our approach.

Social thought
Two points are fundamental to the concrete approach to social thought:

(1)   *everyday* thought and *learned* thought (analytic thought in science, for example) differ both in their nature and in the way they function;
(2)   unlike social thought, everyday thought varies further according to social group. Hence our search for *socio*cognitive structures, cognitive styles which vary from one *social group* to another.

The postulate of dual incommensurability needs to be tested in practice.

Ideo-logic
As regards the *ideo-logic*, component 2 of the diagram, there is no point in proposing an nth definition of the idea. It has been defined in relation to other notions, namely habitus, mentality and social thought. Let us simply state that we are concerned not with the functions of ideology (which have received ample attention from social scientists) but with its *functioning*. As a result, we shall be trying to locate empirically activities such as *ideological work* and *ideological interference*.

Interdiscourse and the typology of discourses
We can now add these two important aspects to the notion of *discourse*. The concept of *interdiscourse* shows that while the different levels of reality distinguished in the general diagram are defined by the relations and interactions, each level of reality itself includes sub-sets which can also only be defined by their relations and interactions.

Although the opposition in the present investigation is between discourses

of supporters of 'xenophobic movements' and their opponents, it would be impossible to attempt any really precise definition of either. In practical reality, the two are indissociable, as each is constructed in relation to the other, and in opposition to each other. They are actually formed in and by their struggle with each other. The two discourses are the result of a struggle between two socio-political groups carried out through the medium of language and discourse.

At the level of discursive materiality, the best indicators of this discursive struggle – this *conflictual and constitutive linguistic interaction* – are to be found in the *polemical form* of both discourses. There are no separate discourses for supporters and adversaries. Each discourse contains the opposing discourse within itself. Each uses the adversary's discourse in its own by changing it, or rejecting it or making fun of it (as for example by the use of partial quotation). Each discourse is materially present in the other. Each performs a *discursive work* on the other discourse, by means of which it seeks to define itself. Each tries to achieve definition and legitimation by a process of discrediting the other. A discourse which is misused in this way will feel bound to respond, and so the process goes on. All discourse is the result of a gradual construction, in this case of a *process of conflictual interaction*, so we can now see more clearly how terms like 'communication' or 'mutual understanding' provide only a very partial account of the true nature of the interactions such discourses give rise to. Hence the concept of *interdiscourse*. By using this concept, we can show that there is no primary, self-contained, autonomous discourse, and at the same time help to dereify social phenomena, in this case language. A way of speaking, like a way of acting or thinking, is defined by its relations and interactions – which may sometimes be conflictual – with the other ways of speaking which operate in a given area.

By using the term *polemical* discourse we have, in fact, already introduced the second notion of a *typology* of discourses. Just as there are no self-contained discourses, there is no single form of discourse. The opposite pole from polemical discourse is generally defined as the *didactic* pole of discourse. In this, the social actor speaker analyses rather than polemicises, analysing the situation by abstracting as much as possible from his own subjectivity and point of view. Such a speaker is not content with passing judgement or condemning, for example, but instead attempts to understand and explain, hence the term didactic. This different attitude on the part of the speaking subject to what he says will find expression in a form of discourse very different from the polemical form. The form is indissociable from the content.

There are, of course, other intermediate forms of discourse between these two extremes, but the exact nature of all these forms still remains to be defined. That is a further purpose of our work.

A type of discourse is not defined solely by one particular discursive form. It

is the result, received at the level of linguistic materiality, of specific relations and interactions between the different levels of reality distinguished in the diagram. A form of discourse always goes alongside a form of thought, or to put it more fully:

An individual is not simply free to do, think or say anything, anyhow, to anyone, at any time, anywhere, for any purpose and with any effect.

The diagram and the guide-formula: outline of integration

By integrating the points in the general diagram with the guide-formula we should start to bring together the subject of our investigation (thought AND language), its methodology, and its main concepts. We can briefly illustrate this integration by breaking the guide-formula down into its main parts:

> *An individual* . . . this part of the formula concerns the conception of the subject, which will simultaneously reflect an idea of 'society', of the 'individual' and of the 'group'. We are dealing with a social actor subject who is both acting and 'acted', both structuring and structured.

> . . . *is not simply free to do, think or say* . . . indicates the primacy of the actionist, constructivist conception (action, practice, interaction, activity, work, process with no end or beginning).

This part of the formula also designates the type of phenomena studied, by simultaneously emphasising their status as practices (social, cognitive and discursive practices), and their *indissociability*. By being linked to the preceding part of the formula, it indicates the *social variation* of these practices (as it is *anybody* who does, thinks and says).

> . . . *anything* . . . the contents of any practice, the type of issue, are one variable factor among many. And *what* is done, thought or said is not something isolated, atomised, and analysable in its own right.
> . . . *anyhow* . . . the content is indissociable from the *form* in which it is said. The discursive form, each type of *discourse*, has its own specific totality, structure, rules and limits.
> A discourse also exists in terms of its interaction with other discourses. This is the *interdiscourse*.
> . . . *to anyone* . . . a given discourse is also a function of the social and other characteristics of the interlocutor.
> . . . *at any time, anywhere* . . . all social, cognitive and linguistic practices are always *situated*, and are dependent on the context, the moment, the situation and, at a more general level, the overall social environment (OSE). Social determinants are micro- as well as macro-social.

...*for any purpose* ... the nature of cognitive and linguistic practices varies according to their aims. The means are a function of the end, even if all means are equally valid for the attainment of an end.

...*and to any effect*... some practices and some cognitive and linguistic strategies are more effective than others. The effect depends on all the antecedent parts of the formula. The word 'effect' thus reminds us of all the *other social functions* of language (besides that of communication). Language is action; to say is to do, and thus to have an effect.

The effect, or the effectiveness, also depends on the *social status* of a social actor subject. Not everybody can obtain all the effects they want to, or even any effect at all. The subjects who have an effect on others by means of language are *agent-subjects*, and those over whom this power is exercised are *patient-subjects*.

The power of a speaking subject is bound up with all the other powers he accumulates, power (or capital) which may be economic, social, political, cultural or symbolic. But because the idea of the social developed here is not at all a purely mechanical and reproductive one, it is obvious that any social actor subject may sometimes be an agent-subject and sometimes a patient-subject, though of course some subjects more frequently occupy one social position than the other. Like all forms of wealth and power, those contained in language can sometimes be appropriated by those whom it dominates, the patient-subjects. Then they rebel, and their complaints make themselves heard, through language. Sometimes they even have an effect. The effect they have will also vary according to the circumstances, the situation and the moment; it also depends on the nature and general state of the social interactions (power relations, for instance) that exist at a given time between the social groups to which the social actor subjects involved in this confrontation of discourses belong.

We can now move on from concepts and theory to our empirical analyses. We shall look at the three topics which provide most in the way of illumination in the following order:

(1)   cognitive centration and decentration
(2)   causality
(3)   perception of time.

Part II

3   Cognitive centration

From the psychology to the sociology of cognition

The main focus of this first empirical study concerns the functioning of thought, or cognition, as we are dealing with cognitive centration and decentration. The terms centration and decentration have been borrowed from Piaget's genetic psychology and epistemology, and transposed into sociology.

This transposition consists of *altering six elements* of Piaget's design.

(1) Piaget was interested in the cognitive development of the *child*, and the different stages of this development. We want to provide an improved understanding of the functioning of *adult* thought, or social thought. Piaget demonstrated that children achieve complete cognitive decentration (complete the transition from egocentrism – a form of cognitive centration – to decentration) at about the age of fourteen or fifteen. After that all individuals are, theoretically, capable of demonstrating cognitive decentration. This is the epistemic subject, which as a subject is theoretical, abstract, general and universal. We, on the other hand, are interested in the persistence of multiple forms of collective egocentrism, or *sociocentrism*,[1] in adults, despite the theoretical possiblity of decentration.

Nationalism is one of several examples of sociocentrism. It is a cognitive centration based on the national; membership of a nation is the criterion that determines the whole of the way of knowing. Everything is thought, conceived and perceived in terms of the opposition between national and foreign.[2] The criterion of nationality transcends all others, and therefore also transcends operational thought. So a social factor, nationality, determines the way of knowing. Nationalism is thus a form of *social* thought, a *socio*cognitive centration.

The multiple forms of sociocentrism are *both* social *and* cognitive phenomena, not purely cognitive ones.[3]

(2) In our approach, *language* does not have the status of a pretext, an instrument that can be used to analyse thought. The linguistic *form* of a given thought is as important as its content.

(3) Piaget was looking for universal cognitive structures; we are trying to reveal sociocognitive structures which have a concrete reality and which *vary according to social group*.

33

(4) In *ideology*, Piaget saw a pre-logical, pre-scientific form of thought, which was bound gradually to disappear in favour of learned thought. We regard ideology as one of the realities constitutive of human thought. Ideology is not pre-scientific: it is Other. It has its own logic: ideo-logic.

(5) Piaget was not interested in the role of *affectivity* in cognitive development. But it is not really possible to analyse political discourses, which are often passionately opposed to each other, without taking emotion and affectivity into account. And the logic of passion does not obey the logic of reason.

(6) Piaget assumed that by the age of fourteen or fifteen everybody has achieved the intellectual capacities necessary for operational thought, as a result of a process of cognitive development made up of a number of predetermined stages. Every adult therefore has *the same intellectual potential*, and his *cognitive development will be complete* by the time he reaches adolescence.

However, if we observe language and thought in use, we will see that all adults do not share this same basic potential.

The classic works of sociolinguistics, the work of Bernstein, Labov, Hymes, Halliday and others, have shown that children from different social backgrounds *do not have the same linguistic and cognitive competence*. They go on to show that this intellectual potential is not static and that even adults are capable of linguistic and cognitive development. In such cases we use the terms *cognitive and linguistic work* and *individuation*, rather than development.

More generally, the cognitive and linguistic practices of the adult world are a function of all the other everyday social practices, both at work and outside it. Thus a broad range of social integrations, many and varied social, cultural and political activities – the various social practices – retroact on cognitive and linguistic practices by activating and intensifying the more narrowly cognitive and linguistic work.

Despite these six alterations, the definitions and characteristics of egocentrism and decentration as described by psychology enable us to have a better understanding of the phenomenon of sociocentrism, and point to areas which need to be taken into account in an empirical approach.

Egocentrism and sociocentrism

It should be said right away that sociocentrism – which is a very widespread phenomenon in everyday social thought – can never be seen simply as a survival of childish egocentrism. The sociocentric nature of any given social thought has to be explained socially.

At a very general level, sociocentrism is a social actor subject's tendency to favour his own point of view within his way of knowing. A sociocentric subject will tend to attribute his own categories of knowledge to other subjects' interpretation of social (and cognitive) practices (i.e. there is a predominance of assimilation over accommodation). He assimilates other

categories of thought, and those of others, to his own categories. This operation often involves:

(1) reducing new elements to already known and familiar mental categories, and
(2) categorisations that are unchanging, or stereotyped. Instances like this are evidence of superficial cognitive work and an individuation process which is, as it were, blocked.

Sociocentric subjects cannot see that other people's – or the Other's – ways of knowing do not necessarily depend on the same categories as theirs. The Other is just the not-self, and has no reality in itself. Perception of the Other is limited to seeing it as different from the self; the self is never perceived as different from others. It is egocentrism or the absence of reciprocity that defines the centred subject.

The sociocognitive structure of sociocentrism is clearly not defined just by centration on the individual's point of view, but by a whole set of sociocognitive mechanisms which we shall be revealing empirically.

The functioning of egocentrism casts some theoretical light on the kind of mechanisms at work in this form of thought.

> It is the assemblage of all the different precritical and consequently pre-objective cognitive attitudes of the child's mind . . . Fundamentally, egocentrism is thus neither a conscious phenomenon (egocentrism, when self-conscious, is no longer egocentrism), nor a phenomenon of social behaviour (behaviour is an indirect manifestation of egocentrism but does not constitute it) but a kind of systematic and unconscious illusion . . . Piaget, *The Language and Thought of the Child*, p. 268[4]

By analogy, we can assume that a sociocentric way of knowing is also unconscious, pre-critical and pre-objective, to a greater or lesser degree. Rather than talk about unconscious attitudes, though, we would say that within such a sociocognitive structure the social actor subject is more 'acted' (by his own categories of knowledge) than actor. The subject has little autonomy, and the cognitive and linguistic work is not extensive. He cannot distance himself from his own way of knowing reality.

By contrast with analytical, learned thought (which, by definition, implies a high degree of decentration and a critical attitude which attempts to understand social phenomena as fully and as objectively as possible), we would expect a sociocentric form of thought to accord little importance to criticism and objectivity.

> Egocentrism is thus in opposition with objectivity, in so far as objectivity signifies relativity on the physical plane and reciprocity on the social plane. *Ibid.*, p. 271

> Egocentrism is . . . on the one hand, primacy of self-satisfaction over objective observation (hence the nature of the early thought of the child, which is halfway between play and adaptation) and, on the other, is the distortion of reality to satisfy the activity and point of view of the individual. In both cases, it is unconscious, being essentially the result of a failure to distinguish between the subjective and the objective. Piaget, *Play, Dreams and Imitation*, p. 285n.

The primacy of *satisfaction over the objective observation* and the *failure to distinguish between the subjective and the objective* represent two other areas which require empirical verification. Sociocentrism would thus be affected by two influences: fixed and inflexible categories of knowledge, and subjectivity, affectivity and emotion.

Remembering the role played by the emotions in political struggles, and the inflexibility of some diametrically opposed, ideological hostilities, we should expect sociocentrism to be a fertile ground and ideal anchorage point for political discourses.

> . . . egocentrism signifies the absence of both self-perception and objectivity, whereas acquiring possession of the object as such is on a par with the acquisition of self-perception. *The Child's Construction of Reality*, p. xii

> [The child] plays in an individualistic manner with material that is social. Such is egocentrism. *The Moral Judgment of the Child*, p. 27

> Childish egocentrism, far from being asocial, always goes hand in hand with adult constraint. It is presocial only in relation to co-operation. *Ibid*. p. 53

It should be possible to locate this characteristic constraint – the slender weight of autonomy *vis-à-vis* heteronomy – in sociocentric thought.

Other Piaget definitions connect with what has already been said about the way of knowing the Other, or rather of mistaking it, the impossibility of knowing it. This impossibility is not a fault or a lack: it is a constitutive characteristic of sociocentric thought.

> Egocentrism in so far as it means confusion of the ego with the external world, and egocentrism in so far as it means lack of co-operation, constitute one and the same phenomenon. *Ibid*. p. 87

> egocentrism being by definition the confusion of the self with the not-self . . . *Ibid*. p. 249

> the inability to differentiate between one's own point of view and other people's . . . *Language and Thought*, p. 267n.

> A factor of primary importance [in egocentrism] is that spontaneous attitude of the individual mind in which thought turns directly to the object without first being aware of its own point of view. *Ibid*. p. 276

> Egocentrism consists in taking one's own perception of reality to be the only possible one. *Le Développement des quantités chez l'enfant*, p. 277

Egocentrism, that is the co-ordination established in accordance with one's own viewpoint and no other. *Ibid.* p. 242

Egocentrism is the denial of the objective attitude, and consequently of logical analysis. It therefore gives rise to subjective synthesis. *Language and Thought*, p. 140n.

Logical egocentrism produces autism . . . Ontological egocentrism produces magic and precausality . . . They both falsify the perspective of logical relations and of things, because they both start from the assumption that other people understand us and agree with us from the first and that things revolve around us with the sole purpose of serving us and resembling us. *The Child's Conception of Causality*, p. 302

Sociocognitive decentration

A decentred form of thought, by contrast, can be defined by the following characteristics:

(1)   a greater general activity of the social actor subject (he acts as much as he is acted upon);

(2)   more elaborated linguistic, cognitive and social practices;

(3)   this generalised work thus leads to autonomy, enables a degree of distance to be established *vis-à-vis* the multiple forms of determinism and heteronomy. It encourages the desire to understand. Analysed as objectively as possible, reality becomes a 'constraint' which cannot simply be denied.

The more successfully he decentres himself, the more active the subject becomes, or, to be more precise, his decentration is actually the measure of his effective activity on the object . . . *Introduction à l'épistémologie génétique II*, p. 15

. . . it is impossible, at any level, to separate the subject from the object. There are only relations between the two, but these relations may be centred or decentred to a greater or lesser degree, and it is in this reversal of direction that the transition from subjectivity to objectivity consists. *Ibid.* p. 16

To decentre means 'to group'. *Ibid.* p. 112

. . . co-ordination of centrations, i.e. decentration. *The Child's Conception of Movement and Speed*, p. 223

Objectivity does not therefore mean independence in relation to the assimilatory activity of intelligence, but simply dissociation from the self and from egocentric subjectivity. *The Origin of Intelligence in the Child*, p. 367

The centration/decentration opposition

In everyday actuality there is no hard and fast distinction between centred and uncentred forms of thought, so the centration/decentration opposition has to be seen as a heuristic tool which enables us to apprehend forms of

thought, rather than as a concrete fact. Any given form of thought will be centred or decentred to a greater or lesser extent.

The difficulty of this approach to sociocognitive centration is that it operates in relation to very different social referents. It can operate by centration based.

(a) on the assimilation of the norms of a particular social category (class, nationality, generation, etc.) Or

(b) on those of much more restricted social groups (reference groups).

It can also be based:

(c) on more abstract models of explanation (theories, doctrines, political or religious ideologies).

Or finally:

(d) it can rely on much more personal systems of reference, derived from specific experiences.

There is a sense in which all individuals or groups are centred. All have an environment, and define their identity through processes of centration, and all centration is a function of an infinity of social factors, as well as of the practices and personal experiences of individuals. Nonetheless we need to separate out the most general and important sociocognitive processes and mechanisms (the social regularities) and try to construct a typology of the different forms of social centration and decentration operating in actual everyday life.

The centration/decentration opposition has something in common with the opposition between subjectivity and objectivity. The egocentrism which Piaget discovered in children is characteristic of a pre-logical mode of thought. Knowledge has its origins in sensorimotor activity and comes to fruition in a system of operations (reversible interiorised actions). But it cannot do without representations (the use of signs, symbols, visual representations, etc.), and 'representational thought' is as much an obstacle as an aid to the development of operational thought because it encourages the static aspects of reality (configurations, states, and so on) at the expense of change (transitions from one state to another). It also favours the individual viewpoint, the consequence of which is an absence of reversibility in this type of thought.[5] In order to grasp the fact that a change (a change of form or a displacement) can happen in both directions (inversion), or that a relationship can be understood in more than one way (x is the father of y, or y is the son of x), the subject must be capable of adopting a point of view other than his own.

Egocentrism in children's thought is in fact linked to sociological egocentrism in two ways. First, because the transcendence of egocentrism in favour of operational thought goes hand in hand with the subject's socialisation (their ability to co-operate); only by taking all possible viewpoints into

account does the subject reach the level of operational thought. And secondly because the threefold division into sensorimotor action, representation and operations recurs at the level of collective thought as, in Piaget's terms, technique, ideology and science. Egocentrism is here replaced by sociocentrism. There is certainly an analogical relation between ego- and sociocentrism, insofar as both stem from representation, which plays a dual role, as both preparation and hindrance, for operational thought and for science.

Looking at actual individuals, though, there is a need to keep the two functions separate, as subjects may achieve a high degree of decentration in their mastery of formal operations (such as logic), yet remain extremely sociocentric in their judgements about the behaviour of the Other.

Generally speaking, all adults are capable of cognitive decentration, but this does not preclude them from being sociocentric as well. This is well illustrated by the following example from our investigation:

> *470007*
> ... the milling machine was going all one Sunday, then every evening for a fortnight. You've got to have strong nerves to put up with that. But to them it's just natural. 'We live here ... we can do what we like.' *So it's really us who are the foreigners.*

This demonstrates clearly that the speaker is able to handle the reversibility implicit in a symmetrical relation of the 'x is a foreigner to y' type. But the ironic conclusion, coming after a series of statements in which foreigners are portrayed as loud and insensitive to their neighbours, in contrast to the politeness and discretion of the Swiss, is an expression of astonishment, or of a sense of absurdity, at allowing a situation which might seem logically possible, and which could even be used as a debating device to justify his own position, to become a Reality. This example is sufficient to distinguish the two different types of centration: egocentric and sociocentric (further proof that we cannot regard sociocentrism merely as a relic of infantile thought).

In sociocognitive centration we again find this constant attempt to 'arrange' new facts into pre-existing categories (assimilation), which works to the detriment of the inverse process (accommodation) with its tendency to identify differences between new facts and the categories regarded as relevant. This conception of centration also brings out the nature of decentration. In the apprehension of the real there are limits to the search for difference. Beyond a certain point, it leads to anomie and the destructuring of reference systems. From that point onwards, decentration cannot constitute an achievable ideal except in the realms of mathematics, logic and science. Considered from the sociocognitive level, it becomes clear that centration is a function of individuals' social experience. A variety of different social factors will affect the nature and degree of centration or decentration. This justifies

the transition from the concept of cognitive centration to that of sociocognitive centration, and shows that in everyday life we are dealing with practical logics in social contexts.

Concrete analysis of sociocentric discourse

The sociocognitive mechanisms characteristic of sociocentrism
We begin by analysing the sociocognitive mechanisms likely to cast more light on sociocentrism, dealing in turn with

the tendency towards essentialism
normativism
false identification
one-dimensionality

Then in a second section we analyse different forms of centration, presenting them in the form of a typology going from centration at its most extreme to its complete absence.

The tendency towards essentialism
Essentialism represents one of the most obvious and familiar characteristics of ideologies. Every system of political and social representation is organised around essences, natures or noumena which are regarded as, by nature, transcendent, unalterable and historical. This is particularly recognised to be the case in philosophical systems where, since Plato, there has been an unrestricted increase in pairs of concepts, one element of which refers to a genuine Reality (the world of essences) and the other to Appearance. This is equally true of ideological discourses concerned with groups and social phenomena. Some aspects of this essentialism are well known; what we are interested in here is their connection with the problem of centration and decentration.

Take the way a speaker perceives himself and identifies himself through his discourse, an example of which can be seen in the following extract from an interview:

540038
A: As I said, I'm patriotic. I like to see the Swiss win, because I'm Swiss.
B: What does being Swiss mean to you?
A: Oh it's tremendously important to me, being Swiss. I'm Swiss. That's something very important to me. I don't know why. It's just that I'm Swiss. I don't know how else you can put it. Despite all the stupid things they do, doesn't matter what they are, I'm still Swiss. But I'm not Swiss to please the government or anything like that, I'm Swiss for myself and for the Swiss people.

In short, the speaker is saying that he is determined by the social identity he expresses. He feels Swiss in the same way as a man feels he is a man or a woman feels she is a woman. He does perceive himself as an individual who belongs to a group, but as someone sharing an Essence (or an Idea, in the platonic sense). This is one characteristic of ideological discourse and its logic. Where formal logic is extensional (because it refers to sets and their relations of inclusion, combination, intersection, etc.), the logic of ideology is usually intentional. The inferences encountered in it are based on associations of meaning.

The speaker quoted above recognised the faults of some Swiss people but did not feel affected by them. National identity is asserted as eternal, inalienable, indissoluble and exclusive. The behaviour of the community, whatever form it takes, cannot affect the sense of identity. In the speaker's eyes, the reality is of little importance: what counts is the affirmation of the Self, which in this case is national.

This discourse reveals the fascination that the idea of being Swiss has for the subject who identifies with it, as well as the difficulties he has in putting it into words: 'I don't know why.' This has that sense of an obviousness which cannot be put into words: 'It's just that I'm Swiss. I don't know how else you can put it.'

The judgements this type of speaker is going to make about social reality, about Switzerland and Foreigners, will owe a considerable part of their sociocentric nature to this essentialist scheme of knowledge

Similarly in the interview with the following couple:[6]

460118

He: You mean there are some people who say Switzerland's image is getting worse?

She: It could well be, what with all the foreigners there are here. They don't all know how to behave.

He: No, I don't think the image of Switzerland is getting any worse, but Switzerland's still making sacrifices, all the same.

She: I agree, but we do still get tired of it sometimes, all these people in the street, talking too loud and arguing. I don't know how many times I've not been able to sleep, and I've looked out of the window and it's always foreigners who are arguing in the street, talking at the tops of their voices in the middle of the night.

So if the image of Switzerland is deteriorating, it can only be the fault of foreigners. If the image of Switzerland is not deteriorating, it is thanks to the sacrifices the country is making. Centration has its own characteristic way of understanding: positive consequences are attributed to endogenous causes, negative consequences to exogenous causes. Later in the interview, the interviewer asked the same question again. This was the reply:

He: No, I can't say it's deteriorating. It's been made worse by all these foreigners. Not that I'm against foreigners, I'm not. I've been in Italy, I've been in France, but when I was there I didn't go painting the houses all sorts of colours, or shouting and demonstrating in the streets. I was a foreigner in those countries so I kept my mouth shut . . .

She: I think they're very noisy, I don't think they should be allowed to have all these demonstrations, especially when they're in a neutral country.

The speaker seems to be unaware of the contradiction between the statements 'No, I can't say it's deteriorating' and 'It's been made worse'. In fact he seems to be talking about two different Switzerlands, one abstract, pure, eternal and unalterable, the other concrete and in the grip of foreigners.

Here we can see something of the content of this Swissness, this attachment to an abstract, idealised Switzerland: Switzerland as a 'neutral country' is contrasted with the demonstrations and political attitudes of foreigners. For the speaker 'neutral' means not only free from all external influences, but also free from any political debate, an aseptic environment which she cannot but see as now being contaminated.

In the following passage, we can see how the abstract Idea of Switzerland reaches a point where it no longer has any content, and thus reaches the level of pure signifier:

Q: What sort of thing would you like to hear in a 1st of August speech? [1 August is a Swiss national holiday]

He: I don't know what I'd like to hear, it's always fine words about the progress of the Confederation.

She: Of course it's always a good speech, it's a holiday.

He: They can't say what you want to hear, that things are quietening down in neighbouring countries, that things will be more peaceful and there won't be any more hostage-taking . . .

She: Oh those hostages, it's dreadful.

The speakers don't answer the question, they can't say. As they see it, 'it's always a good speech, it's a holiday'. So the holiday, which demonstrates and celebrates the Progress of the Confederation, is self-sufficient, creating a sense of belonging to a social group, which is the nation.

It doesn't seem to matter what the National Holiday orator says, so long as he speaks and thereby celebrates the festival: it is speech without discourse. But, for these speakers, that does not matter as long as there is a 'good speech'.

The 1st of August speech, the archetype of the political speech aimed at consensus and eternisation, is therefore only important for its form and the context in which it takes place (bonfires, fairy-lights, fireworks); the personality of the speaker and the content of the speech have no practical existence.

Furthermore the form itself is sacralised: it is 'always' a good speech because it is the National Holiday.

After this brief description of the emotional significance of the National Holiday the speakers try, despite everything, to answer the question. What do they think the 1st of August speech ought to be about? Somewhat surprisingly, it is not patriotic topics, international problems or social questions that they come up with: instead they jump straight from the 1st of August speech to the taking of hostages in neighbouring countries.

Within the in-group the speakers do not see what could be a problem. This is the more surprising as they have been bringing up a series of issues they feel dissatisfied about throughout the interview. They are by no means happy with the concrete reality of Switzerland, which they perceive very negatively. Yet for them the concrete Switzerland is not, in the end, the real Switzerland. The 1st of August speech has to be related to a mythical idea of the eternal Switzerland, not to its practical reality.

Here we have a very good illustration of the way essentialist thought is used, and of its close connection with sociocentrism. The speakers associate the National Holiday directly with the idea of a mythical Switzerland, sheltered from the vicissitudes of history. However justified one might be in hoping for something better in the future, that cannot concern this ideal Switzerland. So they move straight on to the Evil that exists in 'the neighbouring countries' (agitation, hostage-taking). Manicheism, which generates antitheses, encourages oppositions like Good and Evil, abstract and concrete Switzerland, National Holiday (good) and hostage-taking (evil), and finally Swiss and Foreign, all of which overlap within a powerfully sociocentric perspective.

Normativism: an abnormal perception of alterity
The *normative* perception of human behaviour, which is linked to essentialism, is another characteristic of ideological discourse, and an important manifestation of sociocentrism. The group the speaker belongs to is, as he sees it, the only one that represents Normality.

> *470021*
> We ought to isolate ourselves a bit, the only languages you ever hear are Italian and Spanish, you can't really feel at home. If you're on a tram, you talk quietly, you show some restraint. But you hear Spaniards and Italians on every tram. Personally I think there ought to be a minimum standard of education for people coming to a country that's not their own.

In this passage, foreigners are perceived as badly educated. Far from considering the possibility that their behaviour might be governed by other rules of sociability, the speaker regards the education he received as the only sort possible. He is incapable of imagining that there might be other, equally

valid, ways of behaving in society. When he says 'I think there ought to be a minimum standard of education for people coming to a country that's not their own', the speaker is perceiving foreigners not just as badly educated but as completely uneducated. This attitude expresses a much more extreme sociocentrism than the form which effectively asks foreigners to adapt to the ways and customs of Swiss society.

The speaker does not perceive that the norms governing a group's social life are relative. The exclusive valorisation of the in-group's norms of behaviour is to some extent related to the speaker's own situation in relation to these norms. We argue that there are extremely rigorous, inflexible rules which he interiorises and which guide his various practices, dictating how he should conduct himself on all occasions, down to the last detail: 'When we are on trams, we talk quietly'. The speaker reveals himself as constantly on show to others, always anxious for their good opinion, and on the lookout for any departure from 'good behaviour' either on his own part or on the part of those around him. From this viewpoint, it is easier to understand that the centration/decentration problem is not just a question of a particular point of view (that of the knowing subject), but that its roots go deep into the social and unconscious structuring of everyone's personality. This is why the more 'carefree' behaviour of foreigners never fails to arouse hostility among the indigenous inhabitants, a hostility which is also a symptom of anxiety at the prohibitions imposed on them by their superegos.

In the next extract, a speaker explains his feelings about street demonstrations:

460118
I've been in Italy, I've been in France, but when I was there I didn't go painting the houses all sorts of colours, or shouting and demonstrating in the streets, I was a foreigner in those countries, so I kept my mouth shut . . . These people don't do that, though. I never went round making a row in Paris, and I was there during the riots.

The speaker criticises foreigners for demonstrating in the streets because he regards it as wrong. He kept quiet when he was abroad. He puts forward his own attitude as the only possible model, and is strongly critical of anybody who does not adopt it. There is certainly a degree of reciprocity in the speaker's attitude: one should not do in other people's countries what one would not wish them to do in one's own; but this reciprocity is used as an argument in support of the speaker's own egocentrism. On one hand, it is unlikely that the speaker would agree with any street demonstrations, whether they were organised by foreigners or by the Swiss; on the other hand, he does not ask himself whether the foreigners might have a reason for demonstrating, or whether the situation he was in abroad is comparable to other situations. His

attitude is revealed as stemming from a matter of principle. His *condemnation* is inspired by an 'objective' morality which restricts the relevance of the problem to 'hard facts'. The significance of these facts is derived only from their approximation to the nationalist axiom, 'I'm a foreigner in this country, so I must keep my mouth shut.'

This compulsory adherence to the norms of conduct and the value systems interiorised by the speaker is well illustrated by another passage, part of which we have already cited:

470007

Q: What do you think the difference is [between the Swiss and foreigners]?

A: Well, they're always having parties, they never seem to go to bed, they keep us awake. And we just have to put up with it, because if we make the slightest comment to them about it, it's always 'We live here, we can do what we like.' We have some consideration for other people; we wear slippers in the flat, we don't annoy the neighbours, we keep the sound down on the TV.

The milling machine was going all one Sunday, then every evening for a fortnight. You've got to have strong nerves to put up with that. But to them it's just natural. 'We live here . . . we can do what we like.' So it's really us who are the foreigners.

Here we can see the same submission on the part of the speaker to a system of inflexible rules. What is interesting, though, is the linguistic form of this discourse. If we remove the punctuation (which was added in the transcription), we get a series of equivocal statements:

we make the slightest comment to them
we live here
we can do what we like
we have some consideration for other people, etc.

'We' sometimes refers to the speaker and his Swiss friends or family, and sometimes to the foreigners. Only the tone of voice enables us to distinguish the speaking subject from the subject of the statement. This play on the subjects of the discourse tells us something about the imaginary process in which the speaker places himself.

If he had said, 'If we make the slightest comment, *they reply* "We live here, we can do what we like"', the speaker would have been speaking for and on behalf of the foreigners. But he does not repeat their words, he simulates their discourse.[7]

This interdiscourse is all the more ambiguous as it bears on the content,

which the speaker believes that he alone has the right to be able to put forward. It is he who really 'lives here', centred in a self-referential centre, and therefore in the right.

The same irony occurs more explicitly in the concluding words, 'So it's really us who are the foreigners.'

One cannot help seeing an egocentric identification of the speaker and foreigners in this disconnected sequence of 'we's'. The speaker describes the foreigners as objects. He sets them in context and incorporates them into his description of the situation. At no point does he operate a distinction between the subjects thus described. It is always he who speaks, not only because the foreigners are absent, but because they are not regarded as authentic subjects.

So we get the impression that there is only one subject in the discourse, the speaking subject who reveals himself by hiding himself in the equivocal play of reference of the subjects of the statement. There seems to be an imaginary dialogue going on between the speaker and himself, between the speaker as he defends an identity and the speaker as he feels himself to be a foreigner *vis-à-vis* the general development of society.

Yet it must be added that this exclusivity of the behavioural norms of the in-group is not a hindrance to the perception of Alterity. That is just seen as natural, but abnormal. In the passage quoted above, the speaker says 'But to them *it's just natural.*' This means that he regards the fact of behaving differently as natural. This appeal to Nature, or this naturalisation, can be linked with the next extract:

> 450032
> Anyway, they're *naturally* dirty, so if they move into a house they won't keep it clean. And if you gave them clean accommodation, God knows how long it would last.

Alterity is recognised as a fact of nature, yet this does nothing to make it more comprehensible. In the two instances cited above, the appeal to the natural merely expresses the speaker's surprise: 'Do you realise?', and his refusal to envisage change of any sort, either in himself or in the Other. 'Anyway, they're naturally . . .' Alterity is recognised and described, only to be immediately devalorised and marked down as irretrievably incomprehensible.

What we are describing here is the joint functioning (the structural nature) of the different sociocognitive mechanisms: essentialisation, generalisation,[8] moral reification,[9] homogenisation and the naturalising perception of social behaviour.

We can see how important it is to take the speaking subject into consideration. Because, above and beyond what is explicitly said in the discourses we are analysing, we can make out something of the largely unconscious nature

of the speaker's personality and cognitive and ideological universe, the sociocognitive mechanisms which are the instruments by means of which – faced with a complex environment – he does everything he can, often to the detriment of truth, to introduce some coherence into his discourse, or to allay the anxiety he feels as he confronts the dangers of the strange or unfamiliar.

(False) identification

Ordinary social thought is distinguishable from scientific thought by its preference for resemblance rather than difference. According to Piaget, knowledge only achieves objectivity through a constant search for an equilibrium between a tendency to assimilate new ideas into pre-existing constructs (or schemas or concepts) and an opposite tendency to accommodate to them. Sociocognitive centration seems to be an excess of assimilation, characterised as it is by an unceasing attempt to reduce new facts to already constructed categories. This is what we call a process of *identification*.[10] To begin with, there is a system of privileged values, which is normal, but then everything which is regarded as compatible with this system of values becomes identified with it, and everything that is opposed to it will simply be rejected. Ideological discourse therefore only uses what is common to two realities and rejects what is foreign to them in order to be able to identify one with the other. Thus if object 'a' has properties P_1 and P_2, and object 'b' has properties P_2 and P_3, 'a' will be identified with 'b' on the basis of P_2, but by the same token the other two properties will be ignored.

This very common identification mechanism results in the creation of systems of objects, properties and values which can be defined as 'crystallised', as each element in the system is linked to another by ideological association. This identification operates within all social discourse in a variety of forms, the main ones being the creation of individuated abstractions (personification) or abstract individuals (essentialisation): thus we get 'the Swiss', 'an Italian', 'a civil servant', 'the police', 'Switzerland', 'our country', etc.

We shall meet a similar phenomenon in the next passage:

070019

> ... I'm absolutely amazed, I'd like to have one of them here now. Unfortunately, I've got a grandson who's a conscientious objector. I've never had a chance to ask him, 'What would you do if there was a war? How would you deal with that? You've got a family, a wife, children: where's your courage? Could you defend your family? Maybe you couldn't even do that.' Perhaps he'd put up his hands; he could do. Do you think that's courage? I think it's a disgrace.

Q: But what reasons do they have?

A: I don't understand them. Yellow cowards. He's got no courage, feeble coward.

We can say that the speaker's value system is constructed on two closed series of associations:

(1)   Military service – courage – sense of duty – self-control
(2)   Conscientious objection – fear – cowardice – idleness

Not only is each element in these sequences clearly connected with the others by a relation which in some cases can be verified, it is also *identified* with those elements. The implications of this are self-evident. If conscientious objection entails not doing military service, it also entails an absence of courage, which the speaker regards as the same thing, and therefore fear, idleness and cowardice. It is also interesting to note that in everyday thought, negation and contradiction are often confused. In formal logic, the absence of cowardice does not necessarily mean the presence of courage.

This sort of logic induces the speaker to exercise his judgement first on the action itself, not on the situation which gave rise to it. In this perspective, the meaning which social actors give to their actions is not regarded as a relevant factor in evaluating the situation. Whether there might be other value systems to take into account is not a question which is ever raised.

The absence of decentration is further illustrated here by the fact that the speaker tries to convict the objectors (imaginary dialogue with his grandson) rather than to understand the reason for their behaviour. As he sees it, understanding is only to be gained from the objector's answers to the questions he asks. These questions signal the problematic which objectors can raise within the framework of the interrogation. The speaker can only express astonishment: 'I'm absolutely amazed'. And this surprise, far from provoking a decentration in relation to his value system, reaffirms it.

Here is another example, on the same theme:

010064
Q: Why are young people so much more hostile to the army now than ten or fifteen years ago?
A: A lot of young people want an easy life. A lot of them, quite frankly, are nervous. OK, there are some conscientious objectors, but some of the young people are nervous, they're afraid to do national service. I'm convinced that out of every hundred young men (not conscientious objectors, people who'd prefer not to do their service) there are some cases who ought to be looked at by a psychoanalyst, there are some who are uptight or neurotic, and there are certainly a lot who are just plain frightened.

Although the speaker here is more sensitive to the subtler differences (he distinguishes 'conscientious objectors' from 'people who'd prefer not to do their service'), there is still the same process of identification generating

crystallised associations, in the sequence: Hostility – Nervousness – Neurosis, which itself stems from a previous association between an Easy Life and Nervousness.

It is also interesting to see how the speaker ignores his initial percentage formulation 'out of every hundred young men . . .' The desire to relativise is immediately repressed by the tendency towards homogenisation (a special case of identification). Thus, as in the previous example, the speaker's references are the only ones capable of providing a basis for acceptable behaviour. Alterity is shifted into illness. The difference is pathological. There is a biologisation and a psychologisation of the social.

The same speaker has this to say on the subject of the *Paix de Travail*:

010038

Q: You mentioned strikes. In Switzerland there's the *Paix de Travail*; how do you explain the fact that Switzerland is the only country . . .

A: Well, you realise the Swiss are a mountain people, a bit cold perhaps, but always reasonable, they understand things pretty well. Even the ordinary worker is always prepared to discuss things, he's well aware of the benefits of it.

We asked the speaker for an explanation. The one he gave also comes down to an association by identification (Reasonable – no strikes), and a paired opposition (Unreasonable – Strikes). 'Reasonable' itself is associated with 'benefits'. So the speaker's judgement is not the result of an evaluation of the concrete situation in Switzerland, and all the features peculiar to it, but of a pre-existing conviction valid in all circumstances: strikes cannot be a reasonable mode of action, thus if there are no strikes the workers must be reasonable. What is at work here is a process very common in ordinary social thought, and one which is linked to the mechanisms of identification, to wit the reversal of antecedent and consequence in an implication. It is quite plausible that the basic proposition, so far as the speaker is concerned, is: 'If you are reasonable, you don't go on strike'. But in fact he expresses the reciprocal of this: 'If there aren't any strikes, it's because the Swiss workers are reasonable'.

It is noteworthy that the association '*Paix de Travail* – No strikes' does not provoke any surprise. In the context of Swiss politics, it goes without saying. Its normative character is equally obvious. The norm of the majority is seen not as a norm but as self-evident. The sociocognitive centration of the majority is almost invisible, and therefore all the more effective.

Identification, as it operates in the discourses analysed here, is generally concerned with the pairing: Action – Moral qualities. This association recurs too often for it to be possible to ignore the idea of sociocognitive mechanisms. Let us look, for example, at an interview about Jura separatism:[11]

070029

Q: Which category of the population has most separatists, do you think?

A: In the Jura? Well, those who are brave enough are separatists, and those who aren't, aren't.

Q: But do you think they're mostly workers, or country-folk, or the rich? The young or the old?

A: It's the older ones who are the separatists, because I know some of them, I know some people from the Jura here, they're not young, but they are in favour of Jura separatism.

The speaker does not see the relevance of the sociological categories put forward by the interviewer. Instead he assesses the situation in terms of the association: Action – Moral qualities. The other implication also operates: if someone is brave, then he is a separatist, and if he is a separatist, then he is brave.

050033

Q: Why are there strikes in other countries and not in Switzerland?

A: Because French workers never do much work anyway, quite apart from all their strikes and holidays, they're always complaining about something or other. And they don't realise that as long as they keep on going on strike right and left, the country's economy will never get anywhere. And the Italians, well they're on strike pretty well all the time from 1 December to 31 January, and what do they get out of it? Whereas here, because striking is forbidden, more or less, nobody can say they're poor, apart from Geneva which is up to its ears in debt. You only have to look at Germany after the war to see that striking isn't the way to pay off debts. And now they're one of the richest countries in the world. And never a year without strikes in France and Italy.

Q: Why have the Swiss understood this and not the French?

A: Because the French are different. The Swiss are better educated. As long as the French have got their bread and wine and a bit of cheese, they're happy. But the Swiss want Switzerland to stay as it should be. But the young people are turning towards Marxism, and they'd change everything if they could.

Here we can see identification operating at several different levels. At the level of national stereotype, there is the sequence: French – Italians – irresponsibility – idleness – conflict, which is contrasted with the other sequence: Swiss – German – serious – *Paix du Travail*. At another level, the speaker, like the previous speaker, associates strikes with irrationality, and reason with the *Paix du Travail*.

A third level, the most sociocentric one, identifies Switzerland with every-

Level I   Nationalist opposition

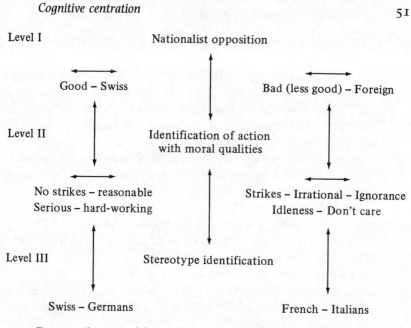

Figure 3.1 Structure of the speaker's social representations

thing good ('as it should be'). There is, as it were, a circulation of meaning, which moves both from the first level to the third and from the third to the first. Dual implication operates as much between levels as among the elements of the same level.

The speaker seems to be assessing each situation of the basis of his a priori system of social representations. The system's component elements are perceived as inseparable from each other. Thus the notion of strike is 'soldered' on to those of 'idleness', 'complaining' and 'ignorance'. Once this system has been constructed on the basis of the nationalist opposition between Swiss and Foreign (strikes are foreign, the *Paix du Travail* is Swiss), it can be used to interpret any set of events.

It is not conceptually possible, in this system, to go on strike and to be reasonable, or to be a good worker and to go on strike. All the components of the structure entail each other. The characteristics of the nation (the in-group) – *Paix du Travail*, the value of work, education, moderation – are taken over and refined to create the basic elements of the structure.

A final example will demonstrate how these crystallised identification systems function as a priori conditions for the way of knowing social reality.

450051
Q: What do think about the unions in Switzerland?
A: I hate them. They do a lot of harm as well. I don't like it when unions encourage their members to go on strike because I'm too fond of order.

Q: But they're not encouraged to strike so much now that they've signed the *Paix du Travail*.

A: Yes, but I think the unions, the workers, get too worked up. Mind you, I'm not trying to run them down, my husband's been a member for years, and he sets a lot of store by the union magazine. Perhaps in this country they behave sensibly, though they do sometimes do a bit of propagandising in the workplace.

Q: Do you think Swiss workers are capable of defending their interests?

A: Yes, though there's no need to defend them, because the employers are more scrupulous than in the surrounding countries. If you look at the French unions, they do a lot of harm sometimes and they support strikes, it's terrible. The same in Italy. Workers in Switzerland have got nothing to complain about. They've all got a car and a flat with a bathroom, they're fine.

Q: But haven't there been some strikes this year?

A: Yes, precisely. Legally, those strikes shouldn't happen. There's no right to strike in Switzerland. Why do they do it? Because they want to be like other countries.

This interview, like the others, contains the crystallised association: Strikes – Disorder – Abnormal, to which is added 'Union'. The latter term is absorbed by the sequence of associations so any judgement about it will be predetermined. In fact, if we define the three main content areas to which reference is made in this discourse, we get:

A an assessment by the speaker of trade union practices
B an assessment by the speaker of employers' practices
C an assessment by the speaker of working-class conditions

If we then compare what is said about Switzerland with what is said about other countries, we discover that:

A does not change – in both cases, unions 'do harm';

B varies according to whether the situation is Swiss or foreign: 'In Switzerland the employers are more scrupulous';

C also varies: 'Workers in Switzerland have got nothing to complain about', which implies that the situation in other countries is not so favourable.

A therefore remains unchanged whatever context it occurs in. Trade union practices are regarded as bad, regardless of the situation they may be working in, because they imply a challenge to the established order. The speaker does not regard the attitude of the employers or the condition of the workers as relevant to an assessment of trade union practices.

As in any process of identification, the concrete totality is dissociated, and only those elements that can be identified in other totalities as well are

retained. The trade union practices are dissociated from their context. The unions are judged and condemned as troublemakers without first assessing the specific situations in which they intervene.

Order also plays an important part in this speaker's argument. The reason why trade union practices are so strongly criticised is because they are identified with disorder. Sociocentrism, with its refusal to enter the realm of difference, frequently appeals to order. Disorder and noise not only upset everyday habits, they also disturb habits of thinking, ways of knowing, especially when the latter are inflexible. Unlike a cognitive process of analysis, all sociocentrism can do is judge and condemn.

So we have defined a very widespread mechanism of ordinary social thought, that of identification. It is a mechanism which throws significant new light on the centration/decentration problem. Sociocognitive centration is first and foremost a defence of the identity against attack from anything unfamiliar, foreign or new. The mechanism which then comes into play reduces diversity to a very small number of entities or even, as in nationalist discourse, to two opposing poles, Swiss and Foreign, and on that basis, by equivalence and assimilation, creates a set of a priori judgements about the whole of social reality.

One-dimensionality

The tendency towards reduction characteristic of identification can also be seen in discourse as a one-dimensional reading of social reality. This characteristic operates in two ways:

(a) The speaker may appeal to a single criterion, or a single factor, to explain any social phenomenon, no matter what. There can therefore only ever be one (moral) reason for breaking the *Paix du Travail*, or for anti-militarism. This is causal supersaturation. Identification, assimilating meanings to each other by dual implication, logically leads to a one-dimensional outlook. In this case, that outlook is determined at the deepest level by nationalist and patriotic categories. We can therefore talk about nationalist centration from this point of view.

(b) The speaker may, on the other hand, put forward his own point of view as a single frame of reference for everybody. This is not surprising. Nothing seems obvious unless it is shared. The objective search for truth proceeds via intersubjectivity. But the chief characteristic of these forms of social thought that are so highly centred by comparison with scientific thought, where this intersubjective agreement is the result of a mutual exchange, is the fact that the subject demands agreement unilaterally. Thus if he comes up against a different system of values, all he can do is devalorise them a priori, or else register surprise and incomprehension that anyone should think differently from him.

We shall deal with nationalist centration first, and then go on to look at the subjective projection of speakers' frames of reference.

Sociocognitive centration based on nationalism. The following passage illustrates this type of centration:

070047

If you listen to 'Les Métiers' on the radio at quarter past twelve it's very interesting, the jobs they do, they manage to answer about 90 per cent of the questions one way or another. I like it when it's a foreigner, some of them are really good, you know, like that Italian from Chêne-Bourg, the tobacconist, he was champion one time, he won 1,200 francs. He had spirit. He said, 'I've lived in Geneva for 25 years so I think of myself as a Genevan.' That's great, I agree with that. He knew the answers, he was witty, he had a Geneva accent and he was . . . he had all the qualities of a real Swiss. But what about the ones that can't even speak the language? Why do people come 6,000 kilometres from Chile to Switzerland?

Q: That's a different question, that's to do with political refugees. That's something different, isn't it?

A: Yes, OK. But these people get here and the first thing they want to do is have three months' holiday. They're just a load of scroungers. They don't seem to have any idea of what work means. I mean, when I think what things were like when I was young, well . . . [laughter]

The devalorisation of the out-group and the valorisation of the in-group which are expressed so clearly here are not our immediate concern. It is clear that, in answer to the interviewer's question which tried to establish a difference between candidates for naturalisation and political refugees, the speaker acknowledges this difference, which he had previously ignored as if it didn't have any relevance to him on its own. Then he reasserts what he sees as the only really relevant factors: the 'idea of what work means', which he perceives as belonging to the Swiss (both in the sense of possession and of characteristic). Where the refugees come from, why, and what they hope to do in the future, play no part in his assessment of the situation. The only important issue is 'the idea of what work means', which, as far as the speaker is concerned, a foreigner cannot – as a matter of principle – possess to the same degree as the Swiss themselves.

This, therefore, shows how all the sociocognitive mechanisms operate at the same time. The nationalist centration derives from essentialism (the ideal Switzerland), which in turn is closely linked with the process of identification (Swiss = idea of work), as well as with the normative perception of the social. The centration on the Norms prevents him from taking the situation into

account, so that only in-group values can be used as a passport: survival, or escape from death, cannot supplant respect for the Norms.

The interview continued by examining the refugee issue:

070049

Q: So, going back to political refugees, you're not in favour of them?

A: Absolutely not. And I'm against that well-known one, Kaiser, the *Terre des Hommes* one, a Frenchman who came to Switzerland because he thought it would be easier to get lots of stories. Why doesn't he go to France, and make his *Terre des Hommes* in Paris? Eh? Because there are nearly 900 charitable organisations in Geneva, and he thinks he can always scrape something together here. And then he wanted to bring over – he wanted to but fortunately the Canton of Geneva wouldn't allow it – he wanted to bring over 50 Tunisians it was at first, then 50 Vietnamese. Can't the Tunisians look after their own kids? Do they have to come to Switzerland to do it? And then most of them end up in court because they don't have anything better to do. If you just look at the case recently of those three lads, four lads, who did a series of break-ins, they got a suspended sentence; the next day they'll be out doing it again.

One of the main assumptions of nationalism is implicit in the statement: 'Can't the Tunisians look after their own kids?'

Put another way, this means: everybody ought to be at home looking after their own affairs. No circumstances, no emergency situation, can justify going against this assumption. National frontiers are turned into demarcation lines within the speaker's mental functioning. This is what is meant by national-cognitive centration.

070070

Q: But it's always been a Swiss tradition to accept refugees.

A: Yes, it is a Swiss tradition, but it needs a bit of sorting out, this Swiss tradition.

Q: . . . during the war, then the Hungarians, etc.

A: Of course. There was some value in that because of the people who came here. Though mind you there were some pretty duff types among the Hungarians, and some of the ones that slipped through probably ended up in court for burglary, but yes, we're very good about it in Switzerland.

We can see here that even traditional Swiss values like welcoming refugees (whose value the speaker acknowledges) has to be subordinated to the nationalist assumption. So even 'tradition' needs 'a bit of sorting out' when it fails to keep out foreigners who don't fit in with the speaker's norms.

Memories of the war seem for a moment to supplant the nationalist assumption, but this is only momentary. The Foreigner–Criminal association re-establishes order.

There is another example of nationalist centration in the next passage. The speaker was asked about favouritism in employment benefiting either Swiss or foreign workers.

> 260035
> If the employer is foreign, and there are a large number of foreign employers in Geneva, then foreigners receive favourable treatment. If the employer is Swiss, then the opposite happens.

The problem of privileges can be defined exclusively in nationalist categories. The employers do not act out of self-interest, but out of some supposed omnipresent attribute. The linguistic form of this statement is also interesting. The absence of centration is clearly marked by its apodictic nature. For the speaker it is not just a matter of fact, in which case he could have said, 'Most employers . . .' or 'If the employer is Swiss, he will often . . .', but a necessary, universal law. According to this statement, it is impossible to find an employer who does not give special treatment to his compatriots.

At the end of his explanation, the speaker mentions the fact that foreigners are prepared to accept lower wages:

> My job was taken over by a Spaniard, I think because he didn't want such a high wage. It's bad when employers behave like that.

The speaker is more repelled by the idea that the employer could act out of interested motives than by the existence of privileges based solely on nationalist considerations. The latter eventuality would seem less unjust to him, because it would be part of the order – his nationalist order – of things.

The question that obviously arises from this, is why the nationality in-group is more susceptible to egocentric identification than other in-groups (such as the working class, for instance), and although it is difficult to provide a complete answer, there are several lines of thought which suggest themselves.

The nationality in-group is not a simple reference group, centred on 'resistance' or common interests. For a thorough-going nationalist, it is a group capable of symbolising important elements of affective experience. It can evoke both paternal and maternal images (which is not the case with the working class). The nationality in-group is self-sufficient; it is possible to live entirely within Switzerland in the imagination, but it is more difficult to live harmoniously entirely within the working class which, by definition, is practically and concretely opposed to other social classes. The nationality in-group enables a turn, or return, or perhaps a *regression from the political to the psycho-familial*, which is another basic sociocognitive mechanism.

It is therefore possible to conceive of Switzerland as a womb. A nostalgia for narcissistic completeness. This does not mean that special identification with the nation arises out of all these images. But it seems reasonable to suggest that only the nation allows a sufficiently large number of affective needs to be satisfied within the framework of a form of thought which stems at this point from sociocognitive centration.

Projection of the frame of reference. Under this heading comes a fairly common type of expression of sociocognitive centration through discourse. From the range of possible criteria, the speaker selects one single criterion of judgement, one problematic, which he regards as his own. This he then projects, and regards as equally valid for everybody.

The following passage cropped up in connection with Jura separatism:

460027

Q: Who would you support, the people who want the new canton, or the ones who don't, seeing that the Swiss people will have to vote on the issue?

She: I think they're wrong, in a way, because after all it's Berne that's responsible for maintaining the roads, and if they want to be totally independent they'll find it very expensive. In fact the Confederation contributes to a lot of things. I don't understand why they ever wanted to be independent, because I've always regarded them as Swiss like us, I just don't see why they need to be independent.

He: I mean, personally, I'm not Genevan, I'm Swiss.

She: That's right, there aren't any frontiers, we're all Swiss.

He: I don't think there are any frontiers. I come from Zürich, I live in Geneva, I'm Swiss.

She: Well obviously there aren't any frontiers, we're all Swiss.

'I've always regarded them as Swiss like us': this comment shows how much the Jura question disturbs the speakers. The desire of the inhabitants of the Jura for independence is an assault on the representation ordered around national identity. The speakers seem to be asking how anyone could feel Jurassian. This bears witness to the difficulty they have in understanding a logic that runs counter to the one they have interiorised. Their hierarchy of values seems to them to be valid for everyone, and they do not consider the Jurassians' desire for independence as enough of a priority to outweigh national unity. The only sociological division they recognise as relevant is that based on national frontiers: 'there aren't any frontiers, we're all Swiss'.

At the heart of the centration is a *limitation of the possible*, a one-dimensional division of reality. Social identity thus appears to be founded on a single criterion; the speakers have no sense of belonging to several social groups

simultaneously. They give absolute priority to the social reference group which they regard as relevant to the foundations of everybody's practice. Hence their astonishment, even incredulity, at the idea that other people are demonstrably involved in a (relative) reversal of these priorities.

It is noteworthy how the speakers' centration in this discourse appears self-evident at the level of linguistic utterance: an individual does not do, think and say just anything, anyhow . . .

For one thing, there are a striking number of first-person personal pronouns: 'I mean personally I'm . . .' For another, the speaker uses himself as an exhibit to support his argument. What looks like a simple juxtaposition of affirmative statements – 'I'm not Genevan, I'm Swiss', 'I come from Zürich, I live in Geneva, I'm Swiss' – is in fact regarded by the speaker as a kind of reasoning. To give coherence to the fact that one may be Genevan by domicile but non-Genevan (i.e. from Zürich) by origin, he reaches the natural conclusion that the important thing is national identity.

There is another example of subjective projection in the following passage:

260046
Q: How do you set about deciding how to vote?
A: I try to base my opinion on logic. What you're voting for is either
      something good or something useless. You can usually feel whether
      it's logical or not.

For this speaker logic, or rather logicality, is a matter of feeling: 'you can usually feel . . .' In the final analysis, the logical/illogical opposition could be replaced by one between black and white, as it is as easy to detect as colour. There is an overlap between the most subjective aspect of knowledge, sensation (used here in its figurative sense) and logic which, as it requires intersubjective agreement, is the most objective. This is why the logical/illogical pairing seems self-evident and unproblematic to him: it overlaps the good/useless opposition, and perhaps even the basic opposition of Good and Evil. Logicality is accepted because it coincides with his own interests, but these interests are presented as equally valid for everyone else as well.

Later in the same interview the speaker gives an indication of the criteria by which he judges logicality:

260046
Where large sums of money are involved, like with that new road, there's no need for any fuss because things are perfectly OK as they are. I've never lost my way, I've never got somewhere and said, 'This is no good, there aren't any roads here.'

The logical, in this speaker's eyes, is what can be shown to be indispensable for the population (for the ordinary citizen). The illogical is something which is not indispensable, and is merely put forward to satisfy what he sees as private or over-clamorous interests.

We can see an association between pairs at work here, and we can trace the sequence of these pairs back, as follows:

Logical/illogical
Moderation/waste
Indispensable/unnecessary
Simple life/modern excess
Past/present

It is plausible to hypothesise a relationship between this view of what is 'logically' acceptable and the speaker's own economic situation. The centration certainly relates to a need to 'make ends meet' at the end of the month. Thus a set of individual demands, based on the speaker's practices, are expressed in the guise of a universally valid norm.

140004

Q: What, in your view, are the differences between Switzerland and the neighbouring countries?

A: Well, language, of course. And I'm on a special diet, so I have to be careful what I eat, and that's much easier to do in Switzerland.

From the first, this speaker situates himself at the level of his own immediate personal practice. He isolates one very fragmentary aspect of his daily life. The totality which his image of Switzerland might constitute is dissociated. Only one particular aspect of it is retained. Again this is typical of one-dimensionality.

So the speaker's image of other countries is a construction. He has never been to these countries, but he has formed a fairly precise idea of them: 'that's much easier', he thinks. For him, Switzerland is somewhere he knows and loves, a place where he knows what to expect. Anywhere else is unfamiliar territory. The centration which derives from immediate practice is anchored in a bi-polar construction:

Here = ease – certainty – security
Elsewhere = difficulty – uncertainty – insecurity

Switzerland is Here, and the speaker seems to feel as much at ease in Geneva as in the Engadine. The differences in way of life, custom, and language between the different regions of Switzerland are irrelevant to his representation. But once over the frontier, everything changes and these differences appear fundamental, permeating the smallest details of everyday life.

It is interesting to note at this point that what at first sight appears to be egocentrism based on individual practice (dietary problems) has in fact been articulated as pre-existing sociocentrism. The dichotomous Swiss/Foreign perception creates the basic point of anchorage for the ego-based discourse. So individual egocentrism does not in itself exist in questions of social judge-

ments or social representations. The speaker cannot centre his discourse on his individual practice except in terms of his social identity. In the example quoted above, he can only talk about his dietary problems in terms of a way of knowing the social which, in this case, is dominated by the criterion of nationalism.

Conversely, a way of knowing the social can only appear relevant through its articulation with individual practice. At the level of content, a social identity founded on the dichotomous Swiss/Foreign representation only ceases to be abstract through individual practice, conditioned in this case by dietary problems.

Typology of the forms of centration and decentration

So far, sociocentrism has been analysed as a general phenomenon, but we can now distinguish different forms of sociocognitive centrations. We know that we cannot contrast centration and decentration in any rigorous way when they involve discourses concerned with social realities, in the way we can with forms of knowledge which are, so to speak, more neutral in relation to the subject, such as mathematics and the experimental sciences. So instead of talking about a centration/decentration opposition, we should think in terms of a continuum in which we can situate the position of a group of subjects according to their *degree* of centration. Despite the slight artificiality of all non-numerological typologies and scales, we can distinguish the five following stages:

(1) Total absence of decentration: complete devalorisation and rejection of the out-group, generalised aggressivity. In such cases the desire to understand the Other is manifestly absent. The subject proceeds by simple judgement and accusation, not by comprehension and explanation. This type of centration has to be in harmony with a high degree of idiosyncrasy in the subjects. The discourse is merely an accompaniment to thought.

(2) Interiorised and deliberate centration, linked more to social situation and the type of social integration than to the various social practices and plans of the subjects. There is a consciousness of centration, and this can even become a strategic tool. The 'centred' discourse acquires a degree of autonomy and can be deliberately 'utilised' by the subjects to defend themselves, situate themselves, advocate a given system of values or an ideology, etc. Sociocentrism is still strongly present, but it is conscious, and thus used for the purposes of personal subjective satisfaction. Subjectivity takes precedence over objectivity. Desires and beliefs are more important than reality.

(3) Acceptance of the Other as fact, but without understanding or dialogue.

(4) Decentration: acceptance and understanding of the Other and its value system. With a concomitant search for dialogue, equilibrium and compromise. Decentration corresponds to the grasp of reciprocity in genetic epistemology.

(5) Anomie: an excess of decentration: governed by doubt, uncertainty, and 'perhaps'; total absence of centration. Anomie has its counterpart in discourse heavily larded with words like 'they', 'there is', 'it' and of course 'perhaps'. Everything is indeterminate. Society is like a kaleidoscope, and the social actors like unidentified flying subjects.

We shall be analysing stages two to four, as the two remaining stages are too extreme for us to have found them in their pure state in the interviews, though there are some parts which are relevant to them.

Many extracts from interviews in the first part of this analysis, where we were concerned with centration and the other sociocognitive mechanisms which accompany it, derive from the first stage, but as these have already been dealt with we shall pass straight on to stage two.

The discourse of interiorised, deliberate, centration (stage 2)

030001

Q: What do think of when you think of Switzerland?

A: The most beautiful country in the world, and that's not just my opinion, it's what other people say too.

Q: So the first thing you think of is the country's natural beauty?

A: Yes. I've never been abroad, so I can't really say, but for me it's the most beautiful country.

The speaker's judgement is not the result of comparison, as he has never been anywhere else, but he holds the opinion strongly for all that: '. . . for me it's the most beautiful country'. Yet he also appeals to the evidence of other people: 'it's what other people say too'. This evidence, however, merely supports his own earlier conviction. There is, therefore, no need for verification and comparison. From the outset, that is seen as vain and useless. The speaker's reasoning could be schematised at the discursive level as:

I DON'T KNOW, BUT THAT'S HOW IT IS FOR ME, SO . . .

The speaker puts his judgement forward as the sole truth. He asserts his freedom to make judgements without reference criteria. He rejects what he sees as the logical process of seeking for objectivity. Truth is founded on the subjectivity of the speaker. This example is interesting as a way of understanding what differentiates sociocentrism from cognitive egocentrism: *the perceived but inexplicable consciousness of subjectivism.*

Here is another example from a speaker whose interview has already been quoted in part in connection with identification:

540013

A: I love everything about Switzerland. I'm proud of being Swiss and I'm even chauvinistic about Switzerland. That's the way I am. When I'm watching sport or anything, I'm a chauvinist. I'm Swiss through and through.

Q: But how do you account for your love of Switzerland when . . . [the speaker had earlier been extremely critical of Switzerland and the Swiss].

A: I love Switzerland and the Swiss people.

Q: Do you think there's a special Swiss mentality?

A: There are various mentalities, depending on the canton. It's a bit annoying, you find different mentalities in different cantons.

Q: Despite the differences between the cantons, do you think it's still possible to describe the Swiss mentality?

A: The Swiss are good people, they've always got their feet on the ground. I . . . that is, the Swiss are hypocritical, too, by the way. You've only got to go to a bistro, everybody's full of their own opinions, jabbering away, 'This is no good, that won't do', but then when it comes to a vote, they're all busy doing something else, they're full of talk when they're sitting round a bistro table, then when the time comes to do something about it, there's nobody there.

This speaker does not reveal the bi-polar representation normally present in nationalist thought. He identifies differences and similarities within the in-group. And in addition to this, the out-group is not used as a negative image for comparative purposes.The presence of a degree of decentration is demonstrated by the fact that the in-group is neither valorised a priori, nor treated as if it were homogeneous. And yet the speaker feels a powerful need to assert his identity: 'I'm Swiss through and through', and his fondness for the group he belongs to: 'I love everything about Switzerland.' We have already seen how this speaker experienced his identity as an unalterable essence which could not be tarnished by the hypocritical behaviour of Swiss people. But in this instance, as in the previous one, we can establish a consciousness on the part of the speaker of the subjectivism of his position. What is at work here is a centration which is both interiorised and deliberate; the speaker seems to stage his identity and display it like a flag, in a rather theatrical way.

This centration is directly related to the speaker's social integration. He was in fact from the Jura, but he had moved to Geneva. It had been difficult for him to integrate himself into the city and into his work. And working on the roads in a strange environment it was his work which became his *raison d'être*. He had been made redundant from his job, to make way, he claimed, for a

foreigner and he was hostile to the unions and to politics. Being an emigrant, a member of a minority, and on the outside, he seemed to experience his national identity as a sort of last resort.

Understanding without accepting (stage 3)

010036

Q: Which people in Switzerland do you think are least attached to the traditions?

A: I've got two sons, and young people don't appreciate the value of Switzerland, they're more internationalist. They don't want to do their military service, they don't accept what I say about letting people into Switzerland. 'Foreigners are just as good as us', they say. As far as I can see, it's because this generation hasn't experienced the sort of hardship we did. Obviously their education isn't the same as ours was, but really young people these days have such an easy time of it that it's made them lose touch a bit with real values.

In this example, the speaker is concerned to understand the reasons which drive young people to accord less importance to patriotic values. His explanation is that the younger generation 'hasn't experienced the sort of hardship we did', that they 'have such an easy time of it' that as a result they have 'lost touch with real values'.

The speaker is decentred in relation to his own experience. He admits that young people have a different mode of apprehending reality because their experience differs from his. But he does not allow that this could even partially justify new values. Genuine values, 'real values', can only be the ones he interiorised in the past, which remain valid for everyone.

The speaker's decentration stops at establishing difference, and therefore does not go so far as the acceptance of a recognised reciprocity with the Other's value system.

The surprising thing, though, is that the speaker retains his allegiance to the old values which, from his point of view, correspond better to the situation in an earlier period than they do to the contemporary world. Because for him values remain the same even if the social situation that created them changes completely. To the speaker the change is not really fundamental. The economic situation, the convenience of modern life, prosperity, and so forth, are all regarded as secondary or contingent factors. Just because there are changes in the material sub-stratum does not mean that there also have to be changes in the behaviour and attitude of the social actors. The speaker therefore accepts the relevance of economic conditions in explaining social behaviour, but refuses to endorse the validity of this determination, because it does not conform to his view of how things should be.

This speaker's way of knowing thus remains largely sociocentric. Admit-

tedly he tries to understand the attitudes and behaviour of other people but by finding *raisons d'être* for them which are derived from personal experience. He cannot conceive that the same explanatory schema could be applied to himself. Indeed, we may ask whether what the speaker refuses to acknowledge is not so much young people's behaviour, which he readily excuses, as the material changes in society, which he regards as abnormal.

We could schematise this speaker's implicit reasoning as follows:

(1) $A_1, A_2 . . .A_n$ recognise B's system of values
(2) $A_1, A_2 . . .A_n$ are arguable

Therefore B's value system is arguable, but I understand that he does have that system.

On the other hand, decentred reasoning in this context would run:

(1) $A_1, A_2 . . .A_n$ recognise B's system of values
(2) $C_1, C_2 . . .C_n$ recognise my system of values
(3)   My system of values is not the same as B's

Therefore my value system has no a priori reason for being more valid than B's, and if I prefer it, it's up to me to justify my choice to B.

Sociocognitive centration cannot therefore exist on the sociocognitive level alone. The mere fact of understanding the reasons which underlie the behaviour of the Other is a necessary, but a sufficient, condition for reaching true sociocognitive decentration, which requires a consciousness on the part of the subject of the relativity of his own value system.

Understanding and accepting: the discourse of sociocognitive decentration (stage 4)

Transcending conflictual situations
Unlike centration, which is so frequent as to be almost a natural phenomenon, decentration is always the result of real *work*, and of sometimes long and arduous experience: experiencing the Other, and questioning one's own certainties. In the following passage, we can make out this gradual process of decentration through contact with foreigners.

230035
Q: Do you think the Swiss have particular difficulty in their contacts with foreigners?
A: No, I don't think so, I don't think so. I've had a few difficulties with Spaniards, but perhaps that was because I was too hard on them. I'm

hard on myself so perhaps I expected too much. Perhaps it's that they aren't used to working the way I do. Perhaps I demanded too much of them.

As I say, there are always differences, it's a matter of education and tradition. Spaniards don't have the same way of thinking as someone from the Vaude.

The speaker is expressing a genuine decentration. The difference between the Swiss and foreigners is accepted for what it is, and there is no special valorisation of the characteristics of the in-group. There is also, however, a sense that this process of decentration only happened after a series of experienced conflictual situations with foreigners. The understanding of relations with the Other is based on a notion of reciprocity.

In this speaker's case, it should be noted that the process of decentration was facilitated by the particular conditions of his work, the practice of which provides a common 'code' between him and the foreigners which enabled decentration and communication to be more easily achieved.

This does not explain everything, however; the speaker also has a much more generalised and deeper organisation, and sociocognitive structure. The discursive structure reveals a way of thinking about relations with alterity which is profoundly different from the previous speaker's outlook. The cumulation of 'perhaps' is in marked contrast to the assertive tone, the proclaimed certainties and the unarguable norms of sociocentric discourses.

This social actor subject has been more searching in his cognitive and discursive work, and this work itself is indissociable from his other social practices.

Non-dissociation of judgement and explanation

In the previous paragraphs we have seen how a subject can explain the behaviour of another without calling his own value system into question. In the following interview, the speaker not only tries to relate the behaviour of other people to their experience, but in so doing admits the relativity of points of view.

040009

People of 25 and people of 50 have very different ways of thinking about their country. That's quite normal. When I was 30 I'd notched up 1,500 days of military service, I'd never even been able to go as far as St Julien because there were Germans there, and my dream was to travel. Even though I was 30, I was still under the thumb of my parents; I wanted to go to Madagascar, but that was unthinkable, at that time everyone thought you were crazy if you wanted to do that sort of thing. But now I look at my daughters who are 25, and they've had a year in the United States, or a year in England, or eighteen months in Spain, and they've been to London and Paris and New York.

They're more detached from their own country, which is something quite different. We think of it in terms of defence, because when we were young we were attacked on the work front by unemployment (there were a thousand people out of work in Geneva). You had to struggle to get work, and inevitably that's left its mark, whereas our children, between 20 and 25, have a marvellous opportunity to discover a whole world around them, so they're bound to have a different idea of this country from people of my generation. My children don't belong anywhere in particular. I'm just stating a fact, mind. I heard one of my daughters say, 'I prefer Rome to Paris.' We could never have dreamed of saying that, it just wasn't possible. But these young people, God knows they're lucky, can look at their country in a critical way that we never could, because they've seen it from the outside. We can now, too, but our ideas are already formed.

For this speaker, ways of thinking about one's country depend on individual experience and concrete conditions. Alterations in outlook are perceived as linked to changes in social reality. Alterity is acknowledged to be inevitable in a changing context. Difference is therefore seen as reciprocal. The speaker completely understands the way his outlook on the world was conditioned when he was a young man. Rather than visible oppression, it was a system of values and norms that made themselves indisputably felt, with all the weight of the Real. 'At that time, everyone thought . . .', 'but that was unthinkable', 'it just wasn't possible', 'We could never have dreamed of saying that'. The decentration is expressed in the discourse itself through the presence of spatial metaphors, which decentration depends on: 'They're more detached', 'they've seen it from the outside'.

At the truly discursive level, the length of the answer is evidence of a more elaborated, worked, discursive style. Explanation is both longer and more difficult than plain condemnation.

We have already encountered speakers for whom differences in experience were a factor in explaining the variation in value systems. But this explanation did not prevent them from regarding other value systems as a manifestation of deviant, rather than different, behaviour.

This form of decentred thought casts further light on decentration itself, which thus becomes a dissociation of judgement and explanation. It can be understood in the following way: either the speaker does not realise that the explanation based on social conditions and personal experience can equally well be applied to his own system of values, or else his 'explanatory' reasoning appeals to facts which he contests on the basis of his value system, which seems to bar the way to decentration even more radically.

The dissociation between personal attitude and interpretation
In cases where evaluative judgement remains separate from explanation, as

in the example we have just looked at, it is because the speaker experiences difficulty in dissociating his own attitude from his interpretation of other situations and behaviour. In the following example, the decentration occurs as a result of this type of dissociation:

500083

Q: What do think about these demonstrations?

A: I told you before that I don't like crowds, I don't like demonstrations, because they're just like a flock of sheep. You have a leader at the front and everyone else follows him.

Q: But why, in your opinion, have there been more of them recently than, say, ten years ago?

A: Because people's attitudes have changed. I don't think things are any worse than they were ten years ago, but people's attitudes have changed, they think about things more.

Q: Yourself, do you disapprove of people who take part in them?

A: No, in fact I read an interview recently with that young student who was arrested because he was carrying explosives and everything. Turned out he'd had to break off his studies, I think for family reasons, and because of that he rebelled against society. When you read something like that you can't help putting yourself in the other person's shoes. It makes you think.

The two propositions that seem most significant for our argument are the following:

(1)   'I don't like crowds (or demonstrations) because they're just like a flock of sheep'

(2)   'There are more demonstrations because people's attitudes have changed. They think about things more.'

There is clearly a sharp dissociation between the personal attitude towards the situation ('I don't like crowds'), and the search for meaning related to that situation. The discourse operates a distinction between what concerns Me and what concerns Others. The criteria on which the personal attitude to the situation is based are not the same as those on which the interpretation is founded. The personal attitude is based on a refusal to follow the crowd or flock, whereas the interpretation functions according to the *amalgam*, or false identification, principle. For our speaker, the fact that the crowd behave like sheep does not necessarily imply a negative attitude towards demonstrations, only a refusal to join them. This type of decentration can only occur if the subject is not exclusively concerned with the external actions of other social actors, but wants to find out what they mean. This entails a shift of perspective

which puts the subject in the other's place: 'When you read something like that you can't help putting yourself in the other person's shoes. It makes you think.'

Search for an equilibrium between one's own interests and the interests of the Other
Decentration does not imply the effacement of the subject and the renunciation of his personal interests and his own point of view. The objectivity of knowledge is a product of the co-ordination of different perspectives (intersystemic differentiation and integration, in epistemological terms). The same is true of social discourse about the social. The Other's point of view is assessed in its own context.

500040

Q: Do you think the workers are capable of defending their interests?
A: I think they can defend themselves as well as anyone can, if the need arises. There's no doubt about that; I'd be amazed if they didn't. But if the situation did arise, they could defend themselves like anybody in any other country. But what scares me really, though, is the sort of thing we saw on TV the other day. They questioned several workers who were very well aware of the situation, they understood the employers, but the employers shouldn't think it's a good idea, or a good solution, to make people redundant just because most people understand them. At a time like that it's too easy just to say, 'Most of the people understand, so we can do what we want.'

The assertion, 'they can . . . as well as anyone' is followed by doubt. But this is more to do with the actual certainty than with the content of the assertion: 'There's no doubt about that; I'd be amazed if they didn't.' This second sentence, which is meant to reinforce the first, actually only serves to weaken it. Then the next formulation comes as a surprise: 'But if the situation did arise . . .' This *but* implies an opposition. Yet at the level of statement, it merely links two propositions of similar intent. What happens is that the opposition remains unformulated, the doubt having been stifled before it could be made explicit.

There is a sense of ambivalence triumphing over certainty. Thereafter, the speaker maintains a distance from each of his assertions. He puts forward a proposition, then retracts it almost at once and changes his perspective, or the angle from which he approaches the problematic. This attitude can be seen even more clearly in the next part of his answer, where he is trying explain the reasons for his doubt: 'They questioned several workers who . . . understood the employers, but the employers shouldn't think . . .' The speaker assesses the situation then wonders what negative effects might be created by the positive

factor he identifies. 'They were very well aware of the situation' is presented in a positive way, but immediately afterwards we are shown the negative effect of what was considered as positive: 'The employers shouldn't think it's a good idea . . .' We can see working here what might be called an intra-discursive dialectic, analogous to the dialectic of yin and yang: positive and negative are both put forward, but there is a negative within the positive, and a positive within the negative. This dialectic seems to be a fairly good representation of the search for equilibrium we mentioned. The speaker seems to be looking for a point of equilibrium on the basis of which the perspectives of both sides will be co-ordinated and explained.

For the speaker, therefore, the truth is never valid on its own. It must be set in its context for its relevance to be verified. The understanding shown by the workers, as opposed to their employers, is regarded as something positive, but in the current socio-political context it could have harmful consequences. This contrasts radically with the assertions based on the identificatory associations we usually find in sociocentric thought and discourse.

Decentration as discursive strategy

Under this heading we can place the type of discourse whose decentration is made explicit by the speaker in the form of a systematic attempt at relativisation, as in the following interview:

500002

Q: Why, in your opinion, have they [the authorities] implemented this policy [on immigration]?

A: After what happened with the referendums, I'd say they wanted to make the people take the blame, because two weeks after that, the redundancies started, they didn't need the foreigners any more, and that's when all the confusion started.

Q: So you're saying they were looking for an excuse to . . .

A: I'm not saying they wanted to, I'm just saying that's the impression you get after the referendum results, and after the redundancies that started happening two weeks later. That's what creates that impression.

After the 'I'd say' in the first answer, which is already fairly cautious, we find another very interesting statement, one which is very characteristic of this discourse:

'I'm not saying they wanted to, I'm just saying that's the impression you get.'

The speaker is drawing a clear distinction between the social actors' categories of meaning, and those on which his own perception of reality is based. He begins by disclosing his interpretation, then he looks at the situation

from the authorities' point of view, and finally (in response to the interviewer's mistaken interpretation) formulates a clearer distinction between the event under consideration, the intentions of the social actor and the impression it produced on him.

This shift of perspective, which is an expression of decentration, can be regarded as the manifestation of a discursive strategy. By using a discourse characterised by a constant sense of the need to relativise, to present the points of views of different social actors, the speaker puts himself permanently in a state of withdrawal, becomes an observer.

There can in fact be no engagement and, in a general sense, no practice without some degree of ego- or sociocentrism, the main effects of which are mistaken generalisations and false identifications. Decentred thought encourages the integration of new facts into interpretations of reality and thus, also, the restructuring of analytic categories. Taken too far, though, it can lead to disengagement and withdrawal on the part of the subject, and to a conviction that, in the end, everything is equally valid, because every situation has its good and bad sides. In that context, decentred thought can equally well be regarded as the expression of a discursive strategy by means of which the speaker adopts the position of observer. The same speaker provides us with a clear set of examples of this *strategy of withdrawal*:

> 500001
> I've been to Canada and America, but I'm always glad to come back here. Personally speaking, I mean, because I don't want to suggest that everything is perfect here at the political level. But as long as human beings are imperfect, society will go on being imperfect too, that's my opinion, that's my philosophy.

> 500006
> I think there's a lot that needs to be done, and I also think that human beings *can perhaps* get in the way of progress, but *perhaps* that may not be such a bad thing after all, because things are already changing fairly fast . . . By that I mean that, *perhaps* unconsciously, because they're afraid of change, they slow down developments that the technocrats would like to see happening more quickly . . . In one way *perhaps* it's not so good, and in another *perhaps* it's not so bad either.

> 500028
> *perhaps* they don't have freedom of thought in Eastern Europe, whereas in the West they do have the Left. But if you take the two extremes, living on credit is just another way of having the knife at your throat, even though you can say whatever you like. I don't think any regime is perfect, I think it's human beings themselves that need to evolve, and *perhaps* become less selfish, but that's another story.

500067
Q: You often hear people say that Switzerland is a sort of model democracy. What do you think about that?

A: Because of its federalism, *perhaps*, but federalism has its drawbacks as well. When you realise that each canton has its own laws, whether to do with schools or education or whatever . . . I think it slows down development . . . More centralisation? No, I don't think so, that's not really a satisfactory solution either.

500096
I think every period has an interesting side to it, as long as you can see it. And the things that disappear, that's just part of life; the wheel turns, things move on.

'Society will go on being imperfect.'
'In one way perhaps it's not so good and in other ways perhaps it's not so bad either.'
'That's just part of life; the wheel turns . . .'
These are not just clichés, they are the actual bases of his way of understanding the social problems he is talking about. The speaker displays his scepticism about any project that aims to change society too radically. 'Progress has its good and bad sides.'

This type of decentration can also lead to a *psychologistic perception of the social*, in which reality is less important to the speaker than the way in which it is perceived: 'so far as one can see' a situation always has a 'good side'. The speaker situates himself outside the issues he is talking about. Even when he is talking about people in the West (of which he is one) he uses the indefinite pronoun 'they' ('in the West *they* have . . .') It is as if the process of decentration itself gives him satisfaction. This might be another way of affirming identity. You feel he wants to emphasise to his interlocutors the unwisdom of only seeing one side of things. The rejection of Manicheism, which is very marked here, becomes an end in itself. Hyper-relativism is presented as the correct model and visibly permeates the discourse in the avalanche of 'perhaps' and euphemistic negations like 'I don't think', 'I don't mean', 'not bad', 'not good', etc. Decentred thought seems to function like a well-oiled machine. Each assertion is matched by a counter-assertion which restores equilibrium. Good and bad cancel each other out and allow a position of neutrality, exteriority and extraterritoriality to emerge from the field of Manichean and conflictual oppositions. The speaker seldom adopts a position himself, acting as arbitrator instead. This type of equilibrium, or non-engagement, is different from those analysed above. The central issue there was the reconciliation of the different interests and points of view of the interlocutors, which were very noticeable. Here, on the other hand, the speaker minimises the differences and seems to want to adopt a neutral, conciliatory point of view. He does not, so to speak, put himself in the Other's place, so much as tidy the Other away.

Consolidation of the theory

Before drawing any more general conclusions from these empirical analyses, we shall need to add the concrete results that emerge from the two other indicators, causality and time, to these preliminary findings. Nevertheless, some important points may be summarised now:

(1)   Although an understanding of the development of egocentrism in the child provides important pointers for the study of sociocentrism, the two are essentially very different. It is now quite clear that sociocentrism can never be regarded simply as the residue of this egocentrism, nor as a purely cognitive phenomenon. Sociocentrism is essentially a social phenomenon and can only be explained by social factors. It is therefore justifiable to talk about a *sociocognitive* reality, this time on an empirical basis.

(2)   At a more general level, we can see how indispensable it is to approach everyday thought and language as they are used, as they are actually put into practice.

(3)   Conversely, these empirical analyses demonstrate the speculative nature of theoretical formulations that aim at universality.

(4)   We can already see how the analysis of sociocognitive reality can extend and deepen a content analysis or a purely linguistic approach.

(5)   The variety of relations between ways of knowing (the various degrees of decentration) and ways of speaking shows that there is also an empirical foundation for the postulate of the indissociability of thought and language.

(6)   An approach like this, which is both relational and variational, leads on to *typology*. Some comment is necessary about the criteria underlying the typology of the five different forms of centration/ decentration, because the problem of the typology of ways of knowing and speaking will become increasingly important.

We chose a particular order, the transition from the most centred to the most decentred forms of discourse. This, however, does not imply any value judgement on our part, or an apologia for decentration. The order might well have been reversed, except that as it stands it does demonstrate one basic point: the different forms of social centration are so numerous and so generalised that sociocentrism might seem to constitute the obvious, inevitable, 'natural' reality. Decentration, on the other hand, appears to be much more difficult to acquire. It requires a long and laborious apprenticeship and a considerable amount of work. It is the result of genuine achievement. So it is not enough to say that the theoretical possibilities of the rational epistemic subject are present in all individuals, because in practical social reality the

epistemic subject is affected by so many opposing individual and social factors that it ceases to be a recognisable entity.

We should also emphasise that this preliminary typology of the forms of centration and decentration does not account for all the possible forms of everyday social thought. There are other forms which can be placed in relation to this continuum. Take, for example, a form of thought not yet encountered, but which might exist. Those sectors of the population who have benefited from an extended education are by definition likely to have considerable cognitive and linguistic ability. This is obviously true of intellectuals, for example. Decentration might even have to be an intrinsic component of their cognitive ability. But it could also happen that this important verbal activity might lead to a sort of verbalism. And in extreme cases we might find forms of thought cut off from any real, concrete experience, the sort which the man in the street dismisses laconically as 'nothing but talk'.

Decentred thought implies developed cognitive and linguistic work, but a hypertrophied development of that on its own can also lead to vertigo. This hasty and simplified – though not therefore caricatured or merely theoretical – example demonstrates how complex and difficult the idea of decentration is, as well as how mistaken it is to take it as the ultimate objective to be attained absolutely and valorised unconditionally.

We have already come across one type of thought which was defined by its excess of decentration. The example above shows that it is not the only one to occupy an area where decentration can be seen as problematic.

The continuum on which our typology is based is not a photographic representation of reality but a heuristic tool to enable us to situate the various concrete, social forms of thought more accurately.

We should also say something briefly about the forms of thought and discourse which are sometimes described as 'pathological'. It is not correct, in our view, to speak of *collective* pathological thought, only of forms of thought or sociocognitive mechanisms that have been taken to extremes. This would be the case with absolute centration or absolute decentration which, in the first case, would be a form of obsession, and in the second, a form of anomie. When some sociocognitive mechanisms are taken to extremes, this may prevent other mechanisms from being put into practice, especially the ones capable of re-establishing equilibrium at a higher level.

We now turn to the concrete analysis of causality, as the next addition to the empirical material analysed so far.

4 Social causality: the types of explanatory discourses

The five logico-discursive forms and the three paradigms of causal explanation

What we are trying to do in this section is to examine, in very practical terms, the different ways in which everyday social reality is explained, not to analyse the phenomenon of causality itself. It is important to make this clear, as a great deal of work has been done on the subject of causality, and problems to do with the rationale of causality or its meaning have preoccupied scholars as diverse as Lévy-Bruhl, Brunschvicg, Einstein, Piaget and Heisenberg. Our object, therefore, is *social* causality rather than causality in itself, although this will not preclude some differences of opinion with more philosophical approaches in connection with particular empirical results.

We have touched on causality in an earlier work,[1] but mainly in order to construct our general conceptual and theoretical apparatus. What we want to do now is test this apparatus empirically by applying it to the various concrete, detailed forms that causal explanation takes on in everyday life. So we shall be looking at causal thought and causal language *in use, in action, in the process of development*, and not at some abstract, generalised notion of causality in itself.

We draw a distinction between the *logico-discursive forms* of causal explanation (of which there are five) and the *paradigms* of causal explanation (of which there are three). The logico-discursive forms are more abstract than the paradigms.[2] They are ideal models of explanation. A single social actor subject may in practice use several logico-discursive forms without, however, using them undifferentiatedly or simultaneously.

The paradigms are the specific concrete modalities of interaction between logico-discursive forms and given contents (the subjects of the discourse).

A logico-discursive form is close to a theoretical model, whereas a paradigm designates the concrete nature of the *dominant explanatory style* appropriate to a real discourse in progress. A single paradigm generally covers several logico-discursive forms. What defines it is the type of combination between those forms and their interactions with given contents.

A paradigm rests on a specific discursive and sociocognitive structure, which explains why, for instance, a given political discourse does not use just any paradigm of causal explanation.

The five logico-discursive forms have been conceptualised as follows:

(1)   segmented causality
(2)   circular causality
(3)   contingent causality
(4)   causal supersaturation
(5)   multiple causality

The three paradigms are:

(1)   the deviancy paradigm
(2)   the materialist paradigm
(3)   the indeterminacy paradigm

   Again, the forms and the paradigms are both collective social phenomena, and have to appear in the discourse of a large number of people to be granted this status. The variation (and the regularities) are social, not individual. The forms and the paradigms, despite being advanced at the beginning of this analysis, were actually constructed gradually, and empirically, out of multiple readings and re-readings of the interviews, and constant comparison between them. They are not a priori categories.

Types of social thought and logico-discursive forms

Segmented causality and associative thought

   Segmented causality, a causalised expression, belonging to a type of thought we call associative thought, *uses the association of ideas to construct cause and consequence pairings linked one to another*, each element in turn being the consequence of the preceding one and the cause of the one that follows. It often happens, for example, that a speaker changes tack in the course of his answer, leaving the original topic for a different one altogether. Then in what he goes on to say after that he may similarly drop all the subjects he broaches, one after the other. The thought is defined by these spontaneous associations of ideas, lacking any leading thread. One idea leads on to another, which leads on to a third, by which time the first is 'forgotten'. Consequently this 'spontaneity' has a discursive form that is characterised by a sequence of pairs of elements. The relation between the elements of each pair may stem from any kind of structuration (and more particularly from any type of causal imputation), but no reasons can be adduced for links between elements separated by more than a single interval. This is what is meant by *associative thought*.

   The most visible characteristic of this kind of thought is a series of incessant *thematic breaks*. The speaker does not seem, at first sight, to be concerned to argue a particular position. *The discourse accompanies spontaneous thought*, whereas in other types of relation between thought and discourse, thought is

channelled (and its spontaneity thereby inhibited) by the attempt to produce a coherent discourse by means of classification, systematisation and structuration.

020022

Q: Do you think the people will say yes this time? [to proposed legislation to deal with the surplus of foreigners]

A: Yes, I'm sure they will. I'm voting 'yes' this time, anyway. Because this week I've had to make do on ten francs for the whole week. I don't know if you could manage on that, it's the first time it's happened to me, but when you've got other problems it's not funny. So if some of the foreigners went, there'd be more work. I've been out of work six months and I can't find anything, you can't pick up a job for two months, you can't do anything. It's the same everywhere, even at Laurence, at Acacias, you know, they wanted someone on the ma-chines, but they had to be under 40, I said why did they have to be under 40? They said 'Because the machines are hard work'. I said OK, but there you are, at 50 you've lost the right to earn a crust. It's not normal. Every day in the papers, average age 40. What does a woman do if she's on her own? When you can't work any more. And then they tell me Switzerland has got a good government. Well that's not true, there's something, I don't know exactly what, I'm not an MP, but there's something wrong somewhere.

The discourse moves away from the first question, the result of a referen-dum on some new legislation against 'the surplus of foreigners', to express the speaker's intended vote, then his difficulties in finding work, the problems of older workers and single women and finally the functioning of the political system. The striking thing is the way it does not return to the initial argument but keeps picking up a new thread, especially as such a return is a permanent possibility (as for example by describing how older workers or women compete with foreigners on the job market). This is thus not a case of 'illogicality' of thought, but an intentional foregrounding of the speaker's everyday practical problems and the factors influencing them, without always being able to articulate that influence. By the end of this statement, the explanation of voting intentions is no longer relevant as he is talking about something else. The statement has no overall causal structure, only causal (or thematic) relations between elements of the discourse taken in twos. Seg-mented causality is not strictly causality, as that would necessitate selecting one or a number of elements recognised as possessing a more important function of logical structuration, whereas in associative thought no one element is picked out as a causal factor. All the elements are a priori able to be treated as causes. We are thus outside of the causal/non-causal dichotomy, in a proto-causal realm whose frontiers are not established.

140021

Q: What do you think about the foreigners' living conditions?

A: They're not badly off, not the ones here anyway. There may have been some who . . . but as far as housing goes they're not badly off, believe me.

Q: We've heard very different opinions. Some people say they're disadvantaged compared to the Swiss, others say they're better off.

A: That's certainly true of housing. We used to do some caretaking, to try and keep the place clean, because it was so dirty, it was dreadful. But then I had to give it up because of my arthritis, I had arthritis in one arm, and my husband had two fingers amputated and they said we couldn't do it any more. Oh no, there's no need to worry about them, they're OK.

Q: Do you think they're at an advantage in all areas?

A: Certainly they always have been as far as housing is concerned.

In strict logic, there is nothing in this discourse to prove the final claim that foreigners are advantaged in housing, nor is there anything to prove the truth of the assertion that 'they're not badly off'. Instead, the speaker's invocation of personal difficulties to do with work and fitness takes the place of proof or demonstration. The *associative slide* from one topic to another one which seems to be unrelated to the initial question or the final assertion nonetheless justifies the latter by the synthetic, undifferentiated invocation of a practical situation from everyday experience. Housing, dirt, job difficulties, health troubles, are all associated with the presence of foreigners in an existential whole, an undefined, indefinable, totality. The discourse, with its linked associations, is the unsystematised, unstructured, linear transcription of this general impression. The various elements making up the sequence are only linked two at a time in the statement, but they all have to do with an overall view of experience of which the presence and housing of foreigners are a part. Segmented causality is a response to the rough incursions of everyday life.

As expressed thus in discourse through sequences of associations, segmented causality corresponds to a *synthetic grasp of reality* (and particularly of experienced reality) which establishes no differentiation between primary and secondary, determinant and contingent, etc., and which therefore expresses a refusal to divide lived experience into analytic categories. It can be postulated that any division of that sort would be felt to be an impoverishment of individual experience, an extreme schematisation of reality, and that social thought, by proceeding through this sort of association, is resisting domination by analytic thought. We shall return later to the sociological significance of this postulate.

Segmented causality can also function by *associations of crystallised ideas*. Particular associations are made constantly. One of the segments of the

causality is thereby rigidly established, and will always be the same regardless of context.

140014–15

Q: How do you explain the fact that a section of young people is now opposed to the army?

A: They're left-wingers, aren't they. They want to destroy the army so the reds can take control everywhere. That's the only reason I can see. That's why, there's no other reason for it.

Q: What do you think about the authorities' attitude?

A: They're just crooks if you'll pardon the expression. As far as I can see, they're paid by the big industries to keep the foreigners here. That's all I can say. They don't give a toss about Switzerland.

Although the discussion begins with the question of opposition to the army, the interviewer's question about the authorities' attitude is not received in the context of the preceding statement, but in isolation. It is not the general or contextual meaning of a question which induces an association of ideas, but an isolated phrase, here even a single term, 'the authorities', which sparks off the association Authorities = Crooks. This direct association is based on hostility to immigration policy, to which the speaker attaches particular importance, far more so than to opposition to the army. This prioritised focus is such that the speaker cannot think of the authorities without immediately thinking of immigration policy, creating a break in the discourse as soon as anyone utters the word 'authorities' (and probably allied terms like 'government', 'federal council', '*dirigeants*', etc). This association is crystallised once and for all, independently of any context. A return to the opening topic is here impossible. The sequence of associations does not operate in relation to an overall grasp of a phenomenon, it is deflected by a general mechanism of automatic association.

In the passage cited above, this crystallised association leads to the total disruption of causal relations as they concern opposition to the army on one hand and immigration policy on the other. The sole transitional point of the discourse is the term 'authorities'. So the discourse tells us far less about the speaker's opinion of the attitude the 'authorities' should take to opposition to the army than about the priority he gives to immigration policy in his assessment of government action: segmented causality is thus symptomatic of the speaker's value system.

Circular causality

When the causal relationship between two phenomena is not adequately established (when it is not considered to be adequately established by the interviewer), the speaker sometimes backs it up with an *a contrario demon-*

stration, in which the opposite of the cause results in the opposite of the consequence of the main causal relation. This second causal relation supports the first, and vice versa: the system of imputing causes can operate without any mediation or necessity external to the cause–consequence pair.

320004

> I don't know if people in Switzerland are more peaceful, but there's less theft and that happens simply because people have got money.

Q: You think that's the main cause?

A: Yes. Look what happens in France, people haven't got money and they go and steal, quite simply.

The causal imputation present in the first statement E_1 is constructed on the basis of a relationship, relative to a specific place – Switzerland – between an observed phenomenon ('there's less theft') and the factor which is regarded as causal ('people have got money'). The causal relationship is a simple one: place – phenomenon – cause.

But this explanation does not satisfy the interviewer, or rather he wants to test its solidity within the speaker's thought. So he elicits a second statement, E_2, establishing a causal relationship with the same structure as the first, place – cause – phenomenon. The second causal relationship has to support the first which has been called into question, *a contrario,* i.e. with each of its elements the reverse of the corresponding element in the first causal relationship.

Place: L_2 'in France' is contrasted with L_1 'in Switzerland', if it is granted that France is treated here as an example of a foreign country, of what is not Swiss. It is a familiar example because it is close at hand and therefore credible, and enables assertions that are acceptable or obvious.

Phenomenon: P_1 'there's less theft' is approximately the opposite of P_2 'they go and steal', although there is a difference in intensity as the first proposition is relative and incomplete (less theft than where?) and the second is absolute.

Cause: C_1 'people have got money' is the exact opposite of C_2 'people haven't got money'. These propositions are not relative or illustrative, they are general and absolute and allow of no discussion. To question either of these propositions would be to paralyse the causal development.

The second statement is negative confirmation of the first: $E_2 = L_2 C_2 P_2 = L_1 C_1 P_1 = E_1$. We thus reach a causal *over-coherence*, because the two statements, presented as being coherent in themselves, are thereby further intended to verify each other.

We pointed out the difference in intensity between the two statements. 'In Switzerland there's less theft', not 'there's no theft': the element of relativity this introduces is used as the basis for the comparison with France in the second statement. But the relativity is restricted to the one element 'there's less theft', and does not apply to the other elements of the statements,

particularly to the cause 'people have got money'. In the second statement, cause and phenomenon are formulated in absolute terms. It reinforces the first by removing its relativity, and so the main point of the second proposition is to back up the first, which is the one the speaker said spontaneously and the one which interests him the most. Reversing the order of the elements between one statement and the next (place – phenomenon – cause then place – cause – phenomenon) shows that the main emphasis is placed on the phenomenon in the first ('in Switzerland there's less theft') and on the causal relationship in the second insofar as it strengthens the first assertion (as can be seen from the phrase 'quite simply' with which the statement ends).

(1) The main purpose of circular causality is therefore the *confirmation of elements which are valorised by the speaker's way of knowing and of explaining.*

(2) Circular causality can also perform a second function, which is the *construction of a social representation* out of social facts which are not the subject of first-hand knowledge.

470157

Q: Some young people prefer living together in groups rather than in couples. Is this normal, do you think?

A: No it's not normal, it's immoral. Living in communes is different, though I don't think they do that much any more. It never works. They may enjoy it for a while, but it always collapses in the long run. Communes like that always cause trouble, there's always some people who don't want to work, sponging off their friends, selling this or that, their watch or whatever. It's OK as long as the money lasts, but when it runs out . . . well, then they start thieving and so you see it gets worse and worse. If you want to be honest in this life, you've got to work. Those who won't work, don't eat, or they steal.

There are a lot of young people stealing things. At Carouge four or five buildings were broken into, and things were taken. They don't report it in the papers because it gives other people the same idea, but in one building they broke into all the flats, in the middle of the afternoon. When we were young nothing like that happened.

In all probability the speaker knows no young people who live communally. The discourse makes up for this ignorance, however, by recourse to the representation of social reality based on the values of work, honesty, marriage and the family, a representation which was amply developed earlier in the interview. These values form a system; it only needs one to be suppressed for the others to collapse: this is what is clearly shown by talking about young people living communally.

Communes transgress the norm which assigns private life to the framework of the marriage-based family. The distinction between 'living together

in groups' and 'living in communes' is never made explicit, and so we do not know the distinction between 'immorality' and 'something different', which in any case does not figure in what follows.

This first transgression is followed by others, against those other norms which structure the value system, work and honesty. The couple is replaced by the mass, in which there are always some who do not want to work, some who are not controlled and set to work by the family. Idleness gives rise to poverty which in turn leads to theft. The thefts are then attributed by a series of slippages to young people living communally, the logic of the reasoning operating as empirical verification: 'and so you see . . .'

The edifice thus constructed is over-coherent as it is composed of two opposite sets, in each of which the same logic is at work, in one case positively and in the other *a contrario*. Both sets are based on the *contrast/generalisation*[3] us/young people. *Associated* with 'us' are the family, work, and honesty; living communally, idleness, and theft are *constructed* into a correspondence with 'young people'. This over-coherence confirms the speaker's own value-system, and allows him to construct a discourse out of social facts he has no experience of, and to perceive this discourse as no less true than discourse about the known.

Circular causality enables everything to be explained. You can have an answer for everything. It is thus the foundation of a logic which for facts derived from first-hand observation substitutes representations based on a value-system which for the speaker is prior, and which it is the function of the explanation to confirm.

Contingent causality

By contingent causality we mean *the establishment of causal connections between phenomena which appear simultaneously in the speaker's field of consciousness*. To put it another way, when two or more phenomena are perceived as emerging 'simultaneously', social thought often associates them by means of a causal connection. Their 'temporal proximity' connects them causally.

320042

Q: One might also ask why there are more people [in Switzerland].

A: Why? Well it's because . . . they keep them alive in hospital till . . . well, their heart has to collapse completely for them not to keep them alive on machines. And because they can operate on so many more things, fractures and all that, and handicapped people.

Then there are more people because they try and keep them alive till the last moment, even when they know there's no way they can save them, when it's their nervous system or their brain, I don't know why

they make them go on living like that. It just means there are more
people.

The artificial maintenance of life ('their heart has to collapse completely')
seems to the speaker to be the reason for the increase in the Swiss population.
The two phenomena appeared at the same time in the field of consciousness.
The problem of euthanasia raised passions, as did overpopulation. Yet these
two problems are far from commensurate, and belong to different social
contexts. The discourse connects them in a causal way, and makes particular
connections between them. The difference in their significance is of no
importance. So overpopulation is simply seen as the consequence of artifi-
cially prolonging life in hospitals.

A word about the function of 'explanation' in this type of social thought. It
appears that its main aim is to understand the 'objective' reasons for a given
phenomenon. Verification and proof are alien to it. Thought seeks satisfying
causes, and satisfaction can be fully obtained without verification. This way of
knowing *identifies* and causally *links* phenomena which in one sense resemble
each other, and most of the time avoids asking questions about other aspects
of the phenomena. Thus 'the artificial maintenance of life' enables people to
live who would otherwise be dead. It is obvious that this adds to the popula-
tion (while the relative insignificance of the phenomena in question is not
regarded as important). The two phenomena are associated in that both entail
'a larger number of people alive'.

070058
Q: What do you think the foreign workers have brought to Switzerland?
A: They've brought their labour. They've brought their labour, then
       they've taken away their money. That's the only reason we've got
       inflation.

The departure of foreign workers for their native countries is here presented
as a cause of inflation, without any demonstration of the economic mechan-
isms or mediations by which this happens.[4] This is a more extreme example of
contingent causality than usual as every other cause is explicitly excluded.
Contingent causality relations are generally less exclusively enunciated,
being closer to association of ideas than strict causality.

010017–18
       Things are still going quite well for us, though there has to be a degree
       of closing in, that's the main issue in Switzerland at the commercial
       level, imports and exports, I don't know if you know M. Jolles, the
       director, I think he's a very talented man, anyway he's talking about a
       trade war, where every country institutes protectionist measures. And
       that's the danger, if we get too closed-in on ourselves.

Q: Are there any signs you've noticed in particular that make you think this is the situation in Switzerland?

A: It arose automatically, over the question of foreign workers, for example. OK, there wasn't much interference, but it's this situation which has caused the closing in. But they're well aware that hundreds of these workers have left now.

The presence of foreign workers is seen as causing a nationalist retreat, which in turn is linked (though with no actual process of cause and effect being specified) with trade protectionism. These phenomena are thus united in a sort of 'closing-in' syndrome, one cause of which is specified, namely the presence of foreigners, but it is not suggested that this is the sole cause. The discourse here is on the boundary between causality and contingency. Simultaneous phenomena are set in an overall framework which postulates causal relationships but does not argue for them systematically.

Causal supersaturation

Causal supersaturation is a form of explanation which uses *a very small number of causes to explain a whole series of social phenomena*. At its most extreme, everything is explained by a single cause; this is generalised causal supersaturation. But that form of explanation would be too rigid and too simplistic to provide a workable grasp of social reality. The usual form of causal supersaturation links a number of phenomena requiring explanation with a single causal factor. This cause tends to be *systematically selected* out of all the possible explanatory factors, while all the other factors are systematically obscured.

Take, for example, the way the arrival of foreigners is used as an explanation:

450001–02

A: Switzerland, my native country, the country I was taught to love, cherish and revere. But young people nowadays don't see it like that any more.

Q: Why do you think that is?

A: Mainly because Switzerland's been invaded by foreigners. These days the Swiss, especially the young, want to ape the foreigners, they think that's the thing to do.

450010–11

Q: So you feel that there isn't the same spirit of neutrality?

A: No, there isn't. You hear our politicians talk, and they'll say 'In France, or in Italy, they do such and such.' But Italy's hardly an ideal model at the moment. I'm telling you what I hear, and what I see on television,

people aren't very neutral any more. It is possible to have opinions without openly interfering.

Q: Why do you think it has changed?

A: We've had too many foreigners here and they've ruined our way of thinking. I've done a lot of travelling myself, but I'm still Swiss.

Q: How has it happened?

A: People intermingle, young people admire other nations, first the Americans, then the Russians.

450029
Everywhere you go these days you find foreigners. Our country used to be a haven of peace, right? It was a small, quiet country, where nothing ever happened, a tranquil place where people could live in peace. But then, there are troubles in their country so they come and seek refuge here. You don't put your own house in order by spreading disorder next door. They should put their own house in order first. They should create jobs for themselves in their own country. They should sod off and leave us alone.

450086

Q: Why is it that the army has changed?

A: Too many people have invaded Switzerland from outside and they've had a bad influence.

Q: Do you think young people have been influenced by foreigners?

A: Yes, I think so.

In these passages the speaker uses the same cause ('Switzerland has been invaded by foreigners', 'We've had too many foreigners here', 'they come and seek refuge here', 'too many people have invaded Switzerland from outside') to explain very diverse phenomena: the decline of patriotism among the young, the deterioration of the spirit of neutrality, the disappearance of peace and tranquillity, the changing ideas in the army. The distance between these statements in the interview excludes simple association of ideas, and clearly implicates a deeper causal structure.

The influx of foreigners is not, however, the immediate cause of the explained phenomena, but a *deep cause, the consequences of which serve as intermediate causes.* Two intermediate causes appear in these statements: imitation of foreigners by the Swiss, particularly young people, and the disorder which exists abroad and is imported into Switzerland by immigrants. The selection mechanisms which highlight one factor and occlude the others therefore operate at two levels, between deep cause and intermediate cause, and between intermediate cause and consequence. This twofold operation can be seen most clearly in the second statement (450010–12) where the reason for citing foreign countries as an example is young people's admiration for them, and this admiration – which is a degeneration of the Swiss mentality – is explained by the influx of too many foreigners.

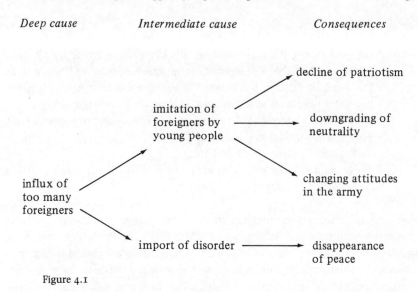

Figure 4.1

The same intermediate cause, the imitation of foreigners by young people, explains the decline of patriotism in the first statement and changing attitudes in the army in the last one. In the third statement, another intermediate cause connects with the deep cause, the disorder brought into the country by foreigners. The structure of all four statements is as shown in Figure 4.1. A similar type of structure is present in the following passages:

> *46006*
> That creates a need for additional schools, for the French, the Italians, the Spanish, they've had to set up a number of them, and that costs the government a lot of VAT, so there has to be this extra VAT, which puts up the cost of living again, so it's us who pay for it, it's our taxes that go up.

> *460034*
> The reason I don't like these street demonstrations is because they have leaders. The Spanish for example have anti-Franco demonstrations, but they have them on our soil, but the thing I think is bad about that people from CERN, the nuclear place, and even State Councillors go on them as well. During the Spanish demonstrations, when they were going on – this is maybe ten years ago – the leader was M. Donzé and he's a State Councillor, they had him so as to encourage the demonstrations, they were in the Place du Pont l'Evêque; and then M. Chavanne from the education department was with them when they broke the windows in the rue de Lausanne, he was there all the time.

> *460107*
> There are a huge number of thefts in Switzerland. It comes from over the border, they're done by Frenchmen.

460118–9

Q: Do you think that the Swiss image is deteriorating?

A: No, I can't say it's deteriorating. It's been made worse by all these foreigners. Not that I'm against foreigners, I'm not. I've been in Italy, I've been in France, but when I was there I didn't go painting the houses all sorts of colours, or shouting and demonstrating in the streets. I was a foreigner in those countries so I kept my mouth shut. That's what foreigners ought to do.

But these people don't do that.

Personally I think they're very noisy, and I don't think all these demonstrations ought to be allowed.

A causal chain is established in the first paragraph: the presence of foreigners requires the setting up of additional schools, which makes an additional charge on taxation revenue, which raises the cost of living. Two successive intermediate causes are inserted between the deep cause and the consequence (the rise in the cost of living). The third answer has no intermediate causes, the presence of foreigners is the cause of the thefts which take place in Switzerland. The fourth answer provides an intermediate cause – demonstrations – for the tarnishing of the Swiss image.

The second answer differs from the others in not taking the deep cause of the presence of foreigners to be a complete explanation; it considers a second deep cause, the actions of politicians. Thus on the one hand the presence of foreigners is the cause of the actions of foreign leaders who provoke demonstrations and, on the other, particular politicians are leaders who co-operate with the foreign leaders in calling demonstrations. However, this last relationship is not really a causal one, as the politicians are seen as leaders by nature rather than because they are pursuing political ends which would explain their participation in the demonstrations. What we are faced with here is therefore a pseudo-cause which is not a second deep cause but which nonetheless establishes an opening in the causal structure, via the intermediate cause 'leaders'.

The causal structure of this set of statements can be represented schematically as shown in Figure 4.2.

On the basis of these two schemata (Figures 4.1 and 4.2), we can put forward a schema for the general structure of causal supersaturation which takes account of possible openings, that is of causal attributions which do not result in the only deep cause (see Figure 4.3).

The 'pure' model of causal supersaturation, however, has no secondary deep cause, and is composed only of deep cause – intermediate cause – consequence sequences, all of which stem from one and the same origin.

The *argumentative function* of discourse based on causal supersaturation is

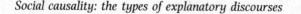

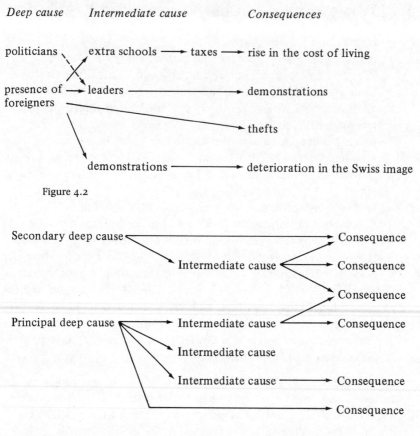

Figure 4.2

Figure 4.3

dominant. One asserted fact is erected into the sole cause of a large number of phenomena, as the basic axis of the interpretation of the social. And it is now quite clear that the choice of this deep cause is a fundamental aspect of *ideological discourse*, of the ideo-logic. This is something we shall return to later, but this is an appropriate point to quote a statement in which the deep cause is definitively established as one which explains everything:

0220030–31
Q: What are the changes you have noticed most?
A: The most striking ones at the moment are juvenile delinquency and
       drugs. That's the biggest change.
Q: So with drugs and delinquency you think there's been a general
       decline in standards?

A: Yes indeed. Because according to the statistics there are 70,000 drug addicts in Geneva alone.[5] That's enough, for a start.

Q: How does it happen that . . .

A: Because young people are too spoiled, they always need more money. We never had so much, but we didn't take drugs, and things were OK. Young people don't want to listen to their parents. Personally I think it all stems from when the Americans announced that children are traumatised if you lay a finger on them; everybody accepted that and parents didn't dare touch their kids. They had to be given what they wanted, given lots of attention and so on. At one time you gave them some kicks up the backside and they were as well behaved as anyone else.

Q: So you'd lay the blame solely on this kind of upbringing?

A: Upbringing and education, and too much freedom, too much flaunting their own opinions. Young people want everything all at once, they're in too much of a hurry to live their own lives. It may also be to do with the fact that the world is in a bad state, they're pressurised into experience, which I can understand. There's nothing you can do about that. In any case it has all been predicted, what has happened has happened, it's a religious matter in a way, what's happening now was predicted, as well as what will happen, everything will happen in accordance with what has been decided.

A variety of intermediate causes are put forward in this statement: juvenile delinquency and drug abuse are due to lax education, too much freedom, incitement to consume, and the wish to experience as much as possible. These intermediate causes all lead back to the general decline in standards predicted in prophecies, and this deep cause explains everything without needing to be proved; 'in any case' whatever happens has been predicted. Causal supersaturation operates here as an unarguable, undemonstrable absolute. No communication would be possible if the deep cause explanation was challenged. The causal explanation is not open to discussion, there is nothing else to be said.

Multiple causality

Multiple causality as a logico-discursive form is diametrically opposed to causal supersaturation. Here a single phenomenon is explained by recourse to *multiple causal factors with no organisational hierarchy*.

> 010056
> I work for a company which does a fair amount of business in the Jura, so I'm familiar with the issue. At first I thought it might be a question of religion because of the North being Catholic and Berne being Protestant. But I don't

really know whether the separation the separatists want will bring many advantages. There was a sense of euphoria, the clock and watch business was doing very well, and now that they're separated from the canton of Berne they'll obviously have to pay taxes for the infrastructure; then there's the language question, isn't there, I know Bernese quite well and there's a lot of German idiom, a kind of invasion which has annoyed the people of the North . . . I can understand that, the area is not big enough for proper assimilation like you get in the cities, where it's much easier. Perhaps you saw that TV programme with Madame Aubry and the secretary of the separatists, Béguelin? The interesting thing about that was that Madame Aubry, who's Catholic and comes from the North, is anti-separatist, whereas Béguelin is a Reformed Church Protestant from the South and he's an extreme separatist. So those two rather suggest that there may be something artificial about the Jura question.

In his attempt to explain the Jura question, the speaker goes over all the possible explanations – linguistic, economic and religious factors, and the actions of political leaders. He does not select or reject any of them, but leaves the question of their interaction, or of their relative importance, open. He offers a range of possible explanations.

230043

Q: How do you explain this change of attitude [among young people]?

A: It's to do with changes in lifestyle, like transport, radio, and television. I went to see a film not so long ago, *Emmanuelle*, and I must say I was staggered by it, it was almost unbelievable, but then times change. It takes us back to what we saying before, that everything has changed, developed. Young people and their ways of thinking have changed. They grew up at a very fortunate time, when they could get what they wanted, when they could buy a nice car, when they didn't have to count the pennies because there was plenty of money about. If you weren't happy with one boss you left him, went across the road and got taken on at an even higher wage.

This statement does not advance a list of explanatory factors in the way the previous one does. Yet its causal structure is comparable, providing a series of causes for the changes in young people's attitudes: transport, radio, television, cinema, higher wages, consumerism, job mobility. These factors could, it's true, be organised into two groups, one centred on the development of communications and the other on living conditions, but the speaker does not do this, he offers a series of different explanations without ranking them in importance or structuring them. The common factor is that 'everything has changed', but this remains an assertion. Everything happens as if, distrusting over-simplification, he leaves open the question of a determining cause, or causes, so that any one or all of the causes mentioned, or one or more deep

causes of which they are the consequences, might play a determining role. The explanation is more like a *kaleidoscope* than anything corresponding to a more precise conception.

020007

Q: So why is there immigration? What are the reasons for it?

A: For one thing, people may like a change of country. I think that has a part to play in it. And are you talking about internal immigration or immigration from abroad?

Q: Yes, let's say Italians immigrating to Switzerland, or Spanish immigration, there's a lot of immigration in the world, in Europe anyway.

A: OK, but the Spanish or the Italians know quite well why they have come to Switzerland, they know there isn't enough work in their own countries, but as for why there isn't enough work there I don't know enough about their countries to say, but there must be some reason for it. There's work here if you want it, but if there are foreigners here then there's bound to be some unemployment. And unemployment is caused by a number of factors, not just foreigners.

What are the causes of emigration? Love of travel, absence of work in the country of origin, a supply of work in Switzerland; the lack of work in the country of origin has its own causes, but these are not known. Then the discourse moves directly from one of the causes of emigration (the supply of work in Switzerland) to one of its consequences (unemployment in Switzerland), which itself has other causes as well which he goes on to talk about later in the same interview (not reproduced here). Multiple causality thus operates very fluidly, by enumerating and constructing a causal sequence capable of being interrupted by the incursion of further, supplementary, explanatory factors. A discourse is established which is based on causal relations but which makes no claim to construct an explanation or prove a hypothesis, merely invoking different phenomena and the connections between them.

But although causal relations are established between analytically distinct phenomena, the general operation of discourse based on multiple causality is not designed to prove anything. Its argumentative function is diffused, rather than being clearly founded. Multiple causality is a logico-discursive form which occupies a place between segmented causality, based on a synthetic grasp of phenomena, and coherent proof constructed out of a necessary sequence of causal relations. We can further postulate that this discourse has a hybrid function, both argumentative and expressive. It may perhaps be a form of self-expression mediated by causal attribution, but in that case it is controlled and carefully elaborated self-expression, which stems from more than a simple emotional impulse. Such an impulse is often accompanied by an activity (or practice) which consists of judging, condemning and making

associations on affective grounds, rather than explaining. Whereas by searching for multiple explanatory factors for each phenomenon, the social actor subject is carrying out an important logico-discursive task, a task which necessarily implies a degree of decentration. It is as if the interviewee wants to show the interviewer, by his practice of causal attribution, that he is somebody who is trying to understand and explain, and is not the sort of person who is content to judge or condemn.

Interaction of forms and contents

In the preceding elucidation of logico-discursive forms, we have already established that the *functioning of certain forms* is indissociable from *the contents* of the causal relation, so that the distinction between causality and what may be viewed as causality (or between causality and contingency) seems indispensable for an understanding of the functioning of certain forms. The function of causal attribution thus also relates to elements of *content*:

–   confirmation of a valorised proposition;
–   construction of a social representation to compensate for the absence of concrete knowledge;
–   selection of one causal factor at the cost of others;
–   self-expression.

This indicates that our initial postulate, that the functioning of causality in social thought is bound up with content and cannot be reduced to a purely formal pattern of thought, remains valid and needs to be extended. The social thought revealed in the discursive practices we have analysed is thus characterised by its necessary application to specific contents. To put this another way, there is no formal social thought with rules governing its operation which can be separated from its content; we are not trying to construct *canonical forms* of social thought, but to examine the interactions between certain logico-discursive forms and the contents of causal attribution. Such forms necessarily function with reference to such contents.

070006
Q: What do you like most about Switzerland at the moment?
A: I think it's a . . . how shall I put it? A kind of peacefulness, a kind of peacefulness about living here which, of course, has disappeared at the moment, because as members of Action Nationale[6] we're ashamed of the way the authorities are sacrificing Switzerland for the sake of foreigners, which is absolutely unprecedented.

The cause adduced for the disappearance of peacefulness is the shame felt by members of Action Nationale for the authorities. It might seem tempting to

reconstruct the statement so that it reads more 'logically', which would give something like: 'The peace of living here has disappeared because the authorities are sacrificing Switzerland for the sake of foreigners. As members of Action Nationale this makes us ashamed.' But the original statement is different, and its formulation can help us to extend our analysis of the form of thought in practice, rather as studying slips of the tongue can reveal mental mechanisms which the discourse is attempting to hide.

It is as if the speaker had embarked on an explanation which would conform to the 'logical' statement reconstructed above until the moment he uttered the 'because', at which point the desire to express his feelings about the authorities interrupted the progress of his explanatory logic. The way the discourse functions seems to be as follows:

(a)   the thought unfolds in accordance with a logic appropriate to the explanatory function;

(b)   the thought moves faster than the discourse, which it precedes; the speaker has already thought about the 'authorities [who] are sacrificing Switzerland for the sake of foreigners', but has not yet expressed the idea;

(c)   there is a judgement associated with the already thought but unexpressed idea, 'we are ashamed', which is further linked to the institutional context of its production, 'as members of Action Nationale';

(d)   the desire to express this judgement takes priority over finishing the explanation;

(e)   once this priority has been satisfied, the discourse takes up the thread of explanation where it was interrupted, but this has now lost its original sense.

The logic of what is desired, what is experienced affectively, is stronger than the logic of explanation, which results in an *amalgam of judgement and explanation*. The feeling of shame at the authorities' behaviour, and the assertion of this behaviour as the cause of the loss of peace, are indissociably linked, intermingled and amalgamated. The affective investment of the content and the demonstration of the speaker's subjective attitudes modify the explanation profoundly. The speaker's affective and cognitive activity is combined into an undifferentiated whole which is projected into the facts he mentions before he actually mentions them. The thought thus functions simultaneously in terms of a logic of desire and a logic of explanation.

140004
Q: What, in your view, are the differences between Switzerland and the neighbouring countries?

A: Well, language, of course. And I'm on a special diet, so I have to be careful what I eat, and that's much easier to do in Switzerland.

This answer is, to say the least, unexpected. Two schematisations overlap without any point of contact between them. Within the logic of the interview, this fairly general question ought to elicit a response that reveals the speaker's representations of his country. But the logic of the interviewee (the speaker) is radically different, as the question is located at the level of practical personal experience, and answered in terms of one, isolated, fragmentary aspect; the issues invoked by the question are broken up as it is seen in terms of the most immediate requirements of practical living. It is this *immediate practice* that provides the criteria of relevance: were the speaker to go abroad, it would be more important for him to make himself understood, and to find the right sort of food for his diet, than to create representations of the differences between the country he was visiting and Switzerland. The content that concerns him is an outcome of his immediate practice, and the *logic of immediate practice* is not the same as the logic of the interview. However, a fuller analysis of the discourse does enable us to identify a comparative representation of Switzerland and foreign countries, by setting the statement once more within the logic of the interview. To do this the statement has to be placed in context, alongside the statement which precedes it:

140002–03
A: We like to spend our holidays in Switzerland.
Q: You haven't been to other countries?
A: No, no. We have such a lovely country it would be a shame to go anywhere else.

The speaker's image of other countries is a construct, as he has never been to any of them. He imagines that solving the practical problems raised by the question is 'much easier in Switzerland'. Switzerland is known, familiar, the site of his immediate practice. Other places are unknown, and fraught with risk and difficulty. This central representation underlies the first statement, and is thus a representation of the characteristics of Switzerland, one which says nothing about Switzerland but does indicate how the speaker thinks about it. In this way we can reconstruct an overall representation above and beyond the fragmentation of reality at work in the discourse.

In contrast to this example of *detotalisation linked to immediate practice* we can now look at a passage in which the explanation of a particular phenomenon is based on a general social representation:

230070
A: . . . there haven't been any problems in Switzerland since we've had the *Paix du travail.*[7]

Q: How would you explain the difference between Switzerland and other
       countries which all have different social relations?

A: Well, here everybody receives an education, everyone can read and
       write, the only people who don't achieve that are the mentally defi-
       cient. Everybody receives an education. But in Italy that is not the
       case, in France it's arguable, and there are still plenty of countries
       where the level is very low, though France is better than Italy.

So the explanation given for the *Paix du travail* is the high level of education,
both elements being highly valued. Conversely strikes and social conflict are
associated with a lack of education and, in the case of Italy, with illiteracy. We
can therefore see that the speaker's values are structured mutually, and their
reciprocal relations provide the basis of their deeper significance. The combi-
nation of social peace, education and a quest for compromise is echoed by the
corresponding but negatively valorised combination of conflict, a low level of
education and social struggle. These two opposed combinations are the
structure of a representation without which it would not be possible to establish
the causal relationship between education and the *Paix du travail*.

The speaker's investment here is effected at the level of an external general
representation which he appropriates rather than at the level of desire or
immediate practice.

In both these instances *the investment of the content governs the process of
causal attribution*. It functions as the *motor of the logico-discursive operations*,
contributing the energy necessary to establish them.

Unlike formal logic, social thought in use, as it deals with causality (or
causal attribution), does not construct a metalanguage applicable to the level
of causal relations alone. The logico-discursive forms and contents of these
statements intermingle and interact. The operation of causality is dependent
on content and its investment. The contents, the subjects broached by the
speaker, are not neutral, or random: they are invocations of material and
symbolic issues which the speaker appropriates, or from which he takes his
bearings, and this investment of content orients the functioning of the causal
relations, and takes them in a direction relevant to the practice of the social
actor subject.

The three paradigms of causal attribution

Introduction

The paradigms of causal attribution are the types of agency effected by the
speaker between forms of thought and content. Three elements occur in
combination: *form*, *content* and *investment by the speaker*. These combinations
are not random: it is not a matter of anybody explaining anything anyhow.

First of all, we need to elucidate *the paradigms of causal attribution present in these discourses*, by an analysis of the discourses themselves. In theory, these paradigms are mutually exclusive, since everyday mental activity functions according to relatively stable sociocognitive systems. To begin with, we shall define the structure and *modus operandi* of each of the paradigms regarded in its own right and as irreducible to any other. It will, however, become clear that the boundaries between them, and their theoretical mutual exclusion, are only relative, and we shall go on to consider the significance of the shifts between them and the ways in which they can co-exist.

The deviancy paradigm

Deviant behaviour as a cause. In its simplest form this is characterised by the fact that social phenomena, such as social change, are explained principally by the *voluntary behaviour (deviant or normal) of individuals or social groups.*

450047

Q: How do you explain the fact that there are so few strikes and so few labour disputes in Switzerland?

A: Because we have order, we take care who's allowed into Switzerland; now there aren't leaders all over the place.

Labour disputes are seen by this speaker as the result of the behaviour
(a) of those (probably the authorities) who are not sufficiently vigilant in controlling the entry of people into Switzerland; and
(b) of leaders. Here the explanation is lapidary. The implication is that they will be foreigners. On the other hand, for the explanation to make sense, the speaker must be acknowledged to be attributing a considerable amount of influence to them.

This type of explanation therefore gives great emphasis to voluntary, deliberate behaviour as a causal factor. Other factors (material, structural, institutional, and so on) do not figure. Here are some further examples to illustrate the way the deviancy paradigm functions:

070010–11

A: Democracy is currently on the decline. The people decide to vote against something, by changing policy, and the authorities talk a lot about it and do nothing. Which makes people think they just do whatever they want (and that's the reason why abstentionism is on the increase). It's a disgrace not to respect the opinion of the people.

I always vote, that's something I never fail to do, and I urge everyone else to vote as well. Especially when I hear a Swiss citizen protesting, 'Are you going to vote? No! you don't have any right to

complain then, you'll have to keep your mouth shut because everyone else went to vote and made their views known, so go and vote, accept your responsibilities.'

Q: But why do you think people don't vote?

A: Because they say, 'Oh, they'll do whatever they want to do anyway.' So, for example, they might want to counteract a law they thought was unjust, OK, but they get angry when they discover after six months or so that the law that was overturned is back in favour, and so they just let it pass.

The phenomenon to be explained here (P) is abstentionism. Let us briefly recapitulate the speaker's propositions on the subject:

(1)   democracy is on the decline
(2)   the people reject a law
(3)   the authorities pass it nonetheless
(4)   the people say: there's no point
(5)   I always vote
(6)   I urge people to vote
(7)   people who don't vote can't complain.

Q: repeats the question

(8)   the people say: Oh, they'll do whatever they want
(9)   the people want to vote
(10)   the authorities decide against them
         thus
(11)   the people are angry
         so the people stop voting.

Or to put it more briefly:

A people do not want to vote because the authorities do what they
         want anyway
B everyone ought to vote, like me
C people who don't vote can't complain

Abstentionism is seen as a *deviant act* with regard to the speaker's expectations about people's roles. The people who do not vote only have themselves to blame; they have no right to complain.

How is this deviance explained? 'People don't want to vote because the authorities do whatever they want anyway.' The *deviance of another social actor* turns out to be at the root of the deviant behaviour of the first social actor. So the overall schema of the causal relations that make up the deviance paradigm is as follows:

AS_1 dev $\rightarrow AS_2$ dev $\rightarrow P$

Key

AS_1 dev = Deviant social actor no. 1

AS_2 dev = Deviant social actor no. 2

P = the phenomenon to be explained (in this case, abstentionism)

This represents the general schema of the causal relations that make up the deviancy paradigm. Whatever phenomenon is to be explained, it will always be a consequence of an imbalance between behaviour and behavioural norm. The explanation would remain at this level if it was not for pressure (from the interviewer) to explain the deviant behaviour itself. When this happens the speaker shifts the responsibility back to another social actor. Some social actor will always be found at the beginning of the sequence:

$(AS_1$ dev $\rightarrow AS_2$ dev $\ldots \rightarrow AS_n$ dev $\rightarrow P)$

Where does this sequence end? In this example we could ask questions about the causes of the authorities' behaviour. Other extracts from interviews show that at a given point the causal sequence is interrupted according to modalities of which we shall have more to say later (the end of the causal regression). For the time being, it is enough to point out this tendency to locate the origin of a negatively judged phenomenon in the deviant behaviour of a social actor, and to note that this behaviour is itself a reaction to the deviant behaviour of another social actor, or to the influence of such behaviour.

Social relations are perceived as determined by specific role expectations. The social phenomenon which is disapproved of originates in the way the behaviour of a social actor fails to conform to the social norms associated with his role. It is an *ultra-codified world* which is valorised, but the codification is interiorised, that is it is implicit rather than recognised as such. The sociocognitive centration is, so to speak, experienced rather than determined. Voting is the behavioural norm of the citizen, and respecting the will of the people is the behavioural norm of the authorities.

The reason the people do not vote is because the authorities do not respect the will of the people. One might therefore expect the speaker, at the end of his explanation, to admit that abstentionism is understandable. It would be logical for him to admit as much from the very beginning of his explanation, as it would fit in with the causal relations he has set up. Yet this is not what happens: the authorities do not do their duty, but this is no justification for citizens to depart from their behavioural norm. In other words, citizens should continue to vote even if it serves no purpose, and yet the speaker himself

constructs the causal relation between the actions of the authority and abstentionism. It is *as if he rejects the dynamic he describes*. For him, the facts and even the relations between the facts, are not enough to justify changes in social relations. The facts are established but *they are still seen as deviance despite being perceived as the logical consequence of another set of facts*.

We can sum up the general logico-discursive form of the deviance paradigm with the help of a *discursive model* made up of three basic sentences:

IT OUGHT TO BE LIKE THAT

IT IS NOT AS IT OUGHT TO BE (which can be explained by the fact
that . . .)

IT OUGHT TO BE LIKE THAT (all the same)

The imbalance between what is real and what is desired has no sooner been stated than the latter is re-established by the discourse and the real is once more regarded as abnormal. There is no way in which the real can become a new state of affairs. To the extent that it does not correspond to the norm it is seen as an anomaly rather than the new reality. In fact, it is more important for the speaker to respect the norm *even if it seems pointless* than to adapt his behaviour to circumstances.

The surprising thing about this discourse is the actual nature of the causality. The speaker refuses to admit the validity of causal relations which he himself takes as verified. Thus, having located the cause of abstentionism in the behaviour of the authorities, he refuses to admit the relevance of it. *A is the cause of B but B should not exist*.

460011–13

Q: Why do you think foreigners come to Switzerland?

A: Well I'll tell you, the main reason is to earn money, save money, and take most of it back home with them. What usually happens is, if it's an Italian, say, he gets home, builds a small house with the help of a friend, so most of them have a house in Italy. They live here as cheaply as they can; they come here to work, and the frontier workers always look at the paper to find out what the exchange rate is or how much they'll get in French francs, so in the end they earn more than we do.

Q: Do you think they would have been able to stay in their own country if they'd wanted to?

A: They wouldn't do so well out of it. I know these French frontier workers, they come here to work, and soon they have a villa and a nice standard of living, better than we Swiss can have, and they do it on exchange rates.

Q: But do you think they could have found work in their own country?

A: They might have been able to, but they'd have to put up with much
       lower wages.

First of all, the speaker emphasises foreigners' desire to earn more money.
Spontaneously, he locates the causality at the level of voluntary action and
ignores other aspects governing the arrival of foreigners, such as unemploy-
ment. This *priority of will over other determining factors*, of free choice over
necessity, is characteristic of this form of social thought, regardless of the
issues involved. Individuals are perceived as free to choose and the behaviour
of social groups is perceived in the same way as that of isolated individuals.
The movement from the particular to the general is resolved by a simple
transposition from one to the other, the generality being considered the sum
of identical individual cases.

By locating causality at the level of voluntary individual behaviour, the
speaker is able to compare his situation directly with that of foreigners: '. . . so
in the end they earn more than we do'. The explanation, which is based on a
sociocognitive mechanism called *voluntarism*, stems partly from a
sociocentric perception and partly from a 'strategy' on the part of a subject
wanting to assert his own identity, which he does by rejecting 'objective'
causal explanations, such as material conditions or the like. In other words,
the speaker ignores external, objective causality, as it is no help in expressing
what he really wants to say, which is his relative dissatisfaction (in relation to
foreigners) with his own living conditions.

It thus follows that causality in this type of social thought does not appear
as a search for knowledge about social processes, but as the search for an
explanation which is capable of expressing his own relation to his
surroundings.

To take another example: after having talked about crime, the constantly
increasing number of thefts and the resultant insecurity, the speaker replies to
the following question:

470042
Q: Why do you think there's so much trouble at the moment?
A: Because there's a large section of people who don't want to work, so
       they steal.
Q: But why is it different now?
A: Because x years ago we were brought up differently, we were edu-
       cated, people were much more honest, we didn't have so much
       freedom, we had a stricter education and led better lives, whereas now
       children today are brought up with much more freedom, otherwise –
       apparently – they develop complexes.
Q: What were things like in your day?

A: Obviously people were stricter, we didn't have the freedom young people have nowadays.

Q: In what ways?

A: We had to be home with our parents by nine o'clock, and there was no question of spending a whole night away from home. Our education was much stricter, so people were better behaved, and they were much more honest.

The upsurge in crime is explained by young people not wanting to work. For the speaker, the cause is to be sought in the voluntary, abnormal behaviour of young people. Again we find the schema AS_1 dev$\rightarrow$P which characterises the deviance paradigm.

This causal factor is itself explained by reference to the deviant behaviour of another social actor, the parents who no longer educate their children in the way they should. Yet what is surprising in this statement is that this second explanation does nothing to alter the perception and judgement of young people. They may be badly educated but they are still responsible. Any expectation that the discourse might present them as victims or absolved of responsibility is frustrated. The determining role of education, despite being fully expressed and explicitly stated ('Our education was much stricter, so people were better behaved'), has no influence on the judgement of young people. They are regarded as responsible even though their behaviour is understood as determined. *In this system of thought cause is dissociated from judgement.* In the end, the stated cause does not really matter. All that is relevant to the judgement is the objective result and the actions stemming from it.

Causality therefore appears as a foreign category, outside the process of evaluation. The judgement only has a bearing on immediate action. The margin of freedom the social actors may benefit from is not a factor taken into account in evaluating their behaviour. Even though they are subject to determination they remain fully responsible.

The discourse proceeds along the causal sequence: $P \leftarrow AS_n$ dev$\leftarrow AS_2$ dev$\leftarrow AS_1$ dev, and the mode of evaluation is the same at each stage. A social actor's behaviour is perceived as the consequence of that of the preceding social actor, but both of these are regarded as voluntary.

This brings us to the question of what 'will' means. 'Young people don't want to work': for the speaker, this means principally that young people do not do what they ought to do; the term does not signify a will to act differently so much as a lack of will. In other words, the idea that young people might demonstrate a will to work less is entirely foreign to the speaker.

The term 'will' does not mean the will to choose any particular value

system, but the will to act in the proper way, in accordance with the norm: young people do not make the necessary effort to behave in the right way; they no longer have the WILL.

Even the idea of freedom does not figure. Freedom is seen as deviant.

As the speaker sees it, young people do not choose: they are deviant. *Deviance can never be considered a choice; it is a state.* To put it another way, individuals can only express their will through actions that conform to the norm. And to possess will is simply to remain true to the norms, and to tradition.

Imitation and the spread of deviance

Imitation, proliferation, contamination and *epidemic* are topics which surface frequently among people who adopt the deviancy paradigm.

460106–07

Q: What sort of thing would you like to hear in a 1st of August speech?

A: I don't know what I'd like to hear, it's always fine words about the progress of the Confederation . . .

They can't say what you want to hear, that things are quietening down in neighbouring countries, that things will be more peaceful and there won't be any more hostage-taking. It's dreadful, these kidnappings. It's becoming an illness, a vice.

Fortunately the French have formed these anti-gang squads, and they are beginning to eliminate it.

Q: Why is there so much of it these days?

A: It spreads, it proliferates, it's like vermin, like cockroaches in a house, it's like rats or mice, it breeds, I think of it like vermin. It starts with just one or two, and then other people start doing it.

The idea that crime spreads like an illness underlies the deviance paradigm like a weird backcloth. Deviance does not need to be explained, or attributed to social causes. It develops autonomously according to its own laws, invading the social organism as a virus invades the biological organism.

There is always a deviant act at the root of the epidemic, which is followed by a process of imitation which is presented in the discourse as the deviant world's natural mechanism. The explanation reveals a radical and clear-cut distinction between society and the world of deviance. And while this may be narrowed down or contracted (by different combinations of the amalgam), it always functions autonomously in this system of interpretation. In other words, it is not perceived as a manifestation of something internal to society, as the product of the overall situation, but as an external phenomenon invading the social fabric like a foreign body.

460127

Q: How do you explain the increase in conscientious objectors over the last few years?

A: It spreads very quickly, like all illnesses. They say 'my friend doesn't want to do it, nor do I . . .'

Here too imitation is put forward as the process by which deviant behaviour spreads. This viewpoint takes no account of any links between society as a whole and the phenomena considered deviant, which simply arise out of the will of certain individuals; the postulate of imitation provides the key to explain the progress of deviance.

450001–02

A: Switzerland, my native country, the country I was taught to love, cherish and revere. But young people nowadays don't see it like that any more . . .

Q: Why do you think that is?

A: Mainly because Switzerland's been invaded by foreigners. These days the Swiss, especially the young, want to ape the foreigners, they think that's the thing to do.

Several connections are inferred between the disappearance of patriotism (the phenomenon to be explained) and the presence of foreigners (presented as the cause of the phenomenon), and are regarded as commonplace and acceptable enough not to require explanation.

'The young want to ape the foreigners': this assertion enables the speaker to make the connection between the disappearance of patriotism and the presence of foreigners. The process of imitation is the central nexus for interpreting social change. We shall be seeing more examples of this. Imitating, copying or aping others is a constant process. Why is there this tendency to imitate? The speaker does not explain. The causal regression is interrupted. Imitation as cause of change is a postulate on which the whole interpretation is constructed.

450054–55

Q: Do you think the *Paix du travail* can continue in the present economic climate?

A: If we want to keep the *Paix du travail* we have to make sure there aren't too many foreigners here. And there must be enough work for our nationals before we give it to the mafia.

Q: Have there been any strikes this year?

A: Yes. And they don't really have any right to strike. There is no right to go on strike in Switzerland. So why do they do it? Because they want to ape other countries.

Q: Why is the army so different from what it used to be?

A: Too many people have invaded our country from abroad and they've had a bad influence.

Q: Do you think that young people are influenced by foreigners?

A: Yes, I think so.

The causes of change are exogenous. The in-group (Switzerland, the army) cannot be changed by an internal dynamic. Any change is implicitly regarded as impossible without some sign of exogenous factors.

Exogenous factor + imitation is the causal schema that belongs to this form of thought. Take another example:

450010–11

Q: So you feel that there isn't the same spirit of neutrality?

A: No, there isn't. You hear our politicians talk, and they'll say, 'In France, or in Italy, they do such and such'. But Italy's hardly an ideal model at the moment. I'm telling you what I hear, and what I see on television, people aren't very neutral any more. It is possible to have opinions without openly interfering.

Q: Why do you think it has changed?

A: We've had too many foreigners here and they've ruined our way of thinking. I've done a lot of travelling myself, but I'm still Swiss.

Q: How has it happened?

A: People intermingle, young people admire other nations, first the Americans, then the Russians.

Imitation is regarded as a fact requiring no commentary. Imitating is intrinsically natural to young people. They are not thought of as motivated by any plan, or by independent needs, or as influenced by objective factors. They imitate because it is in their nature to do so. Hence the danger represented by the foreign presence. Once the postulate of imitation is advanced, the speaker sees nothing to hinder the proliferation of foreign customs, behaviour and ways of thinking. No barrier or obstacle will be able to stand in the way of the evil any longer.

At a more general level, the deviancy paradigm throws up a distinction between *responsible deviants* and *irresponsible imitators*.

The break in causal regression

In the deviancy paradigm, the break in causal regression may take a number of forms.

450017

Q: The Swiss people who take part in demonstrations, why do you think they do it?

A: Why? What do they think they want? In Switzerland we do everything possible for the workers. You have to have lived abroad to appreciate the kind of life they have. Maybe not any more, they've done a lot, they've made a lot of progress, in France, everywhere. These days it's only the worker who counts. What have they got to complain about when they've got plenty to eat? When we got married, my husband earned 300 francs a month; life was hard, and we had a baby.

The speaker *does not answer the question about causes.* She shows her incomprehension; it is difficult for her to call on epidemic imitation as an explanation as that can only apply to certain social groups which are regarded as irresponsible. The incomprehension remains, and explanation gives way to the reassertion of norms and values. 'They've got nothing to complain about, they earn enough money, they have plenty to eat.' The only reasons for contention that the speaker will allow are those she would complain about herself. Yet her frame of reference is the past. 'That was in 1934, and in those days we didn't complain about such minor matters'. Material factors are not seen in their historical context, but in a context of reference which is powerfully invested by the speaker. The result is a sociocentric interpretation which recurs in the causality. The only explanatory factors she allows are ones which she herself considers valid.

450075
Q: Why do you think that they [the Jurassian separatists] wanted to separate from Berne?
A: They said that Berne wasn't interested in them, that Berne didn't build them any roads, that Berne didn't give them anything, that they couldn't evolve, they couldn't develop. I don't believe that. Berne is a very rich canton, and there's every reason why they should take an interest in them.

Immediately before that, the same speaker said:

450074
A: Personally, I would have kicked them out of Switzerland. I was furious. I wept one night watching television when some great imbecile said, 'We used to be French, and we shall go back to being French again if Switzerland won't agree to free us from Berne.' I'd have thrown him out of Switzerland straight away. The Jura makes me sick, same as the communists. It's a canton I take no notice of now. They aren't Swiss, they've done too much harm, it's a disgrace to Switzerland.

Although the speaker explicitly refuses to take seriously the reasons given by the social actors themselves, she does not put forward any alternative explanation. The break in the causal regression comes here, as in the previous instance, through a reassertion of the norms allowed by the speaker.

The deviancy paradigm and logico-discursive forms

Going back to the logico-discursive forms we identified earlier, we can say that to a very large extent the deviancy paradigm is based on *causal supersaturation*.

Of all the social actors whose deviant action is regarded as the cause of a phenomenon deemed to be pernicious, some are selected with sufficient regularity to justify talking about a *system of explanation by accusation*. But there is also sufficiently frequent reference to the deviant action of other social actors for it to be quite inadequate merely to identify the group selected as an omnicausal factor, the automatic scapegoat for all ills, and this radically reduces the paradigm's causal efficacy.

It is true that some social actors appear far more often than others, and it is no surprise to find that these are the non-valorised categories in the discourse of supporters of Action Nationale: leaders and foreigners. But they are invoked both as blameworthy and as objects of causal relations derived from different factors, especially the action of other social actors. A particular system of actors can thus be set up, whose interactions are causes of particular phenomena. This causality does not remove the blame from the social actor or actors responsible, but neither does it allow the issue to be reduced to a simple attribution of blame to one group pre-selected to be a scapegoat.

Additionally, the overall functioning of the deviancy paradigm is steeped in a *negative valorisation*, which involves the phenomenon to be explained just as much as the nature of the social actor and the action attributed to him. And here we find several of the other sociocognitive mechanisms already discussed: *dependence on the past* as negative valorisation of social change, the *devalorisation* of social categories constructed and homogenised by the discourse, and *moral reification* which fixes the system of norms and submits the actors to it.

In contrast to what has just been said, let us look at an example of the explanation of a positively evaluated phenomenon by the positive behaviour of a social actor:

010038

Q: You talked about strikes. In Switzerland there's the *Paix du travail*. How do you explain the fact that Switzerland is the only country . . .

A: The Swiss are a mountain people, a bit cold perhaps, but always reasonable, they understand things pretty well. Even the ordinary worker is always prepared to discuss things, he's well aware of the benefits of it. Even on the socialist side, the left wing of the government, people are sensible and rational.

So the reason for the *Paix du travail* is that the Swiss are sensible. An explicitly positive norm: sensible people are 'prepared to discuss things', to moderate their demands and accept the need for compromise. The social actor

designated in a very generalised, even generic, way as 'Swiss people' acts in conformity to the norm, has the wisdom to conform to it. The happy outcome of this behaviour is the *Paix du travail*. Causality is thus functioning in an identical manner, but this time with a positive valorisation of the elements. Should we then be talking not about a deviancy paradigm but, more broadly, about a voluntarist paradigm, or a paradigm of the norm, with the deviancy paradigm being one particular manifestation of it? The reason for retaining the term deviancy paradigm, and for considering the negative valorisation of content as its constitutive element, is that positive valorisation is much less common. The systematic use of the paradigm remains linked to the negative valorisation of phenomena and behaviour, and to causal supersaturation through the identification of the main 'culpable' groups. Judgement and explanation are intermeshed, so that condemnation of the guilty seems to give the speaker some compensation for the negative situation he is condemning and a discursive power capable of occluding his loss of *real power*. The vehemence of the discourse seems to be in proportion to his actual impotence.

The materialist paradigm

The materialist paradigm is based on *the explanation of social facts*, including non-material facts such as behaviour and ways of thinking, *by material factors*. This does not generally mean that the social actors are excised from the explanation, but that they are considered in terms of the material factors affecting their situation and their practice, rather than in terms of their intrinsic qualities.

The materialist paradigm is a complex mode of explaining the social, and cannot be reduced to a binary relation between a cause and a consequence. To demonstrate how it works, we shall begin by describing such binary relations, the elementary material explanations.

The elementary material explanation

480050

Q: What to your mind are the causes of immigration.

A: Work. When you see Sicilians arrive here, it's because they haven't any work at home. It's normal that they should go and look for it.

Q: Of necessity?

A: Of necessity, precisely.

230062

Q: What, in your opinion, are the reasons why they [foreign workers] emigrate?

A: Simply a lack of work at home. They don't come out of the good of their

hearts, far from it. These people are in a bad way at home, there's no work, just like the Swiss used to do, when they went to work in the service of Louis XV or the Pope, they'll go anywhere.

These two quotations show the construction of a simple relation between two elements, the lack of work in certain countries and emigration from those countries. The cause is a material one, the consequence behavioural, which establishes a simple causality based on a single material explanatory factor, which needs no further explanation.

However, the elementary material explanation is not inevitably opposed to the materialist causal paradigm; it may be its starting point, its zero moment, if the speaker transcends the elementary structure of a relation between two facts by locating them within a more general system, governed by rules of social functioning and social action.

The structural material explanation

(a) *Material causes, material consequences*

230030

A: We live in a small country. It's like an egg, an egg has various possibilities but if it's really full then the shell will crack. That's what has happened to us. And here again, like I said before, it's a question of vested interests. Our big companies have orders, and people are sent out to France, Italy, anywhere, as far as the Middle East, to look for workers. They don't mind where they come from, they've got the capital and it needs to bring in good returns. It's all vested interests and capital that does it.

Here the cause of immigration is 'capital', but this is not an isolated element. The material factor at the root of the explanation is complex, being a *system of factors* which are interlinked: 'our big companies', 'orders', 'workers', 'capital', 'returns'. The connections between these elements are established by the *laws by which the system operates*: 'capital', 'it needs to bring in', and by *actions*; 'people are sent out . . . to look'.

This system has another consequence, apart from immigration, and that is crisis. The speaker offers the same explanation, almost word for word, when asked about the causes of the economic crisis:

230045

Q: Some people say that the crisis is a result of the capitalist system. What do you think?

A: Yes, it's another consequence of it, what you say is quite right because the capitalist system has tried to do too much . . . It's what I was saying

just now, the order books were full, they sent people out everywhere, they produced more and more and more to increase their dividends, but there comes a time when all this production can no longer be absorbed. So, yes, it is a consequence of our capitalist system.

Here we can see another law by which the system operates: consumption must absorb production. The system thus comes into contradiction with this law as a result of its own dynamic which is itself founded on the law of operation we have already seen: 'it needs to bring in'. But this dynamic does not operate blindly, it only comes about through the action of identifiable groups: 'our big companies'. *A system of social actions*, governed by laws of operation and not by static or absolute norms, and functioning through the action of groups, of social actors.

The next illustration puts it more briefly:

500009
Q: Why in your opinion do foreigners come to Switzerland?
A: Well I think it's the employers who get them to come here so that they can affect wages and pay them less. That's how I see it, as simple as that.

The explanation is based on an action ('the employers who get them to come here' and on the laws by which, in this case, the labour market functions ('affect wages').

210017
A: . . . you could say the unions don't demand enough.
Q: Do you think that's changing?
A: Yes it is, precisely because of the current economic recession bringing in unemployment.

This quotation reveals a causal relation between three elements: the economic crisis, unemployment, and change in the unions. In that sense it is already more complex than a binary causal relation. But more importantly it is structured from another point of view: if the cause 'economic crisis' entails the cause 'unemployment' (simple relation), the cause 'unemployment' only implies the second consequence 'that's changing' insofar as it is part of a more general explanatory framework about the way the unions function which the speaker had put forward shortly before. It is never said, either explicitly or implicitly, that change in the unions is a necessary consequence of unemployment. But in the analysis the speaker goes on to make of the way the unions function, it seems that they will develop because there have been changes in their behaviour:

210017
A: We recognise that unemployment, in German-speaking Switzerland

as well as here in the French-speaking part, has hit a lot of people, and our German-Swiss colleagues, comrades, realise that it isn't enough to demand material improvements, we also have to change the workers' power within the companies, if we don't do that we'll get nowhere, because as soon as recession comes they'll take back everything they've given us.

Here again the causal factor (unemployment in this case) is not linked simply to the stated consequence, but cause and consequence are both set against a more general background of the laws of operation and social actions.

Furthermore, the material factors invoked are not just economic, they are *institutional*: the unions are described as a system of actions governed by laws of operation in the same way as was the capitalist system in the previous quotations. An economic cause is thus linked to an institutional consequence by the materialist causal paradigm.

230011

Q: What would you single out as the most important changes in Switzer-
      land compared with 20 or 25 years ago?

A: Well, despite everything there's been great progress from the social
      point of view. And there's no doubt this has been due to the efforts of
      some of the unions and some of the left-wing parties like the socialist
      party, which has grown considerably and now commands a lot of
      respect. The reason why we now have old-age pensions is because the
      old parties, conservatives like the liberals and the radicals had to give
      in on some issues because the demands of the other side were getting
      so strong. We've obtained something wonderful, old-age pensions,
      and that's good. I can remember when I was young, old people had to
      live on charity, while now they're human beings, not animals.

The institutional cause (the increased power of the unions and the parties of the Left) has an economic consequence (the creation of a social insurance scheme) within a system of actions which is that of national politics, in which the social actors are political parties and trade unions. Its law of operation is that of compromise made necessary by changes in power relations: 'the liberals and radicals had to give in on some issues because the demands of the other side were getting so strong'. The *indissociability of system and actors* is clear, the political system functions by confrontations between the 'left-wing parties' and the 'conservative parties'. It is only because of this *system of social actors* that the rise of the Left has led to the creation of the AVS.

Thus we have instances of the explanation of material consequences by material factors which themselves give rise to actions (social actors) and the laws by which these actions operate. The explanation introduces a system of

determined actions, which itself is a function of material factors, between material causes and material consequences. These material factors may be economic, but they may also be institutional, which prevents us from regarding the materialist paradigm as economistic.

(b) *Material causes, non-material consequences*

400008–10

A: People in Switzerland are certainly not as sober and responsible as they used to be.

Q: What do you think this change in people's attitude is due to?

A: Life got too easy, for a time at any rate, maybe not so much now. But life got so easy that people perhaps lost the desire to take trouble and care about their work.

400011

Q: Why did the Swiss have this character trait?

A: I think it's something to do with the smallness of the country, which meant that because there weren't many people, there was no force of numbers, so they put the effort into their work, into the quality of what they produced.

210002

A: It's a country where the population has to work to live, and this means there's a very strong element of . . . of . . .

Q: How do you mean?

A: We know that we need to export in order to live, and to export we need quality, so the only wealth the country has is its labour.

210006–07

A: People are very inward-looking, they're fairly cold, and there are clear barriers between cantons and between linguistic communities.

Q: Why is it like that?

A: It's a historical consequence of federalism. Everyone is very wrapped up in their own federalism, in local attitudes, they cultivate them and support them.

      They tried to make one country out of very different communities but the distinctions are still there, everyone wants to hang on to them to [protect] their personalities.

180015

Everything has gone well in Switzerland up till now, there's been work and we've had seasonal workers coming in, and for a while that was OK because they worked, and then suddenly we see that they're taking up jobs which we could do now. This has been clear for some months now. That's why people have started becoming racist, and not enough changes have been made.

Again we see material factors, both economic and institutional, used this time to explain non-material phenomena, attitudes of mind ('responsible', 'character', 'inward-looking', 'cold', 'racist'). These mental phenomena are explained in terms of behaviour partly determined by material factors: 'we need to export', 'to try to make a country'. But behaviour is not mechanically determined, as the explanation brings in general or specific social actors ('people', 'the Swiss', 'the population', 'everyone', all of which are related in a general way to the 'Swiss' social actor, defined in opposition to the non-Swiss foreigners), and laws of interaction between these actors and the other factors (laws of competition in world markets requiring high-quality production, laws of the historical development of the nation state out of cantonal states).

Yet it is the case that the social actors and the laws of interaction are less precisely identified in these quotations than in those concerned with explaining material phenomena. Thus while the social actors are all linked to the 'Swiss' social actor, this is often only by implicit reference to the non-Swiss, who only figure in terms of their effects (competition), or by implicit comparison (as in 210006–07, where centralised states are implicitly assumed to be inhabited by people who are more open, and less attached to their own particular circumstances, than the Swiss); the quotation 400008–10 has nothing to say on the subject. The laws of interaction, too, remain vague and, for the most part, unformulated. Yet they are presented, implicitly, by the statement of the explanation itself. So from the first statement we can identify the law that says that a hard life makes for responsibility, and from the second, the law that small countries motivate their human resources to withstand international competition. The only law which is explicitly stated, 'to export we need quality', only applies to material phenomena and not their non-material consequence, the enthusiasm for quality.

So non-material phenomena are not treated in the same way as material phenomena: they are given a *greater margin of indetermination*, as much in terms of *specifying the social actors* as of *defining the laws of interaction* (we cannot really continue to use the term 'laws of operation' which seemed justified for the explanation of material phenomena).

The perception of social actors as a cause of material factors

400004–05
A: ...there's been too much development, too much building, there's not enough countryside left. People often say, and I agree with them, that we were too ambitious, that, Geneva was possibly too ambitious.
Q: Why do you think that was?
A: I think it's happened since the war. They were afraid of being overtaken by other countries, so they tried to get a bit ahead, and maybe they went a bit too far.

It is not simply competition that causes expansion here, it is the '[fear] of being overtaken by other countries', i.e. the perception of that competition. The speaker intimates that that perception was perhaps false, the fear excessive, yet he never says so explicitly, leaving the interpretation open. Similarly in the following quotation:

400016

Q: Do you have any ideas about the reasons for this [political] indifference?

A: My view is that we have a pretty good life in a free country. People don't put themselves out when there's a referendum, there are plenty who say that it doesn't make any difference if they don't vote.

The speaker does not make any claims about the validity of the opinion he cites. Admittedly one could connect 'there are people who say it doesn't make any difference' with 'we have a pretty good life in a free country', but the modality of the statement is somewhat different, and includes a criticism of that opinion when it was mentioned a little earlier ('a lot of people don't take much interest in politics, which is a bad thing'). The overall sense is very different from that of a statement which cuts out the perception and only keeps the material factor, a statement of the sort: 'we have a pretty good life in a free country. I think that although people don't put themselves out when there's a referendum, it doesn't make any difference if they don't vote'.

This type of explanation can also be applied to material phenomena:

210020

A: From the political point of view, we've seen a slow progression to the Left, very slow, but it's happened as workers have become aware of their dependence on the economic system as they've looked for an alternative.

Here the social actors' growing awareness of a material reality has material consequences (of an institutional order). This is far removed from simple explanations by means of a material factor, as '[the growing awareness of the workers]' is the central element in the argument, and it is linked to '[the search] for an alternative'. The action is based on the perception of a material reality, but also on a choice, on a decision to act, which does not happen mechanically. An *interaction* is inserted *between the material determinations and the consciousness (the perception and decision) of the social actors* involved.

The construction of complex systems
Structuring argument by using material facts, social actors, their perception of the social and their relative autonomy of decision sometimes gives rise to

very complex schemata. By distinguishing *different levels of reality*, in which the social actors and their laws of interaction can be located in various ways, the materialist paradigm enables us to deal with complex systems linking a variety of different causes and consequences, as in the following joint explanation of immigration and xenophobia:

> *210039*
> The problem of foreigners in Switzerland is shown particularly in the influx in the years after the war, when Switzerland's economic development led to a shortage of manpower, and most employers had to look for labour from abroad. It's not the fault of these invited workers that they're here, they were fed with illusions, they were used, nobody made any serious attempts to assimilate them, the relevant authorities always said they were merely supplementary manpower – a belief which Swiss law reinforced. The problem has been that there were too many of them, too many who came in before the authorities introduced any restrictions on immigration. We in the unions were able to see from the reaction of the Swiss population that the situation would become serious, and at the same time we saw the difficulty of integrating these workers within the factories, where workers from this country were gradually getting angrier about the lack of controls on immigrant labour. The social problems were enormous, because once they had brought over this foreign workforce, recruiting it over there, they made them come and sleep in tents or barracks because they hadn't done anything for them. The employers didn't want to make the necessary investment in rationalising industry (and they're facing the consequences of that now), they just expanded, added more machines, increased warehousing space and shop space, and in fact the new labour served them well because they succeeded in selling all they wanted to sell. And now we're facing the reaction of the Swiss because there's too much, and the whole problem stems from that.

Without wanting to schematise the totality of causal relations in this passage, we can distinguish several connected arguments

– economic development stimulates a demand for manpower which involves a search for foreign labour on the part of the employers;
– the employers do not invest in rationalisation, and are too ready to use foreign labour;
– the authorities do not restrict immigration;
– the consequence of the three foregoing facts is too many foreigners;
– they (the employers and the authorities?) did not make the necessary provision for the immigrants, so there are social problems;
– they did not think about the assimilation of the foreigners, and there are too many of them, so the Swiss workers have reacted.

This structuration sets four social sectors in relation to each other: the employers, the foreigners, the authorities and the Swiss workers. It attempts

to explain immigration policy, the social problems of immigrants, and the reactions of Swiss workers. The fundamental factor is material and economic: the search for immediate profits by employers who do not invest in rationalisation. The second factor in the explanation is the authorities' behaviour in not restricting immigration, not predicting assimilation, and not making the necessary provision, because they regarded the foreigners as a supplementary workforce.

The negative valorisation of the phenomena described here means that causal attribution becomes a search for people to blame: the 'problem of the foreigners' and the 'social problems' of foreigners are caused by the action of the employers and the inaction of the authorities. But the condemnation is not a moral one; the criticism of the behaviour of these social actors is not a judgement; it is backed up by an explanation of the material factors that led these groups to act as they did. The materialist paradigm is *incompatible with the moral reification* we have identified in 'xenophobic' argument and in the deviancy paradigm. The complexity of the explanatory schema is not designed to go back to the defective behaviour of a social actor who can then be declared culpable. It enables one to explain the behaviour which is the object of criticism, that is, to situate it within a general, structured system, and thereby to *bring the criticism to bear on the whole of that system* while retaining its complexity.

The limits of explanation

The materialist explanation, especially when it involves the construction of complex systems, presents the question of causality in a particular light, as the explanation resides more in the *explanation of the operation of the system* than in making a connection between a cause and a consequence. Thus phenomena which at first sight appear to be very diverse can be linked causally in a structured argument. There seems, therefore, to be no limit to the possible ways the materialist paradigm can function, as it is not limited by the nature of the phenomenon to be explained, nor by the cause attributed to it.

Given this, how and where does the explanation stop?

500002

Q: If you had to describe the country to somebody who doesn't know it, what would you say?

A: I think I would give him documentation rather than try to say anything, then on the basis of that he can ask me questions, and I can tell him about what I know myself. Because there are lots of regions I don't know enough about.

Here the speaker does not even begin to broach the subject; he prefers not to

say anything in case his lack of knowledge should cause him to make mistakes. This refusal is noteworthy, as he is being asked to express an opinion about his own country.

But the speaker also links his lack of knowledge to an indifference towards the question, which inverts the previous relation in which his lack of interest is the product of his lack of knowledge.

500075
Q: What do think are the main arguments in the Jura question?
A: I think it's a question of language, at school level. I think that's what it is. There may be other issues now, I don't know too much about it. I haven't read much about it because I think they're stupid. If Berne forced them to use books in German then, sure, there might be a problem, but why they should want separation at any cost, I can't see that that's the right solution.

Here the speaker does tackle the issue and takes up a position. But he refuses to explain (or decides not to explain). The only explanatory element he offers (the language question) would work better as an argument for separatism than for the speaker's position: perhaps he prefers not to know any more about it so as not to have to state his position? At all events, he says himself that his a priori position on the question means that he has not looked for further information. It is not that he is incapable of explaining, rather that his refusal to explain entails his rejection of information. This, therefore, leads us to ask a more general question: how does the speaker manage his *lack of knowledge?* At first sight, he can treat the question as if he knew, refuse to explain and simply state his position, or refuse to say anything about it. We can postulate that the choice between these strategies is linked to the valorisation of the phenomenon to be explained, thus to a personal attitude to its content.

The non-determinacy paradigm

In some discourses of causal attribution we frequently find a reiteration of *impersonal terms* such as 'one' or 'they', 'it' and 'there is'. This causal paradigm, based on *causal non-determination*, occupies a place midway between the deviancy paradigm and the materialist paradigm. It can be distinguished from the deviancy paradigm by an absence of social categorisation, the whole of society ('they' or 'everybody') being collectively responsible for the phenomena to be explained. It differs from the materialist paradigm in that it does not take into account the relation of the actors to material facts or to the workings of the social system.

The absence of social categorisation

200056–57

A: It makes me laugh to hear them talk about the housing crisis. We were
married in 1946, and in those days we didn't have a flat. There was a
housing problem then, too. They offered us a flat at 105 francs a
month, and [my husband] was earning 375 francs. They say it's a
scandal now, but the problem was the same then. They complain
about flats at 500 or 600 francs, 800 francs, but the workers still have
to . . .

Q: Why do you think it's still the same now as it was then?

A: They were too keen to continue building, they ought to have known
when to stop. There has to be some stability, they can't carry on,
because they build two or three houses, then they have to put the
foreigners in them, so the situation is still the same after 30 years.

'. . . hear them talk', 'they offered us a flat', 'they say it's a scandal', 'they
were too keen to . . . build', 'they can't carry on', 'the situation is still the same':
the society represented in this discourse is a game played by anonymous
actors (unidentified flying subjects). Within the network of interactions we
find a few objects with no power of determination over the system: 'us',
'workers', 'foreigners'. The cause of all their troubles lies in what 'they' say
and do, as 'they were too keen'.

Who are 'they' who seem to hold all the power? 'They' are not named. The
context does occasionally provide the information needed to identify them:
thus whoever 'offered' the flat must have been the owner or an agent.
Certainly it is not the same 'they' who nowadays 'say [the rise in rents] is a
scandal'. Yet there is nothing to indicate that these people (or social groups)
have nothing in common: quite the reverse, in fact, as they are designated by
the same term. 'They' relates, in the first place, to *all those who have a degree of
power*, even if that is merely to say something and be listened to. But the
speaker does not know enough about these people to say who they are, he
cannot categorise them, at least not without excessive over-simplification. Or
else that does not interest him, and the only relevant explanation for the
current housing crisis is that the foreigners working in the construction
industry occupy the houses they build. Whatever the cause, the explanation
involves familiar categories, especially that to which the speaker herself
belongs (here, 'the workers'), and in a vague way describes the presence
behind the scenes of *actors who determine what happens while remaining
concealed*. So the play unfolds, in the statement quoted above, with three
categories of characters: the workers (including 'us'), the foreigners and
'them'.

120010–19

A: *It's* changed a lot, Switzerland. Personally, I think *they've* run things badly.

Q: What do you think the mistakes have been?

A: The mistake *they* made was to let a few entrepreneurs, directors and capitalists earn so much. *It* all comes from *that*, because frankly *they* built more and more, and *they* went for more and more expansion. So *there were* lots of people who thought, 'I want to be a boss too, I'll set myself up', and now *there's* all this unemployment.

Other social categories are represented here, 'entrepreneurs', 'directors' and 'capitalists'. But in the first place the designation is particularised, each time concerning only 'a few' members of each category, and secondly these are not the actors directly responsible for the situation as the explanation is based on 'the mistake they made' of 'letting them earn so much'. So the explanation pinpoints neither the system which allows the entrepreneurs so much money, nor the blameworthy action (deviancy paradigm) of some of them, as the cause of Switzerland's negative changes. Responsibility seems to be laid at the door of the people who allowed it to happen, an unidentified 'them'. The number of characters involved, not all of them from the speaker's milieu, increases, but the explanation always harks back to the unknown figures behind the scenes. 'Lots of people' seem to be connected with them, but it is not made clear whether they are actors, accomplices or victims; they are people who set themselves up (or would like to set themselves up) as employers. The laws of operation of the economic system which might justify a causal relation are not explained.

Causal attribution is vaguer in this quotation than in the previous one. It seems that an *unknown deep cause* works through the intermediary of apparent causes (the action of 'some entrepreneurs, some directors and some capitalists', and of 'lots of people who thought, "I'll set myself up"').

400038–39

Q: Is the crisis a logical outcome of our economic system?

A: No, I don't agree with that. Maybe if *they* hadn't gone so high there wouldn't be the danger of falling.

Q: So you attribute the crisis to the fact that . . .

A: That *everybody* was over-ambitious, workers as much as employers and whoever was responsible politically. I think that *everybody* was over-ambitious, everybody thought *it* would go on and on and never stop.

Here 'they' is identified as 'everybody'. Which means nobody. No category

is regarded as particularly responsible, which comes to the same thing as not naming anyone. The causal factor is the mistaken estimate of the man in the street, or whoever, of the possibilities for expansion. The categories he cites (workers, employers and politicians) are only invoked to show that they are not relevant to the explanation, in which each group figures 'as much as' the others.

'They' are everybody, nobody, anybody, other people or somebody.

The naturalisation of the social

The paradigm of non-determination reveals the importance of the mechanism of naturalisation of the social (the perception of social reality as a natural reality governed by equally natural laws which the social actors have no choice but to submit to). This sociocognitive mechanism is at the heart of the causal paradigm of non-determination, and provides it with a general framework of perception in which *the role of the actors is secondary* to that of the laws.

The naturalised laws of social functioning

260011

Q: Was the crisis predictable for a long time?

A: Yes. When I saw *all that* being built, new sites starting up everywhere, I said to myself: 'There's something cooking.' *I don't know* why they're laying out sites, they're doing it everywhere, why they're suddenly . . . so *it's* . . . *I don't know*, as if you did an hour at your office and then got two or three of your friends to do your job, your job would get done, and you could spend all day sitting down doing nothing.

The speaker reduces the explanation of the crisis to a simple calculation, expressed by an example: if you use a large amount of manpower to do a job, it will be finished more quickly than if you use fewer people. The argument is implicitly founded on two postulates: first, that in a given society there is a fixed quantity of work to be done, and second, that the needs of individuals are defined and limited. So the reasoning is that once the work is done it's done, and there is an unemployment situation. Neither the idea of need, nor that of the organisation of work, are criticised or looked at relatively. The labour market is seen as something mechanistic and quantitative, and man (anyone, us) is subordinate to the laws governing this market.

260002

A: As I see it, there isn't any unemployment. There are 80,000 unemployed and a million foreigners, so all you've got to do is reduce the number of foreigners in Switzerland. Then there wouldn't be any more unemployment.

The laws presented in this train of reasoning are extremely simple: supply in the labour market is fixed independently of all other considerations, and Swiss workers have an absolute priority over jobs. The logical consequence of this, 'reduce the number of foreigners', is a simple deduction from the initial statement about the number of foreigners and the number of unemployed.

The naturalised laws of the labour market support the whole explanation, which involves no actual actors even in the practical conclusion deduced from the explanation, 'all you've got to do', in which the impersonal 'you' is of the same order as the 'they' we came across earlier. The naturalised social reality is also depersonalised (there is an absence of actual social actors), so the explanation links abstract phenomena together and deduces abstract behaviour from them.

180071

Q: And the current situation, what's caused that?

A: *It's* because of the surplus, *there are* too many people who've done well out of years of superabundance, too many fat cats. *They've* done too well. Surpluses are not always a good thing, *people* have to pay for them in the end. *It's* because all civilisations have their ups and downs. *There's nothing you can do about it.* Sometimes *you* get there more quickly, *you* rise faster and so *you* come down faster, too. *You can't do anything about it, that's how life is.*

Surplus creates further surplus, so that a surplus in one direction is followed by a counterbalancing one in the opposite direction. History is seen as governed by a general, universal law of balance, as if it were a pendulum. 'Superabundance' gives rise to crises, which then have to create fresh periods of expansion.

All explanation of the causes of the recession is thus reduced to an assertion of this law of the pendulum, in the face of which the (unspecified) actors are powerless: 'there's nothing you can do about it'. The law has a tautological inexorability: the law is the law, and needs no justification, as it is the criterion of legitimacy. *Stating the law* is here the only discursive act necessary for causal attribution.

400027–28

Q: What do you think about this immigration policy?

A: It went much too far. They let vast numbers of foreigners come here, then they complain when the economy overheats, it's obviously one of the causes of overheating.

Q: And the reasons for this policy?

A: They needed to produce everything they could while the orders were coming in. They had to make profits, they had to expand. Whenever there was a chance to export Swiss products, they took it.

'It went too far' but 'they had to': the naturalised law (in this case, the law of expansion) absolves the anonymous actors ('they') of responsibilities for the mistake the speaker thinks they made. The important thing in the explanation of overheating and immigration is not to know who committed the deviant act which caused it all (as would be the case in the deviancy paradigm), nor to discover what overheating means in the context of the economic system (as in the materialist paradigm), but to reveal simple and unchangeable laws governing the economy: 'you have to produce all you can sell'; but also another very general law: 'things should never be taken too far'.

400052

Q: What do you think about the opposition to nuclear power stations, like Kaiseraugst?

A: Well I don't agree with the out-and-out opponents. I don't mean they're backward-looking, but it always makes me think of the first cars, when people said, 'If they start going any faster they'll die at the wheel, the speed will kill them', when in fact of course they were able to go far faster without dying behind the wheel. So I think you have to move forward. Life evolves, technology changes. You can't go against them.

The law of progress governs all social evolution: technical innovation is necessarily good. Actors who do not accept this law are 'backward-looking', i.e. they have not understood that this is a fundamental law of evolution. There is no choice between one technique and another, there can only be submission to or disobedience of the naturalised law of progress. The naturalisation of the social, in the final analysis, rests on the meta-law which states, 'You must not go against' the laws governing human activity.

This causal paradigm's 'natural laws' are therefore not the behavioural norms of the deviancy paradigm (norms providing the basis for moral condemnation of those who transgress them), nor the laws of interaction of the materialist paradigm (which do not exclude the conscious will of the actors): they are presented as objective laws (independent of social actors and of the speaker) which determine (or should determine) the action of individuals, but which carry the consequences of their violation within them. Thus, too much production results automatically in overheating; casting doubt on technological progress is to stand in the way of inevitable progress. The unspecified social actors are neither autonomous nor guilty; they are all objects who are automatically induced to behave in an acceptable way by social functioning.

Laws without courts, and powers with no material form, are the general, abstract principles of a vast *social mechanism*. Merely to pronounce them is enough to make anybody submit to them.

020007–10

A: There's work here if you really want it, but if there are foreigners here then there's bound to be unemployment. In the last analysis, unemployment is caused by a number of factors, not just the foreigners. And they do a lot to help the young people today, which they never used to do. They spend huge sums of money on young people, through apprenticeships and suchlike.

Q: So what connection do people make between that and unemployment?

A: Well that's hard to say, it's probably not directly related to unemployment, more with the money which they naturally have to spend on young people, on all sorts of things, like motorways, which may not always be necessary; but I don't know, I can't give you the full answer, I'm not a sociologist.

'I don't know' what the law is. It must be related to 'the money they have to spend . . . on all sorts of things' and which is no longer available for creating jobs. But the relationship clearly cannot be as simple as it is in a household where buying a TV set means not being able to afford a holiday. There must be a comparable, but more complicated, economic law, which specialists (both sociologists and others) are familiar with. The laws are not deduced from observation, they are presupposed. Ignorance of the law does not mean it does not exist; *there are laws* in the naturalised representation of the social, even if you do not recognise them.

The social hierarchy

If there are laws, there must be somebody with the authority to ensure they are respected. We have seen that these are laws without courts, and without authorities specifically designated to deal with violations of them. But instead of judges there are *responsible people*, people in authority whose function is to prevent the laws being broken. And these responsible persons are, 'naturally', the actual rulers of society.

400028

Q: And the reasons for this [immigration] policy?

A: They needed to produce everything they could while the orders were coming in. They had to make profits, they had to expand. Whenever there was a chance to export Swiss products, they took it.

Q: Did the government influence this one way or the other?

A: The government? Yes, of course. The government has to be responsible for immigration.

Q: Do you think they could have acted differently?

A: They could have set limits to it sooner, but then it's always easy to be wise after the event.

'The government has to be responsible', that's what it is for, it is there to be responsible, and to take the necessary measures at the right time so that the naturalised laws of social functioning will be respected, which is what the government failed to do in connection with immigration – 'They could have [done it]'. Despite its mistakes, though, the government is vindicated by the difficulty of the task: criticism is easy, while taking the right action is hard. The naturalised laws are not a code of good conduct which has to be followed to the letter, they are general laws whose practical effect has to be assessed in advance; the government has to be aware of them and understand how they work, it has to unite knowledge and power, it has to know and decide for the majority of the population who do not have the means to assess what will happen or to decide what steps should be taken. Thus power is justified and, at the same time, those who possess it are regarded a priori as legitimate, and, in any event, their responsibility is always limited, because 'it's always easy to be wise after the event'.

400044
Q: What is the government's policy in this [crisis] situation?
A: They try to salvage what they can. I think they try to act for the best. They try to take the best measures.

The speaker, a plain citizen with no specialist knowledge, does not know 'the best measures' for improving the situation, nor does he know (or if he does, he does not say) what measures the government is taking. He trusts them to know what needs to be done, and to do it. In the naturalised view of the social, possible errors in management do not threaten the confidence they have in their ruler. Everybody, rulers included, is trying to do their best. Rulers are hardly ever identified as a precise category: the 'they' which designates them is similar to the 'them' which explains social phenomena.

180037–38
A: You can't respect people at the top of the ladder when people at the bottom are treated as if they have no importance at all. Every human being is valuable. There's no need to be a director to be respected. There are some people, even in my family, all you have to say is 'He's head of this or that' and people are immediately nice to the person, but if it's somebody who's got nothing, then the way he's treated is terrible. The Swiss are very easily impressed by titles and labels.
Q: And how do you think this can be overcome?
A: You can't really do anything about it, because that's the way they think. I don't think there's anything you can do.

This criticism of exaggerated respect for hierarchy also includes a legitimation of it, or more precisely its justification as an unchangeable natural reality. Hierarchical relations are acceptable as long as they do not result in the creation of unpleasant attitudes of mind. It is not the inequality and privilege of a hierarchical system which is seen as important, but that everybody should be respected regardless of their hierarchical position. Attitudes are thus causes of behaviour, but unlike in the deviancy paradigm, they are not treated as an independent cause and condemned as a source of evil. The attitude is explained by its social context, the hierarchical structure. It is a vicious circle: the hierarchical structure explains hierarchical behaviour (differentiated by rank), which in turn reinforces the hierarchical structure. 'There's nothing you can do' to alter that state of affairs. The naturalisation of society and social hierarchy *removes responsibility*, at the level of causality, from the people who are to a greater or lesser extent defined as responsible; it legitimates their superior position. More than that, it excludes the problem of their legitimation. The current state of affairs is only the consequence of itself, and any factor that might lead to change is excluded, and if not unthinkable is at the least perceived as unrealistic.

The absent subject

400046

Q: What if you were made redundant?

A: My first reaction would be one of tremendous disappointment. I think that if a company can no longer survive as it is, you've got to put yourself in the place of the boss or the manager who has to keep it going somehow.

Q: You wouldn't try to oppose it?

A: I'm not against redundancies in principal; I think it's better to make a percentage of the workforce redundant than risk everyone losing their jobs. At least it protects the wages of the people still in a job.

A 'tremendous disappointment': social action is impossible or pointless. You don't fight against the laws of nature, nor against the naturalised laws of social functioning. You don't go against the decisions of people in authority because they are there to decide, they are the only ones with the knowledge and the legitimacy to do it: 'you've got to put yourself in the place of the boss'. Any self-assertion, or attempt to find alternative solutions based on a defence of self-interest are a priori unthinkable. The naturalised world is a mechanism of inexorable laws, where the rulers oil the cog-wheels and everybody else, the non-leaders, are simply objects.

400031

Q: What do you think about the living conditions of foreign workers in Switzerland?

A: They're pretty poor. I think what they want to do is spend as little as possible so they can take the maximum amount home with them: that's what they're here for. We live here, so we spend a good part of our income in rent, but they try to spend as little as they can on it. It's difficult to provide maximum comfort if they don't want to pay for it.

The present state of affairs is presented as an inflexible fact, with no antecedents and no possibility of changing. The law of the market (which is seen as a natural law) sets the prices, and foreigners want to spend as little as possible on housing; given the price they pay, they cannot get anything better. The wishes of individuals, in this case of foreigners, can only be satisfied within the exact limits of the naturalised laws. Responsibility for their poor living conditions falls on to the immigrants themselves, because the market is not responsible for anything, nor are those who 'supply' housing as they are also subject to the laws of the market. Individuals are therefore just the medium for supply and demand, never conscious subjects acting on their own decisions. This is why they are presented in such a vague, impersonal manner, as 'we' or 'they'. Everybody behaves in the same way, no matter who they are. In this social mechanism, people are just interchangeable units who ensure that an unchangeable state of affairs goes on functioning. They are objects, not subjects.

400059

Q: Should the decision [to build a nuclear power station] be taken by the people as a whole?

A: No, I don't think so. I think that if the need for electricity continues to grow, they have to provide it; they don't ask the Swiss to vote on it when they build a dam, so why should they have to do it before they can decide to build a power station? When they build an electric power station, or a dam, or when they divert a river, they don't ask the people, it doesn't happen after a vote, it is decided in accordance with what's needed.

Nobody decides, even 'the Swiss' *en masse*. 'It is decided': the process is anonymous, impersonal and to some extent automatic. 'They' build, and do not ask anybody's advice. 'They' are different from the Swiss, but are probably not foreign, they are really nobody so much as 'the need' itself. How can you be opposed to 'need'? Nobody has any say in a decision which is taken automatically in the absence of electricity consumers who are reduced to the fact of their meters.

Conscious, acting subjects are the major absentee from the naturalised representation of the social, which only recognises the interaction of 'us' and 'them' within limits fixed by the great, unarguable laws of social functioning. Some people, the leaders, have a bit more responsibility than the others, but in the last analysis they are not responsible for anything except making people respect the great laws to which they too are inexorably subject. They are hardly more like subjects than the others.

Use and limits of the causal paradigm of indeterminacy

Neither cause nor subject: the bypassing of causality. Comparing the paradigm of indeterminacy with the other two paradigms, one cannot but be struck by *how little causal functioning* it has.

(a) In the deviancy paradigm, the cause of all ills is the deviant action of a clearly identified social group or groups.

(b) In the materialist paradigm, a material causal factor is assigned to the phenomenon being explained, and this causal relation is fundamental to the explanation, even if it is relativised by relating cause, consequence, social actors and laws of interaction within a general, structural framework of reasoning.

(c) In the indeterminacy paradigm, the relation between cause and consequence seems almost insignificant beside the *general laws of social functioning*; the social actor subjects, too, dissolve into the indeterminate generality of the social whole: 'we', 'they', 'everybody'. Causality is general and unspecific. It can be applied to any object. It is also distant: the aim of any speaker using the indeterminacy paradigm seems less to explain a causal relation or attribute a cause to a phenomenon, than to establish a *distance* from the phenomenon in question and to present it as normal and inevitable. It seems to be more to do with *justifying a state of affairs*, whether permanent or transitory, than with explaining how it arose, how it functions, and how it will develop. This *causal vagueness* makes it easy to move from this paradigm to one of the other two: designating one social group as 'they' eases the transition to the deviancy paradigm; defining the particular material circumstances of the situation to be explained, and the relation of the actors to these circumstances, the explanation connects up with the materialist paradigm. But the discourses out of which we have constructed this indeterminacy paradigm generally avoid these shifts, which the speakers tend to find awkward, towards more precise relations of causality. The indeterminacy paradigm is also the paradigm of prudence, or 'wait and see'. Perhaps it reflects something in the sociocognitive deep structure that underlies the notion of the 'Swiss compromise'.

If the social actors are absent as active, conscious subjects, the speaker is

doubly absent from the discourse: as an active, conscious subject intervening in the situation described, and *as a speaking subject* explaining the situation. The omnipresence of 'we' enables the 'I' to remain hidden, out of reach. The naturalised general laws obscure the specific historical situation of the phenomenon and that of the speaker himself. The justification of a state of affairs removes any question about the position of the speaker at the level of the discourse as much as at the level of social practice. The causal indeterminacy paradigm seems to be a mode of explanation that perfectly suits the speaker's disinvestment, his disengagement and refusal to act.

'There must be . . .': designation of a solution or of impotence. 'There must be stability'; 'there must be a reduction in the number of foreigners'; 'you have to move forward'; 'they could have set limits to it sooner'; 'it's better to make some people redundant than to risk everyone losing their jobs'; 'they have to provide the electricity'. The discourses we have quoted are not short of conclusions about what should be done in practice. But the practice is usually expressed in impersonal terms, in accordance with the logic of this type of explanation. Somewhere, somebody (some-'one') ought to do what the explanation seems to show is necessary.

200012
Q: What solutions would you propose to remedy that? How do you see it? What do you think needs to be done?
A: It's complicated because it involves so many . . . so many areas. I think in the end it's building, because there's going to come a point, soon, when this using up every bit of green land for building reaches saturation point. I think it's building that they'll have to stop now, because the more they do, the more they build, the more people there are and the more problems there are.

Although the *solution* of the problem is precise – to halt building – the practicalities of its application remain unknown. 'They'll have to stop' building: who will have to stop? Entrepreneurs? property developers? the authorities? The discourse has nothing to say on this question, which turns the announced solution into a mere wish or a general principle. The absence of social categorisation, the absence of the speaker as subject, the legitimation of the social hierarchy, all come together to remove the question of how the suggested solution should be put into practice. If the causes are indeterminate, so necessarily are the solutions. Because 'they' have done this or that, and the outcome is not what was wanted, all 'they' have to do is whatever is necessary to rectify the situation. Because it is based on the naturalisation of the social, the indeterminacy paradigm subjects the realisation of the speaker's wishes to the play of anonymous forces and naturalised laws that it

describes. But in order for the speaker to be absent from the discourse, he also has to be absent from the production of the discourse. We may wonder, therefore, what function the discourse can have for the speaker.

Through this causally indeterminate, naturalised discourse the speaker articulates his *impotence*, which he presents as inevitable despite the fact that he may occasionally *pretend to a power* without saying how it might be exercised ('It would be better to', 'they could have', 'they have to'). The only power the speaker exercises is the power to put forward solutions which he knows he has no way of applying. The naturalisation of the social shows a strong tendency to legitimate the state of affairs it presents as unchangeable. The solutions put forward are only credible to the extent that they correspond more or less to what is actually happening. This legitimation does not necessarily signify approval of the action of the people in authority, but it does at least indicate acceptance of it. The discourse expresses a degree of confidence in the 'responsible authorities', who are presented as doing the best they can, 'they try to take the best measures'. Legitimation of the authorities. In some instances, however, the indeterminacy paradigm is just used to justify inaction and resignation in the face of a situation which is what it is and cannot be anything else.

020014
A: There's nobody to tell us that we have to do this or that, we have to find our own way of sorting things out, it's as if we were each on an isolated island. Being in Switzerland is like living on an isolated island.

If the laws of functioning are not clear, the effectiveness of the paradigm in producing possible solutions is, to say the least, minimal. There is uncertainty as well as indeterminacy. The speaker has no means of resolving practical problems which require an explanation of social functioning. He does not even have a way of finding somebody who can explain the situation and advise him how to act: 'There's nobody to tell us that we have to do this or that'. The world is a complex, incomprehensible desert in which the speaker feels and expresses a situation of dependence which he can neither explain nor overcome. This is an extreme example of an almost total absence of causality and intelligibility.

Action is impossible. It is pointless, too, as in the statement already quoted:

180037–38
A: You can't respect people at the top of the ladder when people at the bottom are treated as if they have no importance at all . . .
Q: And how do you think this can be overcome?
A: You can't really do anything about it because that's the way they think. I don't think there's anything you can do.

By putting the emphasis on the inertial force of the existing state of affairs rather than on changes that could be brought about by the naturalised laws of social functioning, by essentialising the social rather than naturalising it, the speaker ends up not by putting forward solutions but by expressing *resignation*. We move from pretended power to real powerlessness. But are these not, in fact, the same thing?

Semantic shifts and boundaries between paradigms

0070030

Q: Why do you think foreign workers come to Switzerland?

A: Because they get conditions of a sort they've never had in their own countries. What do you think!

How does this, at first sight simple, explanation of immigration relate to our three paradigms of causal explanation? Does it belong to the deviancy paradigm (foreigners always want to get more money)? Or the materialist paradigm (foreigners emigrate because of unemployment)? Or the indeterminacy paradigm (wages are better in Switzerland)? The extract quoted above fits neatly into none of these. Does this mean that they have only limited analytical efficacy? Our view is rather that the *polysemy* of discourses remains to some extent irreducible to generalisations. Identical statements may have similar but different meanings, and vice versa. This *vagueness of expression* occurs frequently in everyday linguistic practice, whereas one of the chief characteristics of learned discourse is an attempt to eliminate it by a careful definition of the terms used, and by formulating general laws underlying the relations between these terms.

To define the different possible meanings in the statement quoted above, let us construct a series of sentences whose meanings differ but which can all be taken as equivalent (but not identical) to this sentence based on it: 'Foreign workers come to Switzerland because they find conditions better than anything they have ever had in their own countries'.

Foreign workers come to Switzerland because:

(a)   there is unemployment in their own country

(b)   they don't have any work in their own country

(c)   they can't find work in their own country

(d)   it is difficult to find work in their own country

(e)   they don't earn much money in their own country

(f)   they earn more money in Switzerland

(g)   they want to earn more money

(h)   all they think of is earning money

We have moved gradually, by a series of shifts, from a simple materialist

explanation to one based on voluntarism. The stages of the process are as follows:

(a)   unemployment regarded as a social phenomenon in itself ('there is unemployment')

(b)   the introduction of the notion of a social actor determined by objective conditions ('they don't have any work');

(c)   transition from the notion of determination to one of subjects acting in a given social context ('they can't find . . .');

(d)   relativisation of the subjects' action ('it's difficult to find');

(e)   relativisation of the context itself ('they don't earn much');

(f)   once the relativisation has been emphasised, there is the introduction of a comparison between social contexts ('they earn more');

(g)   transition from the comparison to the idea of choice ('they want to earn more');

(h)   elimination of the comparison, with only the will remaining ('all they think of is earning').

In this series of reconstructed statements, the first sentence (a) can be ascribed to the indeterminacy paradigm, the last two, (g) and (h), to the deviancy paradigm, and the sentences in between – with varying degrees of precision – to the materialist paradigm. The variety of potential meanings within one statement seems considerable enough on the basis of this example alone, yet it is based on a fairly narrow definition of 'conditions', taken as meaning receipt of a waged income. If we were to take into account other possible senses of the word, we could multiply the meanings of this statement still further.

At the methodological level, this polysemy suggests caution in interpretation and consequently we have analysed the discursive elements by setting them in their *general context*, which is first that of *the complete interview*. The statement we quoted above needs to be analysed in terms of other causal relations established by the same speaker, most frequently in accordance with the deviancy paradigm (see the quotations whose reference number begins 07, in the section on the deviancy paradigm, pp. 95–6). This information enables us to analyse the sybilline 'What do you think!' which follows the sentence we have been looking at, and to interpret it as 'Of course they come to Switzerland to earn lots of money.' So the analytical unit cannot be restricted to the sentence, nor even to the paragraphs from the interviews which we have cut up (and numbered). The functioning of causality only emerges after (repeated) readings of the complete interviews. This can be seen from the study of causal supersaturation, which we developed from an accumulation of elements linking a variety of consequences to a single cause.

On the theoretical level, the fact of polysemy, not only at the level of topic

but at the deeper level of the functioning of causality, is of great interest for the question of *the acceptability of an ideological discourse*. Without going into that question here, we can say that the gradual aspect of a semantic shift, as identified above, renders it much less perceptible. A deliberately polysemous discourse can claim to represent opinions which are actually governed by relatively different logics. The discourse of Action Nationale includes as many statements arguing that the presence and behaviour of 'foreigners' are the source of all Switzerland's current ills (the deviancy paradigm), as statements assessing the Swiss population as excessive in terms of the 'laws' of demography (indeterminacy paradigm), which allows people who accept the first type of statement (whom we have labelled 'xenophobic nationalists') to belong to it as well as supporters of the second type of statement (whom we have called 'technocratic nationalists').[8]

That is, it is not necessary to be xenophobic to find something satisfying about the *Action Nationale* discourse.

The co-existence of different paradigms

480036–37

Q: Why has it [the recession] happened?

A: It's very simple. The government has put a stop to what the banks were doing. What I'm saying may seem ridiculous, but they started to discover that the workers were earning too much, they were beginning to make inroads into the comforts of the upper class. So they decided to put a stop to it.

Q: Do you think this recession was inevitable?

A: No, I don't think things could have continued as they were going. They couldn't have done. Building luxury blocks of flats. It's a vicious circle, you have a worker who earns fifteen or sixteen francs an hour, he demands twenty or twenty-five, the employer charges the client ten or twenty francs extra, it's a vicious circle, they had to stop it. That couldn't go on any longer.

The answer to the first question presents a voluntarist explanation of the recession, following the deviancy paradigm: bankers and political leaders created the recession in order to stop the workers' standard of living rising any higher. The answer to the second question explains the recession in terms of the indeterminacy paradigm: runaway inflation was part of a vicious circle, which had to be stopped. Two different and competing explanations are provided for the same phenomenon, each following a different logic. Their co-existence does not seem to pose a problem, *no principle of exclusion* intervenes to necessitate choosing one explanation rather than the other. Although a choice of this sort would be necessary in formal logic, no logical demands impose it on this type of ordinary social thought. In the interview, the last

word went to the voluntarist explanation. The interview continued as follows:

480038
Q: Did somebody take the decision?
A: Of course. It was the banks, I told you, it was the government. The government and the banks. Anyway what can a politician do without money? Nothing!

140017–18
Q: Why do you think these foreigners come to Switzerland?
A: They come to earn a living, they can't help it, they're poor. But I think that, now, they should send them back, most of them, what else can you do, there's no work for the Swiss.
Q: Do you think the foreigners who come to Switzerland could find work in their own countries if they wanted to?
A: I don't know if they would want to. Judging by the people in our block, I'm certain none of them would want to go back.
Q: What gives you that impression?
A: That's what the young people say, that they don't want to go back to Italy. Well, fine, they take over our flats, they take jobs away from the Swiss, that's charming . . . and there are seven or eight hundred thousand doing that.
Q: Why don't they want to go?
A: Because it's better here and they're better off here.

To begin with, the speaker asserts that the foreigners came to Switzerland out of necessity, 'to earn a living', so 'they can't help it'. In answer to the other questions, he says that the foreigners do not *want* to look for work in their own country, that they do not *want* to give up being 'better off here'; the clear implication is that there is plenty they can do about it ('Well, fine . . . that's charming'). The first explanation is a materialist one, the second a 'deviancy' one. They are not competing, they are obviously contradictory, but this contradiction does not hinder the production of the discourse. To understand the reason for this *tolerance of contradiction*, we have to look at what is constant in both answers. Quite clearly, this is the idea that 'they should send them back, most of them' in order to free jobs for Swiss workers. The assertion of this principle of nationalist priority is more important than developing an explanation of the presence of foreigners in Switzerland. It is this assertion that dominates the argument, first by dissociating the explanation from the practical solution ('they can't help it . . . but . . . they should send them back'), then by associating them ('they don't want to go back to Italy') so they will have to be sent back, the second half of the sentence remaining implicit.

The practical solution of the problem of 'foreign overpopulation', in short, is

regarded as more important than a causal explanation of the presence of foreigners. *The explanation is made to serve the solution*: any explanation can therefore be used; all explanations, even if they are contradictory, can be used for that purpose. Causality is not invoked on its own account, for the pleasure of explaining something, but in pursuit of a practical aim. An individual cannot explain just anything . . . for any *purpose*.

Limits and uses of causality

Why explain?

We can conclude from the foregoing that causality is more than the simple expression of static causal relations, regarded as a priori facts, and involves a process of constructing causal relations relevant to the speaker. The process of causal attribution is thus effected in terms of the other social practices of the social actor subject, not by using a causality external to the speaker.

In other words, explanation is always explanation for something. Causality is only invoked in relation to the speaker's own aims and interests, as a possible modality of discursive strategies. We shall not be considering discursive strategies as universal and standardised, either, but as another issue that needs to be elucidated by research. But to stay with causality, the fundamental question is still: who is explaining what, how, and to what end?

To answer this question in any detail we must first ask where explanation *stops*: some things are explained and others are not explained. We shall then be able to compare the *discursive function* of the use of the paradigms we have identified and attempt to locate the discursive strategies in which they intervene and relate them to the conditions of acceptability of a discourse. We shall finish with some more theoretical comments on the social use of causality (causality in use), where causality will be treated as a function of the logic of the other social practices of the social actor subject.

Where explanation stops

Explanation and the speaker's value system

470036–37

Q: Do you think the government always maintains the spirit of neutrality?

A: We always hope they do, but deep down we're a little sceptical. I reckon the government ought to intervene and forbid all these demonstrations. They don't mean anything in this country because we're neutral, they mean absolutely nothing. They make the laws here . . .

Q: Why do the demonstrators have these marches, in your opinion?
A: Well, because they've got problems with their own countries, but
       we're neutral, so why do they allow it? We don't have anything to do
       with them.

The question which needed an explanation is swiftly glossed over. The speaker has nothing to say about the reasons why some groups (of foreigners, although this is never made explicit) demonstrate, and refuses even to speculate about it: 'We don't have anything to do with them.' The refusal to admit the legitimacy of the action leads to the refusal to consider an explanation of it. The speaker responds with silence to questions about the reasons for the 'problems' he mentions, and their nature, and about the usefulness of public demonstrations as a solution to these problems. Instead of looking for explanations, as the interviewer invites him to do, he reaffirms the values of his group ('we are neutral'), and the perfect right this group has to impose them on others ('They make the laws here'). Explaining would mean admitting the problematic of the Other. In this situation sociocentrism operates through the denial of causality which is, in fact, a means of decentration.

400062
Q: Why do some young people argue against military service?
A: If it's because of non-violence, then that's the way some young people
       think. But if it's just to oppose the established order, then I don't agree
       with it. I can accept the idea of civilian service for conscientious
       objectors. But I think this goes further. You ought to be broad-minded
       with genuine conscientious objectors, but if it is just somebody who's
       opposed to the army, I wouldn't give him any leeway.

The speaker distinguishes between two kinds of criticism of military service: pacifists or conscientious objectors, and opponents of the established order. These two categories are amenable to fundamentally different logico-discursive treatment. Pacifist objection is explained as 'the way some young people think', and one should be tolerant of them, at least if they are 'genuine'. The objection to the 'opponents of the established order' is not explained, indeed does not have to be explained, only condemned. *Explanation and disagreement are mutually exclusive.* Explanation is felt to be the first step towards justification. What is rejected ought not to be explained, as to do so would be to neutralise the absolute and radical nature of the rejection.

Explanation and absolute disagreement are regarded as incompatible. Explanation is felt to be more or less a kind of legitimation. When it is applied to values opposed to the speaker's own, it is rejected, repressed or denied. Things that are wrong cannot have reasons, at least within the framework of a sociocentric logico-discursive structure.

Explanation and the position of the speaker

540000–04

A: Anyway, personally I think there's one thing in Switzerland that really disgusts me, especially now when there aren't any jobs, they get rid of the Swiss and keep the foreigners. That's what happened to me, by the way.

Q: In the same firm?

A: In the same firm, the O. Company in Geneva. I was the only Swiss crane driver, but I was the one they sacked.

Q: Do you think there's a reason why the employers prefer foreigners?

A: Sure, maybe because of pay. I don't know if I was paid more than them or less, but it doesn't seem right to me, when you're a Swiss citizen, you've done your time in the army, and everything. I'm not racist, not a bit racist, I like everyone. But I reckon that in a country, there's lots of countries, say Germany, it doesn't matter where, they got rid of the foreigners before they kicked their own countrymen out of a job. The people whose country it is should come first, right?

The speaker begins by outlining an explanation for an employer's preferring to keep on foreign labour. The explanation is hesitant, uncertain, and second-hand: 'Sure, maybe . . . I don't know', and comes in answer to a precise question. But before he has completed the explanation, the speaker breaks with any causal intention in order to assert his Swiss identity and the right which, in his eyes, this gives him to keep his job as long as there are still foreigners in the firm. The speaker seems to feel that causality, the need to explain, is in some sense foreign to him, alienating; it leads him into a system of thought where he is no longer himself, which he cannot control and in which he cannot express his most strongly held convictions. At this point he effectively starts again with 'it doesn't seem right to me', and goes on to express what is most important for him to say about jobs, redundancy and foreigners.

This ending of explanation by refusal differs from the instances we saw earlier. It is not so much a confrontation between opposing values, it is the occupational position of the speaker which makes him abandon causality and start asserting concrete principles about national priority in employment. The speaker does not want to know why he, and not a foreigner, has been made redundant, he wants to denounce a situation which he regards as unjust and of which he is a victim. One certainly cannot imagine what answer the same speaker would have given if he had kept his job.[9]

What one can say is that the end of the explanation and the transition to the assertion are linked to a concrete situation, which he states 'by the way' is his own.

020063–64

Q: What's the recession due to, in your opinion?

A: It's a problem that's a bit beyond me, because it's difficult to say. Firstly, there's unemployment because of the foreigners. Personally I always come back to that point. Basically the recession is unemployment.

Q: Do you have the impression that the current redundancies are inevitable?

A: If the employers haven't got any work for their employees, what else can they do except lay them off? It's a matter for the employers. I don't know enough about their business to discuss it. But there must be a way out that doesn't need so many redundancies. I mean, why do the employers have to make people redundant, really, you wonder. Some people have got ideas about it, but I haven't got much to say at the moment. All the same, when three quarters of a firm's workforce are foreigners there's bound to be recession. It's normal. But even if that concerned me, what do you suggest I do about it? I'm an individualist too. What concerns me at the moment is to be able to do a bit of work, and I can't.

Q: Were you made redundant?

A: No, I can't work because of my health. But I could work for two or three months, all the same. But where does it come from in the end, the recession, it comes from the foreigners. If they got rid of a few more there would be less unemployment.

Here the explanation is stopped by a renunciation, not a refusal. The speaker assumes that it is possible to find an explanation for the recession, even if 'it's difficult to say' because he does not have the necessary information. But he renounces any more lengthy discussion of this general explanation and contents himself with a partial explanation which he is familiar with, namely explaining unemployment by the presence of foreigners. One element of the recession – unemployment – is identified, and a single cause – the foreign presence – is assigned to it. This does not mask the speaker's awareness of the complexity of the phenomenon of recession and the probable multiplicity of its causes. But looking for this general explanation is not relevant, whereas attributing unemployment to the presence of foreigners is. And the criterion of relevance is the personal situation of the speaker who is trying to find work but finds that all the jobs he wants are taken by foreigners. 'What concerns me at the moment is to be able to do a bit of work.' For the rest, there is no point in looking for an explanation, as no action of his can remedy the situation: 'But even if that concerned me, what do you suggest I do about it?'

The explanation only seems to be relevant to the extent that it refers to phenomena and causes which are already part of the speaker's practical preoccupations.[10] Explaining the unattainable is seen as a pointless, perhaps even a threatening, exercise. The search for causes is indissociable from the search for solutions.

Using causality as a discursive strategy

The discursive function of the three paradigms: the status of the speaker

(a) *The deviancy paradigm* subjects the social actors represented in the discourse to a system of valorised norms, in a kind of moral reification. Judgement and explanation intermingle. The speaking subject[11] plays a part in the explanation. Admittedly this part is seldom in the first person singular, the speaker preferring the use of 'we', designating a generality which includes the speaker: we Swiss, we adults, we decent people. This 'we' may be implied, or it may be based on a category opposition (such as us/foreigners; us/young people; us/criminals) which is made intelligible by the single category 'other' (foreigners, young people, criminals). Condemning the behaviour of these 'other' categories thus works to justify and valorise the category which the speaker, explicitly or implicitly, belongs to. In all these cases the representation of the social that is built up in the framework of the deviancy paradigm is polarised round a speaker who presents himself as *active subject* (social actor). The speaker claims simultaneously to be an arbiter outside the behaviour being judged and a guardian of norms used to pronouncing sentence on the guilty. The speaker creates a court which is the site of the power he exercises as *speaking subject*, speaking in the name of THE law (which in fact is HIS law), a law which is established beyond argument and which he declares himself to be subject to as well. Taking on the functions of prosecutor and judge, he alone is the judicial power. The legislative power does not exist, because the system of norms is forever defined and beyond discussion. All that is lacking is the executive power, the police who have to take the accused away. It is an unreal power which lasts only as long as the discourse.

It may be assumed that the use of the deviancy paradigm is therefore a discursive strategy designed to hide the speaker's *absence of real power* as a social actor behind a *discursive seizure of power* by the speaker as speaking subject.

(b) *The materialist explanatory paradigm* leaves open the question of the speaker's status both as social actor and as speaking subject.

The speaker is of course the subject of the statement. It is he who speaks and explains. But the speaker may very well be absent both as social actor subject and as speaking subject.

It is the characteristic attitude of the materialist paradigm, the distance the

speaker maintains from his own discourse, which explains the absence (or at any rate, the lesser importance) of evidence of the *speaking subject* in the statements he makes. In fact, the speaking subject can choose whether or not to present himself as speaking subject, and whether or not to go beyond what is strictly explanatory and give his own point of view about the phenomenon in question.

The speaker's position as social actor subject is a similar one. As well as offering his explanation, he can choose whether or not he wants to take sides, become involved, or intervene as a social actor subject.

The use of the materialist paradigm can thus correspond to different discursive strategies. If the speaker does not implicate himself at all, he will elude any possible attempt on the part of the recipient to gain a hold over him: this is a strategy which acknowledges an absence of real power (or in some cases the simulation of real power). If he includes a representation of himself in his description of social relations, he assigns himself the status of social actor, in a strategy of involvement. However, the discursive strategy aspect is not given much prominence, as the functioning of this paradigm leads the speaker to stress (external) material facts rather than asserting his own subjectivity. The materialist paradigm carries the requirement of a certain amount of decentration.

(c) *The indeterminacy paradigm* implies the effacement of the speaker both as social actor and as speaking subject. It also causes the other social actors to disappear behind the mechanical functioning of general, naturalised, social laws, and enables the speaker, having escaped from the interplay of social relations, to legitimate his own powerlessness by the impossibility of altering the situation. Solutions are often put forward, of course, but the conditions of their implementation are vague: 'They should', or even 'It would have been better if they had . . .' Most important of all, the speaker is never himself involved in the solution he offers, has no investment in it (unlike the speaker who uses the deviancy paradigm). The solution remains impersonal, and therefore external to him. This might perhaps be seen as a strategy for legitimating inaction.

We can now say, therefore, that the speaker's dual status as speaking subject and social actor subject differs fundamentally with each paradigm. In the deviancy explanation, the speaking subject is very much present (he pronounces the law and declares some social actors guilty). The subject as social actor is present, but only implicitly or symbolically because of his powerlessness to act in real terms. In the materialist explanation the speaker is free to choose whether to represent himself as social actor or not, and has no important part to play as speaker. In the indeterminacy paradigm, the speaker cannot be present as social actor and tries to efface himself as speaking subject. The first paradigm thus seems to belong with the speaker's vehement

Status of the speaker Paradigms	Speaking subject	Social actor subject
Deviancy paradigm	Strongly present Vehement discourse Discursive seizure of power	Powerless social actor
Materialist paradigm	Absence Exteriority of the analysing subject	Choice between involvement and non-involvement
Indeterminacy paradigm	Absent The speaker actively effaces himself	Impossibility of action Legitimated inaction

Figure 4.4 Diagram showing the status of the speaker, the speaking subject and the social actor subject in relation to the three paradigms

assertion of himself and his system of values, the second with a choice between involvement and withdrawal, and the third with legitimated inaction.

Some of the elements identified above can be brought together in Figure 4.4.

Sociocognitive centration and causality: main links

Having completed our analysis of the practical functioning of the different forms of causal explanation, it becomes immediately clear that there are connections between causality and the subject of centration and decentration.

The different degrees of sociocognitive centration and decentration were analysed primarily from the standpoint of their cognitive form (sociocognitive structure and mechanisms), even though those cognitive aspects could only be apprehended by analysing the language through which they operated.

With the discovery of the logico-discursive forms and paradigms of causality, however, greater emphasis has fallen on the discursive aspects, on linguistic functioning. This gradual shift is part of our overall project of giving increased importance to form as against mere content, though without ever dissociating the two.

The sociocognitive mechanisms are still present in the forms of causality,

but we have not had to demonstrate their existence as we are familiar with them. Nonetheless the forms of causality we have identified are logico-discursive forms, i.e. indissociably cognitive and discursive.

Closer analysis of the discursive level assumes extreme sensibility to the specifically linguistic nature and functioning of a given text. This is worth stressing, because it is not automatically recognised by sociologists who are used to dealing solely and directly with content. Reading a text, for a sociologist, is discovering its content. Furthermore, the understanding of this content is often in terms of pre-established sociological categories, for sociology, like other disciplines in the social sciences and like the man in the street, has its own categories of knowledge, ITS way of knowing social reality.

In that sense, one could say that our project to use the discoveries and frames of reference of a number of disciplines is itself an attempt at decentration, or a co-ordination of different centrations and a search for a new and richer equilibrium in the knowledge of social phenomena. This equilibration process is fundamental as decentration cannot be obtained just by juxtaposing different centrations. Piaget has, after all, shown that the development of scientific knowledge provides many analogies with intellectual development.

Our greater emphasis on linguistic functioning is best illustrated in the *discursive* model we constructed to take acount of the deviancy paradigm (the three basic sentences).

If we briefly set the results of our analysis of centration and decentration against those of the analysis of causality, certain connections will be apparent:

(1)   The logico-discursive model of the deviancy paradigm also takes account of the *form* of the most sociocentric social thoughts. If we went back to the statements quoted to illustrate the forms of centration, we would see that they also provide perfect illustrations of this model.

(2)   We can also see that the materialist paradigm is bound to imply a form of thought which is really decentred.

(3)   We can assume that there are certain relations between the indeterminacy paradigm and what we have termed the excess of decentration, a form which, at the cognitive level, is close to what sociologists mean by the term 'anomie'. One has only to think of the absence of social categorisation, indeed of any analytical categories, and the attitude of withdrawal and lack of direction which characterises the indeterminacy paradigm.

The concrete analysis of the paradigms of causality allows us to verify some of the other arguments that are basic to our work.

The simultaneously structured and flexible nature of sociocognitive struc-

tures can be seen in a very practical way in connection with phenomena such as:

> *the break in causal regression*
> *semantic shifts* between paradigms
> *co-existence* of different paradigms within one social actor subject
> and *the aims* of the causality

It will be remembered that every social actor subject can be defined by his membership of a given sociocognitive structure, but that over and above that general dependence, all concrete social practice is a function of other factors (particularly the matter with which the practice is concerned, the actor's value system, its immediate concrete situation and the ends it is hoping to achieve). These various factors will, to some extent, force the determinisms of the sociocognitive structure to bend to their requirements: an example of this would be the speaker who used the materialist paradigm to explain conscientious objection on religious grounds ('genuine' objectors), which he accepted, but who was quite happy to condemn (deviancy paradigm) objection for political motives, which he criticised because it contradicted his own value system.

Or, to take another example, there was the speaker who began to explain the reasons why foreigners emigrated, but who stopped the explanation and had no hesitation in using two different paradigms to justify their expulsion. The end he was pursuing became more important than rational explanation and dictated the cognitive and discursive form. The cognitive mechanism necessary for a proper explanation was there, but the subject's immediate aims required something else.

This, therefore, verifies the fact that there is no formal social thought. No purely formal analysis can account for this sort of phenomenon.

The interaction between logico-discursive form and content (in the broad sense) is fundamental. The nature of this interaction will vary from one form of thought to another. A speaker whose dominant mode is the materialist paradigm, unlike this last example, would not interrupt his explanation, as he would abstract from his preferences and his subjectivity in an explanatory practice. Explanation and judgement would thus be dissociated. And that sort of logico-discursive practice would also be defined by a different cognitive and discursive style, as well as by different discursive practices.

We can therefore understand more fully why a discourse that aims for efficacy is characterised by a greater tolerance of the co-existence of different paradigms within it, and of semantic ambiguity. The logic of efficacy has reasons which reason does not recognise, but which the end may render necessary.

More general significance of causality

The concrete analysis of the logico-discursive forms of causal explanation at work in everyday social thought reveals several more general points:

(1)   The almost 'natural' character of explanation by deviance, because this form is so widespread, and applied almost automatically.

(2)   The important and constant cognitive and discursive *work* necessitated by the transition from the deviancy paradigm to the materialist paradigm. This work is not in any sense self-evident, it inevitably implies the process of individuation it involves.

(3)   When we talk about explanation we need to be aware that explanation in the strict sense is rare, indeed exceptional, in ordinary social thought. We might, therefore, ask whether it was necessary to choose causality to reveal the workings of social thought. But the reason we did was not solely for what it reveals negatively. Posing the problems in terms of causality has enabled social thought to reveal its deep structures, because the assignment of causes is a *constitutive* dimension of social thought, despite the fact that this process of assignment consists as much of judgements, condemnations, uncertainties and ignorance (whether admitted or dissimulated) as of explanations in the proper sense of the term.

(4)   And then concrete analyses of the forms of causality have unforeseen repercussions, which extend as far as learned thought. If we take into account the importance of the cognitive and discursive work needed for the transition from the deviance paradigm to the materialist paradigm, we can say that the explanation by deviance constitutes a *more primitive* cognitive form (primary causality) than the materialist explanation which is closer to the kind of explanation found in the analytical procedures of science (secondary causality). The latter is, admittedly, more worked and more elaborate. But it is a mistake to set up a clear-cut dichotomy between primary and secondary causality, and to valorise the latter by attributing its use exclusively to scholars.

In actuality, we *all*, in both our daily and professional lives, use *all the paradigms* of causal explanation we have identified. What is variable is the relative importance of each of them in any given kind of thought. We therefore approach them in terms of *variable combinations* and of *degree*, not in terms of clear-cut dichotomies. We are not saying this in order to exculpate those for whom explanation is primarily a matter of condemnation, and to blame those for whom explanation is a job, but because that is how, in reality, the practices operate.

The most unexpected aspect is certainly our 'attribution' of the explanation

by deviance to scientific discourses as well. But no lengthy analysis is needed to establish the fact that scientific debate between opposing 'schools' is not conducted in a purely analytical way. There is such a thing as scientific polemic, and polemic is not governed by the materialist paradigm. We only have to look at the logico-discursive procedures used in scientific refutation. Granted that scientists, in their written discourse, use more restrained language to talk about their rivals than they would in private, spoken conversation with others who shared their viewpoint, there is nevertheless no doubt that analogies exist between the repertoire of such statements and the language of the deviancy paradigm. For once we shall not use concrete statements to illustrate our argument. The nature of scientific language, like any other discourse, depends on the moment, the situation, the requirements of immediate practice and the ends being pursued, even if its dominant style is by definition that of the materialist paradigm.

This statement of the omnipresence of the deviancy paradigm might be compared, by analogy, to the thesis of the 'later' Lévy-Bruhl:

> Let us expressly rectify what I believed correct in 1910: there is not a primitive mentality distinguishable from the other by *two* characteristics which are peculiar to it (mystical and prelogical). There is a mystical mentality which is more marked and more easily observable among 'primitive' peoples' own societies, but it is present in every human mind.[12]

If this reasoning were extended to scientific thought, within the limits we have defined, we would not have any difficulty in accepting it.

There remains the problem of the origin and *raison d'être* of primary causality and thus also the explanation by deviance. We cannot, and would not wish to, tackle a problem which has preoccupied so many scholars, and will not attempt to outline even an embryonic synthesis. All we shall do is discuss one of the empirical results under this heading: a development of linguistic and cognitive structures is accompanied by a diminished tendency to use the deviancy paradigm, but nobody is completely free from it.

There is no contradiction even between this conclusion and Piagetian rationalism. It is a matter of those 'exceptional circumstances in which, without thinking, the average man takes up an attitude (in relation to causality) characteristic of primitive peoples'.[13]

If we take the 'average' man to include the scientist, and if we put the term primitive in quotes, we can accept this statement, too.

We know that from his genetic viewpoint Piaget defined egocentrism particularly in terms of the lack of differentiation between subject and object. Cognitive development brings with it a gradual dissociation of subject and object; the object takes on an external reality, hostile to the subject, at least in the early stages. Poliakov has suggested an analogy between Piaget's argu-

ment and the discoveries of Freud.[14] He compares the notion of the external object to the Other experienced as a hostile or dangerous force. By adding the affective level based on the love/hate or like/dislike opposition and then taking it one stage further he discovers the first manifestation of 'spirits' or 'demons'. The bad or the hated is sought in what is foreign to the Ego, external, Other: we only need add the term 'deviant' to bring in the deviancy paradigm and begin to give it a psychogenetic and affective basis. The mechanism is prepared for the most varied social categories to be placed in the role of demons,[15] diabolic forces, or deviants, depending on the moment, their situation, the type of society and the ends pursued by the social actor subjects.

The relation between cause and effect in the deviancy paradigm is not always a simple or direct one. Individuals governed by the paradigm do not, for example, attribute all ills immediately and directly to foreigners. An *intermediate cause* is often introduced into the explanatory chain. Thus the decline in patriotism is attributed to a change in the Swiss mentality, and only this change is attributed to the imitation of foreigners by Swiss youth. There may here be another analogy with the way in which the savage mind sees witchcraft as a cause. A misfortune is not attributed directly to witchcraft. If a house collapses and a person is killed then the collapse of the house is perceived as the cause of death. But it is witchcraft that causes the house to collapse when the person is inside it. The *primary* cause is always attributed to evil or diabolic forces. Primary causality is extra-temporal and extra-spatial; it is dependent on the principle of participation.

Beyond the search for deviants is the phenomenon of deviance itself. It is this that is the primary cause.

As we have seen, it is hard not to speculate about the origin and *raison d'être* of the phenomenon of causality, even when one tries to keep the analysis at an immediate and concrete level. All we want to do in these brief notes is to provide a reminder of the existence of a problem which comes within the scope of the many questions which inevitably arise from this sort of research, but which are doomed to remain unanswered.[16]

We move on now to an analysis of the discourse of the social representation of *time*, the third of the areas we regard as particularly revealing about the nature and functioning of ordinary social thought and of language in use.

5 The perception of time

Introduction: some problems and sixteen important points

The subject of time presents certain similarities with that of causality.

(1)   It too has been the subject of a multitude of studies across the whole range of scientific disciplines.

(2)   It is not our intention – nor do we have the capability – to present any sort of synthesis of that work.

(3)   Our main aim is therefore restricted to analysing, as empirically and concretely as possible, the different ways of knowing time to be found in everyday life.

(4)   These results will be compared with those obtained by other researchers in the social sciences.

(5)   Of the more general questions to arise in connection with time, we shall discuss those which can be derived from empirical bases.

A concrete analysis of time in use in everyday life should expect to reveal several forms of time-perception. We shall thus be looking for the *social* variations in time-perception, i.e. the *sociotemporal structures*. And according to our postulates every social perception of time, each sociotemporal structure, must have its own specific cognitive and discursive style. The subject of time therefore introduces some new analytical dimensions concerning *other logics*. Time seems to lend itself particularly well to the projection of affective, symbolic and mythic elements, all of which, as we know, play a central role in political discourse.

Alongside the discursive and sociocognitive structures there will also be *socioaffective* structures, as every individual or social group has an *affective, symbolic and mythic capability*.

An interviewee like the one who, when the interviewer brought up the subject of 'Switzerland', became unable to speak and burst into tears (upset at what had become of his 'once fine Switzerland', his 'little Switzerland that he loved, that he had been taught to love') is influenced more by emotion than by analytic reason.

It is understandable that the producers of effective political discourses should use the potentialities in this reservoir of affective symbolic and mythic

144

capacities. These capacities, or dispositions, are themselves capable of being politically invested and used *parasitically* for ideological ends. To promise the fulfilment of a desire, when that desire is expressed passionately, or even demanded by entire social groups (a desire, for instance, to find, or recreate, a mythical, ideal society) is bound to be effective in that situation, with those social groups. Effective ideological discourses absorb, or else become parasitic on, everything which can help them attain their objectives: cognitive, sociotemporal, affective, symbolic or mythic structure, they can all be used to feed the longing for the desired end.

Briefly, the important points are the following:

(1)   Time is one of the areas where the affective, symbolic and mythic capacity can take a particularly good hold.

(2)   This capacity is not the prerogative of so-called primitive societies.

(3)   Everybody, and every society, has this capacity.

(4)   In modern industrialised societies the capacity is often latent. It is frequently withered and atrophied.

(5)   But the capacity is virtually always there, and can be reinvested at any moment, even after long periods of dormancy.

(6)   Some social groups are more sensitive to this capacity than others.

(7)   Political discourses, of the sort we are analysing, invest this capacity in a very big way.

(8)   Some of the terms used above (affectivity, symbol, myth, projection, investment) explain the new and particularised approaches we shall be setting alongside disciplines such as psychoanalysis and the study of myths and symbols.

(9)   We postulate that the different ways of knowing time can be situated on a continuum from the mythic perception of time (or mythic time) at one extreme, and the linear perception of time (or linear time) at the other.

(10)   There is nothing surprising about the existence of a linear conception of time in Western industrialised societies, as they are based on an evolutionary vision of the world (which implies belief in linear evolution and continuous progress).

(11)   The existence of mythic time, on the other hand, may come as a surprise. For this reason we have analysed it at greater length.

(12)   We postulate that a perception of social reality based on the past (with a fixation on the past, which is valorised and idealised) goes hand in hand with a mythic perception of time. This is the myth of the Golden Age (situated in the past, unlike ideologies which situate it in a 'radiant future'), or of Paradise Lost.

(13)   We postulate that the mythic conception of time is found more often in the discourse of those who support the 'xenophobic movements' than of their opponents.

(14)   The direct and fundamental correlative of the preceding postulate is that the affective and mythic capacity can never be regarded as a sort of passé, conservative, or reactionary residue. If that is how it appears, it is because of the alteration and *ideological parasitism* it has been subjected to by the political discourses which have used it for their own ends.

(15)   In itself, however, the affective and mythic capacity present to a greater or lesser degree in every individual and in every social group has no 'natural', ideological coloration.[1]

(16)   Political discourses which claim to be more 'rational' than other, rival, discourses merely appeal less to the affective, mythic capacity. This is doubtless why they are less politically effective.

The differences between the two types of discourse are not, however, the result of a conscious, deliberate choice. They stem from different underlying predispositions, different sociocognitive structures.

Any sociocognitive structure is not predisposed to just any particular conception of time.

The empirical analyses that follow are subdivided as follows:

(1)   The discourse of mythic–cyclical time:
       (a) the concrete working of mythic–cyclical time;
       (b) outline of sociocognitive and socioaffective interpretation.
(2)   The discourse of linear time.

The discourse of mythic–cyclical time: how it works

Tension between the idealised image of Switzerland in the past and a sense of deterioration

> 450001
> Switzerland, my native country, the country I was taught to love, to cherish and revere. But young people nowadays don't see it like that any more ... I'm nearly seventy. I feel this is my country, the land that my ancestors fought so fiercely and so bravely to defend. I was brought up to love it, we celebrated our country on all the patriotic festivals. We loved our country.

This statement, which came right at the beginning of an interview in answer to the question 'What does Switzerland make you think of?', provides an excellent illustration of what we have called the *tension* between the ideal image, which is intensely interiorised (as the subject himself recognises: 'the

country I was taught to love, to cherish and revere'), and consciousness of a deterioration.

Here is another example which expresses the same tension (and which also comes from the start of an interview).

> *260001*
> [Reply to the same question] The speed things change in a man's life. I can remember Switzerland in 1922, when I was eight or ten. It was more peaceful then, not quite so agitated; we weren't so well off then. Some things are better now, socially speaking, but looking at it overall I think we were healthier, our lives were better, we weren't so enervated, we had countryside all round us. I think it's gone too far now, these new buildings right on top of each other with a few square yards for each one, it's pretty suffocating.

And finally, here is the opening of a third interview:

120001
Q: What does Switzerland represent for you?
A: It's my country, which I used to love. I love it much less now. I was born in Les Grisons. Even at school we were taught to be patriotic and to sing patriotic songs, and I've always loved my country . . . because it's clean and orderly, and because of the spirit of the people. What I mean is that I always thought everything was right in Switzerland. Now I love it much less, there are a great many things that aren't well-ordered.

Let us take the two extremes of this tension and examine their characteristics in more detail.

The myth of an ideal Switzerland

The image of a small, self-enclosed community
Such an idea fits in with the sociocognitive mechanism of regression from the political to the psycho-familial. Switzerland, as an entity, is thought of as if it were a family or a household.

> *450009*
> Listen, our country used to be a haven of peace; it was a peaceful little country where nothing much happened, it was calm and we lived in peace.

This vision introduces the idea of a world where people are a closed group, living in a kind of blessed state of narcissistic fulfilment,[2] well-expressed in terms such as 'haven of peace', 'little' country, and in the undisturbed tranquillity of 'nothing much happened'.

> It was more peaceful then, not quite so agitated; we weren't so well off then. Some things are better now, socially speaking, but looking at it overall I think

we were healthier, our lives were better, we weren't so enervated, we had countryside all round us.

This sort of idea is unarguably linked to the countryside and to nature. Several of the subjects we interviewed, describing this ideal Switzerland, nostalgically recalled their country childhoods:

> 230001
> For me Switzerland represents something beautiful but, in the end, deceptive. I was brought up in the country, and that really gave me an elevated idea of Switzerland.

A little later, the same person adds:

> 230003
> Well, it's like I was saying just now, I went to school in the country where everyone was very patriotic. They're much less so now, far less. But then we were taught at school by really patriotic teachers. Switzerland was history . . . and it's true, it was something fine, but the things that have happened since the war have been a great disappointment to us.

'Switzerland was history'. We shall have more to say about this pseudo-mythic valorisation of forefathers and founding fathers in the discourse of many supporters of 'xenophobic initiatives'.

> 300001
> Personally I'm very fond of Switzerland, my country, because I'm from Unterwalden, our family has always lived there, and I think we have a fairly developed patriotic spirit.

A little later:

> 300008
> I think our country ought to be a neutral state, as it is at the moment, that's obvious, but we should live . . . it should be more like a family, more like the way the German Swiss live. You go to Sarnen, or some other part of German-speaking Switzerland, and there's a sort of folklore, a mentality and roots, whereas in Geneva everyone treats each other like strangers.

This is how the following interviewee describes national holidays in a country environment:

> 450000
> It's very moving there, very simple, it's in a natural setting, in Switzerland, with everybody from the surrounding villages, you really feel part of the population.

There are several glimpses of nostalgia for childhood in this interview:

> The one thing that hurts, though, is to see Switzerland invaded by foreigners,

like a house infested by bugs. It makes me upset that it's impossible to go back to the past. When I was little I formed a quite different idea of Switzerland, the land of William Tell and all our ancestors, it was wonderful. But it's not like that any more.

In reply to the question 'What do you like most about Switzerland?', she said:

First of all, its form, its geography. I think it's the most beautiful country in the world. And then, you see, I was brought up in a very close-knit family, with grandparents who'd raised lots of children and given each of them a trade, you see other countries complain, but every government should give work for its own people.

Nostalgia for childhood and for a united family goes hand in hand with a regression from the political to the psycho-familial: the ideal Switzerland is a close-knit family that has to provide work for its children, just like a paterfamilias. We can also see in these two quotations the connection between Switzerland (the 'true' Switzerland, bequeathed us by our ancestors) and the countryside, where life is simple, social relations are more direct, and people do not treat each other as strangers.

Another interviewee had this to say:

070000

Before, we had a better system of doing things, because the point of a system is find the best way of living, so in Switzerland we had orderly ways and customs which we were fond of and which were passed on from family to family. We liked a peaceful life, with plenty of work to do. In those days (I'm talking about when I was young) we didn't look for great banquets, we lived simply, with the occasional celebration. I remember my mother used to ask us what we wanted as a special treat on Sundays, and we used to say 'Please can you make us sweet eggy bread.' We lived very simply, you see, but young people nowadays wouldn't be able to put up with that.

The same characteristic terms are here: orderly ways, customs, peacefulness, simplicity, all linked to a nostalgic recollection of family celebrations.

The image of the ideal Switzerland is constantly linked to ancestors and founding fathers, and to the qualities they had to develop in the course of their patriotic struggle.

540026

What I like about Switzerland is its history, which I love and have always loved, the old Swiss and everything they went through in order to be Swiss. And if the Swiss nowadays had half the character they had then, there wouldn't be any more of these troubles.

The same subject regarded the old Swiss as

540029
more direct and when they wanted something they had it, they made it or they
fought to get it.

Ancestors, in this perspective, are invested with qualities and values which
turn them into real mythic heroes.

300000
Our forefathers showed us they could successfully fight an Austrian empire.
They would not be able to fight against any kind of invader now because they
are all so changeable and divided.

To sum up, then, the ideal image of Switzerland, which is strongly
emphasised and valorised, is embodied in the small, self-enclosed community,
where the living is good and the relations between people are marked by
simplicity and tranquillity. Additionally, this ideal Switzerland was built by
the heroic actions of the ancestors, the founding fathers, who are invested
with every positive value and good quality.

Time and change as a process of deterioration. People who have recourse to this
sort of mythologising in their description of time and change constantly refer
to this ideal image in order to say that things are not like that any longer. They
obviously never stop to wonder whether they ever actually were. They are
happy to register change as deviance from or violation of an order which
ought to be immutable.

The factors involved in this change are of several orders, and we shall see
later how they are articulated in discourse.

Mixing of mentalities, mixed neighbourhoods, the attraction of foreign mentalities.
This argument is mostly put forward by supporters of 'xenophobic move-
ments'. They see the mixing of mentalities, of social outlook, as closely linked
to the presence of foreigners in Switzerland, as they introduce different ways
of life and thereby necessarily contribute to the disintegration of Swiss
culture.

450002
... Switzerland's been invaded by foreigners. These days the Swiss,
especially the young, want to ape the foreigners, they think that's the
thing to do ... We've had too many foreigners here, and they've ruined
our way of thinking. I've done a lot of travelling myself, but I'm still
Swiss.

Q: How has it happened?

A: People intermingle, young people admire other nations, first the
Americans, then the Russians. There are too many communists in
Switzerland these days, that's something I think is terrible.

This mixing of mentalities leads to the country becoming more open and more divided. At the level of social relations it introduces tensions and intermixing, which are seen by xenophobes as evil.

300001

I'm very happy in my country except for the social phenomenon we're talking about; to my mind, this intermixing is the most serious current issue.

It's a pity people don't talk about it more. That's why people are getting more and more neurotic, there's no communication between Swiss people, and with foreigners all over the place, that makes it even more difficult.

Q: Why is there this lack of communication between Swiss people?
A: Because of all these differences in mentality.

The mixing of mentalities and the resulting anonymity are particularly linked to the city and the urban atmosphere, and in the minds of our interviewees were closely related to the opposition between town and country.[3]

300008

You go to Sarnen, or some other part of German-speaking Switzerland, and there's a sort of folklore, a mentality and roots, whereas in Geneva everyone treats each other like strangers. You feel that everybody suffers from the environment, the intermixing.

The enormous growth of the city. Juxtaposition of mentalities and social mix go hand in hand in this discourse, in which the representation is closer to the mythic pole than the linear one. And both are linked to the enormous growth of the city, a topic which crops up in several of the interviews:

200008

In the end, Switzerland is a small country, with its own limits, and they can't go on building and clearing the whole surface of the country . . . not surface, what would you call it? greenery, nature, destroying nature for the profit of a few, because this pursuit of profit ends up diminishing democracy.

In the eyes of this interviewee, the people who have profited from the situation are:

200039

. . . all the capitalists, the large amounts of foreign capital that have come in, the foreign money that has come in, and then advertised in countries where there isn't any work; they encouraged them to come.

Here a connection is established between the growth of construction work on the one hand and foreigners on the other, by means of the double

mediation of (foreign) money and the (foreign) workforce. This creates a vicious circle:

> 200039
> They wanted to do too much, they should have been stopped from going on building. There's has to be some stability, you can't go on, because you build twó or three blocks, and then those are needed to house the foreign workers, so the situation will still be the same in 30 years' time.

This dimension of the discourse is even better illustrated by the following example:

> 260001
> I think they're going too far, with these new buildings right on top of each other with a few square yards for each one. People feel suffocated, at least I do. Heaven knows what it will be like for young people in 20 years' time if it goes on. It will be OK if it stops. But it looks as if there could be a population explosion, and that wouldn't be anything to do with the Swiss. According to the statistics, the Swiss birth rate is just right, so it must be to do with the foreign workforce they brought over here as building workers and who are still here despite the unemployment. Only the other day it said in the paper that when a foreigner leaves it's just a question of money; they don't care whether the people are comfortable or suffocating. But what shocks me is the way industrialists seem to rule Switzerland and the government, the government is just an intermediary for the industrialists . . .

Here we can see one of the basic topics of this discourse: the speed of change and of building; speculation; and the need to bring in foreign labour.

The foreign labour both provokes a population explosion and creates a vicious circle:

Q: What have the foreigners contributed to Switzerland?
A: Their hands. What I always say is it seems to me that the foreigners are like a state within the state, because the foreigners haven't just built for us, they've built flats for themselves, too. They bring the workforce over here, so they have to build flats for them, then once the flats are built, they need shops, and then they need people to work in the shops, so they have to import foreign workers. Then they have children, the children need schools, so it's a vicious circle, because the people who work in the shops need somewhere to live too, and it's foreigners who build the houses.

Building and the arrival of foreigners thus provokes a self-fuelling vicious circle.

Speculation, money and the search for profit are often seen as elements in this negative evolution.

260003
The bad thing is the way mankind thirsts after . . . I mean, they never stop building, they do it to make money. Now I don't know whether they're right or not, but to go by the figures in the papers there'll soon be a time in Switzerland when one square metre will be used for building every second, that's what makes my head spin.

540005
They wanted to build everything at once; in Switzerland they wanted every-thing at once, you can go to any modern village in Switzerland and it'll have been built in ten years, it's incredible, don't you think? I went to Geneva, I went to one part that if you went back three months later you wouldn't recognise it, there's so much building going on everywhere. But what I'd like to know is why it's being built, why it's all being built at once. Either there was too much money around or, I don't know, building takes a lot of cash, and who's got it afterwards . . . well, it's not the employers at all events. These people are billionaires, they've become billionaires in ten years.

Money, well-being and change. In a more general way, money and material well-being appear in this discourse (for the most part exemplified by support-ers of the xenophobic movements) as negative factors of change. Obviously they realise that there are advantages to increased purchasing power but, say the interviewees, taking everything into account, people used to live healthier lives, because they had an ideal, and were able to develop moral qualities.

300008
I'd like to see a return to the way things used to be, I don't mean living in caves, but the pace of work needs to slow down, wages should maybe be lower, with everyone living on less, and everyone having an ideal, which is something that's been lost. The only ideal at the moment is to earn a lot and look after number one. Deep down, the Swiss will always be concerned about the problem of foreigners, but nobody says anything because they're afraid of losing money.

Money makes people amorphous and lacking in will; taken to its conclusion therefore this means that there has to be an economic crisis before they can rediscover the courage and other qualities of the founding fathers. In some cases we can even say that the overt idea is to provoke one by wanting to expel the foreign workers.

260007
There's a kind of failure on the people's part because they don't react and the government knows that the people won't move, whatever happens.

260008
Q: What's the explanation for that?
A: It's just to do with comfort. I know people don't care about what might

happen as long as they're earning a bit of money, they've got their chalet and they can go out on Saturdays or Sundays and eat what they want with their friends. That kind of well-being stultifies you, it's like being in a feather-bed. It puts a man to sleep. It will take a more serious crisis than this one to wake the people up, so for the moment we have to think everything's fine as it is.

Money, individualism and the destruction of Swiss cultural unity all go together.

Q: What do you think the Swiss are particularly fond of?
A: Their dough, their personal and material rewards. But this mentality has changed over the last 20 years or more, because they think of themselves now, they don't think about the country any more. What's the point of safeguarding something when it's not even for the Swiss? So they defend their living, which they're quite right to do, more's the pity. The Swiss used to defend the common good, and now they've become individualists and you can understand why.

The presence of foreign money in the Swiss banks is also seen as a negative factor, and one that leads to the destruction of traditional values.

450036
Too many large sums of money have come into Switzerland, they had to use them productively, they opened factories and businesses and so then they had to get workers as well.

300007
They don't care enough about Swiss workers, and about the poor, at the social level. I'm involved in the social services, and I see the cases that come to me, people who haven't anything to eat, the poor old men who get the worst deal out of this social mixing and who've become xenophobic because they fought to have a country. Our people are on the retreat but you have to remember they were mobilised during the two World Wars, and now they can see the country opening up and becoming divided, that's the slightly negative side, and at the economic level, I think all the money invested here doesn't give the population . . . I won't say nothing, but the whole problem needs looking at.

540028
Q: What, fundamentally, do you think has changed between the old Swiss you were talking about just now and Swiss people today?
A: I don't know. For one thing, there's too much money in Switzerland, too much money, but not Swiss money, it's all foreign money here. It's all foreign money here! All the capitalists and the kings of God knows where put their money here. And the government uses it. That's one thing. And then, oh I don't really like talking about Switzerland, it gets

me down. They're like sheep, they let them do what they want, they let them walk all over them.

And one more example:

240005
Bit by bit our environment is going, and soon there won't be anything left. And why? Whose fault will it be? Again it's those big foreign companies that come and set up here and make lots of money, but don't care a toss about our fields and mountains and forests as long as the dollars keep coming in, and when the money stops they'll go. That makes me angry. They're talking about nuclear power stations and everything that goes with them, but it won't benefit the Swiss at all, the ones who'll profit will be the big American companies.

Here ecological concerns are linked with money but, interestingly, only with foreign money and foreign – particularly American – firms.

After this basically descriptive section, we need to pull all these elements together in order to show:

(1)   the symbolic matrix which generates and unifies them, and
(2)   their functions in relation to the individuals in whose discourse they appear.

The discourse of mythic–cyclical time: an outline of sociocognitive and socioaffective interpretation

The idealised image of Switzerland, or the quest for an originary symbolism

Within the context of this way of knowing social reality, all observations about *time, change* and *evolution* are measured in terms of an ideal image of Switzerland which has a strongly patriotic centration,[4] as well as a deeply narcissistic viewpoint, showing all the marks of a projection encompassing all the narcissistic desires that the present mode of existence leaves unsatisfied. In that respect, the creation of a symbolic ideal Switzerland is comparable to the myth of the Golden Age or of a lost paradise. As Wunenburger puts it, for example.

This topic can be seen as one of the most central mythemes, as far as density of imaginative investment is concerned. It is at the heart of most primitive affabulation, and a complex symbolic history and geography are organised around it. The construction of an ideal place is the main function of the adamic nostalgia which runs through the domestication of ancient man's imaginative world.[5]

The constant references, in this origin-myth, to a garden of delights and to an exuberant and beneficial nature are so suggestive that looking at them in

an admittedly very simplified psychoanalytic perspective it is possible to see a genuine maternal archetype at work.

> The fact that paradise is often localised in the originary period has also encouraged psychoanalysts to see it as a symbolic form of foetal and oceanic regression.[6]

Psychoanalysis tells us that man experiences a profound desire to return to the prenatal state, where he has not yet become a subject and the object world does not exist, and where he is still undifferentiated, immersed in the amniotic fluid. This state of bliss is upset by the trauma of birth, and the consequent need for the individual to adapt to the limits of the external world and to define himself in relation to it. Primary narcissism would thus be characterised by an absence of tension and a sense of limitlessness and infinity which man spends the rest of his life trying to recapture, notably through the symbolic creation of ideal worlds, set in the dawn of history, on to which are projected narcissistic desires and aspirations in the form of a quest for complete fulfilment and perfect wholeness. The dream is of a universe beyond the limits of space–time, and of a society where all relations with other people and objects are direct and straightforward, unmarked by the symbolic dimension and its concomitant notions of distance, absence and alterity, all of which are foreign to the narcissistic quest. We believe that this narcissistic desire is exactly what is found in the image of an ideal Switzerland situated at some point in the past.

Because Switzerland is an inward-looking country, sheltered from international tension and conflict (a notion which gets elided with that of political neutrality), it becomes, in these mythical terms, a haven of peace. The maternal symbolism of nature and the land are important in this, as we have seen, insofar as the 'real' Switzerland in this mode of understanding is a rural, rustic Switzerland. Relationships between people are simple, straightforward and direct, untouched by tension or ambivalence. Each individual recognizes his own image reflected in the other (which provides the definition of narcissism).

Against this idealised image of a bygone Switzerland, this type of discourse puts forward the existence and omnipresence of *tension* and *alterity* in current social reality. This alterity is partly the product of the interaction of different ways of thought, the influx of foreigners into Switzerland (which destroys the cultural unity of the country and tears apart the protective shell of narcissism), and the Swiss desire to imitate foreigners and compare themselves with something other, but partly also of the lust for monetary gain, which distracts people from their real identity and introduces an element of mediation into all their relationships.

And the *tension* is seen as the corollary of alterity. It is bound to be present in a de-narcissised mode, in which relationships with other people are mediated

instead of straightforward and direct, and are thereby subject to ambivalence and equivocation.

Seen in this perspective, the other appears as a threatening figure, a rift in the narcissistic.

The status of time and change

In the context of this ideal and idyllic image of Switzerland, set in a mythical past, time and change cannot help but seem deviant, as the derogation of an immutable order, as degeneration, or entropy.

> Both the great eastern or middle-eastern religions and the oldest Greek myths have made us familiar with the fourfold temporal cosmology, the ages of which are designated by different symbolic metals. Jain and Mazdean texts for example describe a succession from golden age to silver, steel and steel mixed with iron. Each of these microtemporalities is governed by a fixed timespan, and together these make up a great cycle of decay, often reckoned to take 12,000 years. Each period is itself subdivided into phases measurable in centuries, repeating the ages of life in a sequence running from dawn until dusk. The end of one of these major Cycles of world decay, as it rushes headlong into darkness, is marked by a cosmic cataclysm, a universal conflagration in the course of which the world is simultaneously destroyed and regenerated.[7]

Cyclical conceptions of time of this sort, traces of which we found in our interviews, are characterised (as Gabel[8] and Ruyer,[9] among others, have shown) by a *mechanism of spatialisation and reversibility*. Time and change are not experienced as inevitable factors, but are perceived as a kind of space in which it is possible to move around, both forwards and backwards, and even to go right back to the beginning, thereby negating the movement, making it seem as if nothing had happened. Every form of nostalgia for origins tends to adopt this way of representing time. For is it not, after all, an attempt to abolish time, to fix it forever in the ideal moment, and an attempt to abnegate the distance separating it from this ideal so as to restore it in all its splendour?

Certainly this demand for its re-establishment is something we find throughout this discourse.

> *300008*
> I think our country ought to be a neutral state, as it is at the moment, that's obvious, but we should live . . . it should be more like a family, more like the way the German Swiss live. I'd like to see a return to the way things used to be. I don't mean living in caves, but the pace of work needs to slow down, wages should maybe be lower, with everyone living on less, and everyone having an ideal, which is something that's been lost.

> *450009*
> We're lucky enough to still be a small, almost neutral, country. I say almost because they do meddle too much in matters that don't concern us, in other

countries' affairs. We need to keep ourselves to ourselves, and not take too much notice of other countries' politics.

We can get on fine in our country without meddling in foreign politics. And Switzerland can remain independent if that's what all the Swiss really want.

We reproduce these quotations to illustrate the overall direction of the measures recommended, which involve an attempt at re-establishment in one case ('a return to the way things used to be'), and at conservation or preservation in the other.

The narcissistic aspect[10] is particularly noticeable here, in the valorisation of neutrality, and the insistence on the need for family life (keeping to themselves, 'without meddling in foreign politics'). In both cases, the actors of the desired change are not defined. The imperative ('we need to keep ourselves to ourselves') expresses the idea of a collective, generalised effort, which can only be done 'if that's what all the Swiss really want'.

In this kind of reasoning, it is always as if Switzerland could be abstracted from any form of external determinism. There is no mention of the political, historical or social context of which the country is part. Beyond the frontiers, nothing exists, an illusion which is unarguably characteristic of narcissism. The foetus does not recognise any differentiated objects, and can live with the impression that it is at the centre of the world as all its needs are instantly satisfied without the intervention of frustrating intermediaries. The *voluntarism* we encounter in these discourses is shot through with the illusion of narcissistic omnipotence and the external emptiness represented by the absence of determining social factors.

Let us now look at the proposed economic measures in greater detail:

Apart from sending the foreign workers back to their respective countries (which we find in the majority of interviews where there is a tension between past and present, though not in all, as we shall see later), the subjects emphasise a return to simplicity and frugality, along with a reduction in the amount of money in circulation and an effective campaign against speculation and the desire for monetary gain.

> 240000
> Well it's a big problem, Switzerland's future . . . I think about it. We need to safeguard our values. That could mean putting an end to speculation altogether. It's a big problem. Some laws would have to be changed to give the authorities more scope, and make sure they are respected, in areas like speculation and profits. I mean, what's the point of accumulating fortunes, what good do they do you? The important thing is to work and be able to live fairly comfortably. Why have fortunes? The time for that sort of thing is past.

From this standpoint, what the Swiss need to do is regain a taste for simple things and, most importantly, give new status to manual work to minimise the impact of the foreigners' departure.

450031
Yes, but we'll make up for them with Swiss people, they'll just have to get used to getting their hands dirty. They can't all be doctors or lawyers, not everybody's an intellectual.

450036
The Swiss'll have to start doing a decent day's work. If you go into town, you see these groups of young people sitting around in bars from morning till night, when do they do any work? Too many foreigners have been brought into the country, it's happened gradually, since the war. Too many large sums of money have come into Switzerland, they had to use them productively, they opened factories and businesses and so then they had to bring in workers as well.

A return to the way things used to be goes hand in hand with the revalorisation of manual work:

300011
Maybe they'd appreciate our country more if they lived on the land. Everybody goes off to be a student, they talk about democratising education, which is all very well except now they are realising that things aren't going the way they wanted. As I see it, this democratisation of education is partly to blame for the problems of the workforce and overpopulation, because everyone wants to abandon manual work to become intellectuals, so ordinary jobs have lost all their status, which I think is a great pity. When I was young, younger anyway, being a barber was seen as a good job, it meant you'd done an apprenticeship. The same with a mechanic, or a sales assistant. But people have abandoned these jobs now, and it's hard for the Swiss to go back to them because they're regarded as jobs for people without any qualifications. Why do they belittle us? Jobs like that have lost all their prestige.

Some of the people interviewed were not altogether dismayed at the prospect, if need be, of a serious economic crisis affecting manual jobs, as a way of forcing the population, particularly the young, to work hard, like they did 'in the old days'.

200024
Unemployment ought to make young people realise there's more to life and happiness than just filling their faces and going to shops whenever they want and buying what they want. I don't think it's got anything to do with that, in fact the opposite, because that just makes people selfish. As soon as they start having to tighten their belts, they'll refuse to accept it, and they'll do everything they can to find true values.

200030
If you want everyone to change, people to stop taking the easy way, to do it democratically, there's always going to be injustice, it's not enough to say I'll be unemployed for two hours each month, what can you do? At that point you have to stop going out in the car, a whole

load of things. That's the only way we're going to reach a stable situation.

Q: So the current economic difficulties may actually have beneficial consequences?

A: Exactly.

This kind of proposal reveals a quasi-ascetic perspective. In this discourse, a serious economic crisis ought to have the power to lead the population back towards hard work and simple living, forcing them to give up 'over-consumption' of material goods, and, in the long run, making the young see 'true' values and initiating them into the hardships of life.

There is no doubt that this tenor of argument is one held by old people who experienced the economic difficulties and unemployment of the 1930s, and who are reluctant to see young people having access to a material well-being from which they are excluded.

At all events, they derive a degree of pride from their own past problems. The sufferings they endured are regarded as having shown them the true values of life. Alongside this they see young people no longer having a proper sense of work, and so they want to bring back a state of crisis so that the young will realise that 'there's more to happiness than just filling their faces and going to shops whenever they want, and buying what they want'.

There is an apparent contradiction between this perspective and narcissism, as it envisages the re-establishment of a state of poverty and frustration. Yet we know that, at the level of individual lives, these states too can give rise to idealised nostalgia and become moments of as much importance as those of intense pleasure. In fact the process of idealisation can even confuse moments of pleasure and moments of pain and, in some cases, pain can provide powerful libidinal satisfaction.

In addition, a subject's pride at having survived difficult times may be a source of comfort to him and give him the illusion of possessing a sort of power which is indirectly reminiscent of the narcissistic myth of omnipotence.

In short, voluntarism, moralism and asceticism are the sociocognitive and socioaffective mechanisms we encounter in the kinds of measures proposed for the preservation or restoration of an ideal state of Switzerland.

They are linked to the illusion of a narcissistic omnipotence, expressed as the idea of a neutral, independent Switzerland, abstracted from all its determinants, where everything is possible, even overcoming the most powerful social determinants, so long as it is what the citizens want.

On the political level, the re-establishment of an ideal order would manifest itself via greater vigilance on the part of the authorities and the police in respect of any elements that might disturb it. There are clearly analogies here with the deviancy paradigm.

Mythicisation of the image of Switzerland and status of the foreigner in the discourse

Taken as a whole, the interviews concerned with this way of understanding time establish a connection between the notion of some current disorder and the presence in Switzerland of a large foreign population. This connection can be seen at several different levels of the discourse:

Enforced contact between different outlooks and the dismantling of Switzerland's proper cultural unity are both assimilated, in the minds of the interviewees, to 'invasion', or simply to the presence of a foreign body in Switzerland, which if you follow the logic of the discourse, acts like a cancerous cell. Foreigners increase promiscuity and make human relations more difficult because of the mixing of languages and mentalities.

> *300047–48*
> There's such a lack of communication, it's bad. That's why people are more and more neurotic, there's no communication between the Swiss any longer, and having foreigners everywhere as well, that makes it even worse.

Some of the individuals interviewed regard foreigners as factors in the disintegration of Swiss public order, believing it to be them who organise and take part in the public demonstrations which they forcefully condemn.

> *450018*
> There are too many workers demonstrating now. And there are too many demonstrations about things of no importance. And there are too many foreigners on these demonstrations, especially the leaders. When there's serious disorder, like there was in town not so long ago, then they're the ringleaders.

240013
Q: What other important changes do you see in the way the country is evolving?
A: Demonstrations by foreign organisations. The foreigners aren't allowed to have demonstrations in their own countries, so they come here and have them. And, fools that we are, we Swiss not only put up with it, we protect them as well. Then when the police start getting hit, and they try and defend themselves, it's the cops who are in the wrong. I don't agree with that. If I was in the police I wouldn't be throwing tear gas, I'd be letting bulls loose, like they do in Spain, to disperse the crowds.

This is the same speaker who, a little later in the interview, asserted that most teachers in the schools and universities were foreign and were corrupting Swiss youth, an argument which cropped up several times in our interviews.

In a more abstract way, foreigners come to be accused of constituting a frame of reference for part of the Swiss population, who try to identify with the sort of thing that happens abroad, which results in the destruction of the country's identity.

> 450002
> The Swiss these days, especially the young, want to ape the foreigners, they think that's the thing to do. Now I know a bit about these things and I'm totally against it, I'm seriously afraid of communism. The way this country is at the moment reminds me of the frog who wanted to look like the ox, and puffed itself out so far it exploded.

But the most substantial connection in this type of discourse between the perception of a degeneration from an ideal Switzerland and the presence of foreigners is provided by the theme of construction and speculation, which give rise to a vicious circle which can be expressed by the following phenomena of circular causality: speculation and construction → need for foreign workforce → construction of shops, schools and houses needed for this workforce → necessary influx of a new workforce, thus fuelling the vicious circle.

But although foreigners are at the centre of this process, they are not responsible for it. From the standpoint of the interviewees, the 'fault' is fundamentally that of the authorities who agreed to bringing in the foreign workforce, and to the entrepreneurs and speculators who profited from it.

This in turn is unarguably linked with the presence in Switzerland of too great a quantity of money, which a number of those interviewed regarded as if it were entirely foreign money.

> 540028
> For one thing, there's too much money in Switzerland, but not Swiss money, it's all foreign money here. All the money here is foreign money.

> 240005
> Bit by bit our environment is going, and soon there won't be anything left. And why? Whose fault will it be? Again, it's those big foreign companies that come and set up here and make lots of money.

The foreign trouble-makers, in this discourse, are not immigrant workers but big businessmen and the people who deposit their money in Switzerland.

We can see, therefore, that in this type of reasoning the relationship between foreigners and the various factors responsible for the degeneration of the ideal image of Switzerland is a many-sided one, and one that cannot be reduced to a single element; foreigners appear in the discourse at a number of different levels. They may be only tenuously present in some interviews, and constitute the most significant element in others. These different types of relation are internally connected, and make up a *complex logico-discursive*

structure in which some relationships may remain in isolation in the interview, or only appear infrequently.

The question arising out of this concerns the attitudes of the people who share this type of reasoning towards the 'xenophobic initiatives'. How do these subjects behave politically? Possible responses might include the following:

Rejection of the initiative in the absence of any causal connection: it is not foreigners who are really responsible for the degeneration process.

Rejection in the name of moral values: the foreigners ought to be sent back, but humanitarian and moral values are against that step. Here we encounter another characteristic of a way of thinking which is common in Switzerland and which can counterbalance acceptance of the initiative.

Acceptance of the initiative despite the absence of any direct causal imputation between the presence of foreigners and the perception of a degeneration process. This is in fact the way we can approach the reason for acceptance, as all except two of the interviewees whose representation of time corresponded to mythic–cyclical time (the subjects we classed under the heading of 'mythicisation of the image of Switzerland') voted in favour of Action Nationale's initiative.

Let us look quickly at the arguments advanced by the two exceptions (S_{20} and S_{12}) before going on to a more general interpretation of the great majority of the subjects classified under this first form of the social representation of time.

> *200083*
> It's an issue of conscience, I didn't want people to be expelled, and I didn't want people to say it was OK for them to carry on coming here to do these jobs, so I thought about it until the last minute for voting, and I won't tell you the arguments against. We got them to come here, and so to tell them they've got to be gone by a certain time, it's inhuman, I mean it's not very nice, is it, they were taken on by the employers, it was money in the end, what they could earn, and nothing else.

> *120039–30*
> I think the Schwarzenbach Initiative [in 1970] was much more humane, much more reasonable. It was much more humane because he wanted to restrict the number of settlement permits, whereas the other one was just grotesque, if you see what I mean. It's like that guy in Uganda, whatshisname, Idi Amin, same idea, kick out the foreigners. Personally I think it's disgusting. I don't know who could put their name to something like that.

In both cases the refusal to vote for the initiative is based on moral and humanitarian values, while the first has an additional thread running through it to do with working-class solidarity and an argument that in effect lays the whole responsibility for the situation at the door of the employers.

However, the majority of those whose discourse expressed a tension between an idealised image of the Swiss past and the degenerate present said they were voting for the Action Nationale (AN) initiative, even though they seldom attributed responsibility for the process of degeneration to the foreigners. How is this apparent paradox to be understood? First we need to remember that a vote for the 'xenophobic movements' cannot be explained in terms of the sorts of xenophobic, or even racist, predispositions characteristic of various individuals or social groups, but only by the more fundamental elements of sociocognitive structures. Acceptance or rejection of this sort of initiative depends on a whole sociocognitive universe. The sociocognitive structure that predisposes a person to accept such an initiative is defined by sociocognitive mechanisms like moralism, asceticism, normativism, voluntarism, centration (in this case the nationalist centration of which we can see primary narcissism as a particular concrete manifestation), spatialisation of time (as for example in mythic–cyclical time), false identification (the fact of regarding foreigners as responsible for Switzerland's current situation, while explicitly saying it is really, say, the authorities who are responsible, is one example of this process of false identification), etc. To this sociocognitive structure we need to add the role played by other logics, and it is in order to throw some additional light on these other logics that we have applied René Girard's thesis on the scapegoat to the 'paradox' mentioned above.[11]

For many of the people we interviewed, the signs of the current situation in Switzerland included loss of identity, tension between people and, to some extent, a destruction of the cultural and symbolic order of Swiss society. Such a destructuration is conceived as a serious threat. René Girard suggests that every cultural order establishes an economy of violence, an attempt to channel the forms of violence into ritual procedures and operate a distinction between legitimate and illegitimate violence. According to him, the function of ritual sacrifice and the immolation of scapegoat victims is to redirect the concealed violence inherent in a community on to some external object.

> In ritual sacrifice, the victim who is really immolated turns violence away from its more 'natural' objects within the community.[12]

In other words, the scapegoat enables the impulse towards internal violence to be projected on to an external object, and social relations within the community to remain peaceful, by drawing off their aggressivity and directing it elsewhere. If we apply Girard's approach to the AN initiative, can we not then see its acceptance as an attempt to exteriorise this violence and project it on to an outside group, as a way of checking internal violence? Does not the attempt to re-establish simple and direct relationships between people, in place of the current ones marked by tension, ambivalence and promiscuity, operate by means of a similar removal of violence, and a channelling of that

violence on to an external object? Why does the scapegoat have to be *outside the community*? Why cannot the violence be channelled on to a section of the society in question? In our case, why is the violence not directed against the groups that the people we interviewed regarded as responsible for the current state of Switzerland, such as the political authorities, or entrepreneurs? This 'paradox' is not another 'logical absurdity', due to a lack of 'logical' reasoning. It can be seen as a measure which is part of an economy of violence, and which seeks to project violence on to an external victim in order to prevent its mimetic effects. If the violence were directed against one of the categories that constitute Swiss society, there is always the risk that it might rebound against its instigators, or provoke a contagious mimetic effect as well as chain reactions which would destroy the cultural order. What the supporters of this initiative seem to want, on the other hand, is to protect the order threatened by concealed internal violence by exorcising it, projecting it on to an external object.

From this standpoint, therefore, it is no use attacking Swiss authorities or Swiss industry. They are both part of Swiss society and, however responsible they may be for the current situation, are thereby unsuitable objects for rechannelled violence. Far from it, in fact, as that would automatically fuel the process of internal violence which the supporters of the initiative want to stop at all costs.

Obviously, we are not trying to justify the choice made by supporters of this initiative, only to understand some of the deeper mechanisms at work at both the socioaffective and sociocognitive levels. The discourse of AN supporters also involves desires (narcissistic desire, connected with the myth of a lost paradise), fears and tensions (stemming from awareness of the degeneration inherent in the current situation) and an attempt to halt the degeneration process by exorcising the tension and violence from it and projecting it on to a scapegoat, in the hope of purifying and 're-narcissifying' internal social relations. By extension, we might say, therefore, that what we find in this kind of discourse is *an instinctive and affective economy and semantics*. The instincts involved are in this case narcissistic (looking for an ideal state) and are bound up with the consequent frustration and tension, as well as with the need to redirect this tension on to an external subject.

It may seem a misuse of terms to talk about economy and semantics on the basis of so few elements, but our use of them is not in any way designed to lay the foundations of new disciplines, merely to try to conceptualise the new dimensions introduced above. The word 'economy' simply refers to the mechanisms by means of which the flow of psychic energy is channelled, and 'semantics' is meant to convey the objects thus energetically invested. Economy is to semantics as form is to content, the concrete nature of a discourse in use (in this case a type of discourse in which affective and mythic elements

play an important structuring role) always being defined by a specific interaction between form and content.

The process of ideologisation also operates at these two levels:

(1)   by investing, being parasitic upon and polarising dispersed affective and energy forces and capacities, and bringing them together in a single focus, thus playing a basically negentropic role;

(2)   by indicating objects of semantic investment, poles of energy condensation, to social actor subjects.

In other words, to put it perhaps more metaphorically, what we find are some of the elements of a sociocognitive mechanism constitutive of any ideologisation process, namely identification, albeit false identification. Similarly, the unification of dispersed energy forces, and their polarisation, can be seen as a parallel to the mechanism of homogenisation. The only difference is that these mechanisms also include an affective dimension.

Part of the effectiveness of the discourse of the leaders of these 'xenophobic movements' would thus result from the fact that it provides a surface of semantic investment for subjects suffering from unsatisfied desires and frustrations connected with the present situation in Switzerland.

As for the two social subjects who shared this affective, instinctive logic but did not vote for the initiative, we may assume that there were other sociocognitive mechanisms at work there that were stronger than these socioaffective mechanisms.

And we shall see how those individuals who do not have to create this sort of mythicised Switzerland, and who do not reveal signs of a tension between an ideal past and a degenerate present, also have a much less significant level of narcissistic desire and consequent frustration, which renders the victimisation of a scapegoat unnecessary; hence the absence in this second type of discourse of a connection between perception of time and the status of foreigners in Switzerland. As we shall now discover.

The discourse of linear time[13]

From centration on the myth of a lost paradise to the real world

The second type of discourse differs from the first in that it contains no reference to a glorious past whose values have been largely destroyed by the current situation. Nostalgia for the past does not figure in it either; changes in relation to the past are primarily expressed in terms of development, or even of progress. Even where individuals express concern about aspects of the present situation, this is done not in terms of comparison with a past state of affairs, but in terms of a general evolution in a linear time-scale in which a return to the past is neither possible nor even desirable: time here is regarded as

irreversible. This characteristic is absolutely central to the linear conception of time and change.

The impossibility of return to the past, and the absence of any nostalgia for it, can easily be seen in the following extracts, where the interviewees talk about the changes they have observed during the last ten years.

190069

> The ways of getting information we now have, even the kids, and then there are people who have had the means to create situations and to develop particular sectors. That was profitable for them, but now the economy has started to slow down.
>
> Granted they had the means to do well out of it, and to get the things they wanted, but that was really the positive thing about it.

Q: And the changes that weren't so positive?

A: Of course there were some, but that was the case everywhere in Switzerland, and abroad, because of the way the policies accelerated on all levels, not on the level of . . . well, if you look at leisure, there's certainly more of it, but I suppose that's something positive too, in a different way, let's say there's more time when people aren't working, but this creates its own problems and means you have to run harder just to keep up.

Even when it comes to less positive kinds of change, the interviewee slips into a positive approach; satisfaction seems to override dissatisfaction.

Change registered as something positive

320035

Incredible changes. So many more people. Oh it really has changed! I remember ten years back, I was much younger then, but I think though there are more people now, there isn't so much gossip. Which is quite a significant change, because Swiss women are more independent because they can work.

Here even the word change [*évolution*] takes on a positive connotation; change seems almost synonymous with progress.

480017

Things are always changing. There used not be any motor cars, now there are. There used not to be any aeroplanes, now there are. But it doesn't happen with blinding speed. I don't even know if you notice things really changing. On the social level, I get a few more benefits, that's something that's changed, but that didn't take ten years.

500065

I don't know what to say. Consumers' rights, tenants' rights: I think these are useful things that we didn't have before.

500067

Q: Are there any changes you see as negative?

A: I don't know how to answer that. This sort of question really needs time to think about it first. And the other thing to realise is that not answering some questions straight off may be because they take you by surprise, or you haven't thought about them.

One incidentally interesting aspect of these responses is that most people who display this sort of discourse, when asked about the changes they have noticed over ten years, take that to mean 'positive changes'; and the interviewer often has to go back and ask them again about less positive changes they may have noticed.

Compared to mythic time discourse, the difference is striking: there is a clearly defined contrast between the two patterns of thought when it comes to change. For one group the term means deviance, alterity (and mythicisation of the past), while for the other it is equivalent not only to evolution, but to positive evolution.

The relativisation of tradition

In the second type of discourse, the changes that are noticed are generally not regarded as inferior to the values of the past. Similarly, there is no fondness for the past and for Swiss traditions.

> 210034
> [...] tradition, there are some people who think we ought to play all the alpine horns, everyone ought to speak *Schweizerdeutsch*, and that if we lose that, we lose our souls. I think that's completely stupid, but if tradition means maintaining three separate languages and different religions without killing each other, then that's a tradition we shouldn't lose, in fact we should develop it and extend it to the rest of Europe.

In terms of discourse analysis, this extract reveals the *distance*[14] the speaker adopts towards the discourse: 'there are some people who think that we ought', which is in marked contrast to the speakers in the first type of discourse, who identify strongly with their discourse and implicate themselves in it.

The speaker quoted above also maintains a degree of distance from the various stereotypes which, in the traditionalist view, define Switzerland. Thus for people who think of time and change in a linear way, the national holiday, for example, does not represent a great deal.

> 180016
> The first of August? It's a patriotic holiday that's no longer very important . . . [it] stands for the origin of Switzerland.

320022–23
The national holiday? When is it? . . . there's no need for it . . . it's just pretty lights for the kids, that's all.

On the question of any regrets at the changes and things that were lost:

500069
There are interesting things about every period if you can see them. Some things disappear, but that's part of life, the wheel turns, things move on.

These extracts confirm a detachment from any desire to retain a traditional image of Switzerland.

The last quote especially illustrates this tendency to think of time in a linear way: 'Some things disappear, but that's part of life, the wheel turns'. Change is 'natural'.

From catastrophism to optimism

When we asked individuals to say what changes they would like to see in Switzerland, their replies were similarly forward-looking, none of them making reference to a return to the past. They did not perceive change as catastrophic. Evolution was inevitable, linear, and positive.

180025
I would like there to be more unity in Switzerland, at least among cantons speaking the same language. A greater degree of unification. For a small country, there is an awful lot of diversity.

500070
. . . education, by which I mean schools and colleges, should all be organised on a national scale. I think these are reforms which will have to come gradually. And on the social front, I think tenants' rights and the rights of consumers are very important, too.

The changes they want to see are related to current problems; the diversity of the country and the fragmentation of education are not things that have deteriorated over time, merely elements that haven't yet been adequately dealt with. Change seen as positive linear evolution, no nostalgia for the past, and time regarded as irreversible, these are the central elements in this second type of discourse.

The absence of mythicisation of the past is bound up with a degree of confidence about the future. Despite some concern over issues like pollution, overpopulation or inflation, there is nothing really worrying about Switzerland's situation:

Fears about change:

180000

None about Switzerland, at all. Because as I see it, the way we're going, Switzerland'll be able to look after itself.

Switzerland in ten years' time

190000

Your guess is as good as mine. It all depends on how things turn out, but if it carries on as it is now, they'll have done their best to reduce inflation, but there'll probably still be [a crisis], though not such a serious one, but I don't think things will have improved much in ten years.

In ten years:

210000

No danger. There will be some very interesting situations, because we'll be able to take up new positions, but I don't think there will be any danger.

The speaker brings different elements into his explanation while at the same time relativising his statements: 'it's one of the things . . . that's difficult to say . . .' (once again, we can see the distance between the speaker and his discourse).

500008

Q: Worries?

A: No, I wouldn't say I'm worried about anything, but of course it does give you something to think about. But it's not worrying. Like I might say perhaps there are all these conflicts people are trying to put an end to, but war still goes on. These are questions you think about sometimes.

Whereas the first discourse is characterised by a very noticeable loss of confidence in the future, where the only remedy for this degeneration is action by the authorities to restore the values of the past, the second discourse does not present any indications of a desire to return to the past. Some aspects are, it is true, seen as disturbing, but they are regarded as inherent in developmental change, and the action envisaged to deal with these events is always seen as part of an ineluctably positive and linear logic of temporal development.

From voluntarism to social determination

Awareness of the determining social factors is another basic characteristic of linear time discourse, and is a radical antithesis of the ubiquitous voluntarism of mythic time. Social reality (or determining social factors) is resistant to individual will. It cannot be moulded at will merely to satisfy desires, to realise them subjectively. The reality principle (the determining social factors) cuts across the pleasure principle (limitless voluntarism). And we may further

note, *en passant*, that the absolute primacy accorded to the subjective satisfaction of desires is, in effect, a denial of evident reality, and that it operates through the mediation of the sociocognitive mechanisms which define that way of knowing – or perhaps, more appropriately, not knowing – reality.

The idealisation or mythicisation of an ahistoric Swiss past is thus very like an illusion, in the sense in which Freud uses the word:

> Thus we call a belief an illusion when wish-fulfillment is a prominent factor in its motivation, and in doing so we disregard its relations to reality, just as the illustion itself sets no store by verification.[15]

Let us now leave this avenue of interpretation for the time being and return to linear time and some illustrations of the primacy of social determination over voluntarism.

190054

A: The current economic situation? It's a device on the part of the employers. That may not be the whole story, but as I see it that's certainly part of it.

What I mean by a device is unemployment, which began with the famous oil crisis. Suddenly the message started coming across loud and clear, and that's where it all started. That's when people started to get worried. Was there going to be a crisis like in the thirties, I didn't know, and I think the employers probably took advantage of that period to turn the screws.

Profits had been too high and there'd been too much prosperity for too long, the bubble was bound to burst one day, so that was the beginning, and I suppose it's better for it to have happened like that than for it to have gone on for years and years until the whole thing blew up.

Q: How do you explain the fact that there's been some kind of conflict for the last ten years or so?

A: Difficult to say, perhaps it's because young people have more educational opportunities and more free time. Years ago they had to work longer hours and when they got home they were tired out and didn't have time to get involved in these sorts of problems. Whereas now the fact is that they have time to think, and they have access to information and the means to become involved in problems like that.

210024

Q: Why do the Swiss have a different attitude from the Italians?

A: In other countries, and this is what my workmates say too, they have always lived with insecurity, with unemployment, and a degree of workers' struggle, because they are constantly facing social problems.

But in Switzerland, first of all we've had social security which has meant that there has been no unemployment since the crisis of the thirties, so people don't know what it means, and they don't want to risk it by challenging the status quo. And secondly, from the political point of view, as we've seen, because we've always lived with compromise to find ways . . . in any kind of project on the social level the Swiss are affected a bit by that . . . I mean, the way we live, the way we are able to live, always taking the middle of the road, without that Switzerland wouldn't exist. And unfortunately that leaves its mark, and sometimes it's a heavy burden to carry.

320038
Q: What are these changes due to?
A: Maybe the new generation, maybe it comes from them, or from the schools even, because the schools aren't like they were in my parents' time, there's no comparison. There's much more information and that sort of thing. Then you just had your radio and that was that. Now you find out things from television and newspapers.

500020
Q: I asked whether you thought the number of votes for the initiative would be different today. You said the situation was very different. In what way is it different?
A: It's different because of the recession. I can't put the problem any other way. Sometimes there are things you feel but you can't put into words satisfactorily, there are things you feel in relation to change and to the situation, when things can change from one day to the next. You see, I'm not really involved in the politics of it.
      I mean, just before the last war, we had unemployment, and we don't want to go back to that. It could happen, of course, the changes we've seen, because of the crisis, were aimed at that, but they still haven't succeeded in controlling society's problems the way they wanted to, and so you get conflict starting.

This last statement also illustrates the non-voluntaristic aspect of this type of discourse: 'the situation, when things can change from one day to the next'.

These different extracts show how explanations within the linear perception of time take account of social determinants. And alongside this awareness of these determinants there is a capacity for decentration, in contrast with the multiple forms of centration present in the first type of discourse.

From hypostasised mythic time to a generalised awareness of social determination

Where the social determinants are taken into consideration, it tends to be in a

generalised way. Thus we no longer see any elements of an ideal, mythical Switzerland, with an absolute, irreducible reality of its own, nor is it autarchic, but becomes dependent on the surrounding countries. Switzerland as a unique, independent, and powerfully mythicised entity is not even conceivable; it is in contradiction with the sociocognitive and discursive structure characteristic of linear discourse about time and change.

180002
Q: If you had to describe what strikes you most when you think of Switzerland, what else would you say?
A: Switzerland sets too much store by, I don't know really, but for a small country it seems to have rather a high opinion of itself in relation to other countries. It would not be much fun if the only people in Switzerland were the Swiss, would it? A civilised country needs all sorts of exchange to enrich itself, it needs to understand other ways of thinking, other structures, I mean Switzerland, it's like your own life, if you always do the same things you stop deriving anything from them, you need to do other things as well.

190004
Switzerland's a nice country, but like everywhere else nowadays the cost of living is rather high in relation to what you take home. But although we're socially not as advanced as in France, there is one area where I think we are ahead, and that's wages.

210009
Q: Do you think there are some areas where Switzerland lags behind?
A: Yes, in the development of a social strategy, particularly as regards health insurance and accident insurance, because of federalism, where referendums have defeated the more progressive initiatives, and also because in the country as a whole people haven't given much thought to those problems. We're behind in education, schools, the whole problem of learning.

   Other countries either organised their welfare laws in the aftermath of the war, or else they were set up by a government which didn't ask the people what they thought, but just decided for them, which is a lot easier. Here we asked men if they wanted to give women the vote, so it still hasn't happened.

320037
Q: Are there any other changes you feel strongly about?
A: One important change is that women in Switzerland have more independence because they are able to work.

480035
Q: This recession, why do you think it has happened?
A: It's worldwide, it's not just in Switzerland!

500003
Q: To go back to the present situation, what do you think about the attitude of the government?
A: I think the government is doing what it can to salvage a difficult situation, and as it's an international problem, we can't exist on our own any more, or look at it simply as a Swiss problem, we have to take everything around us into account as well. So I don't know, I think they're trying to salvage what they can.
Q: Do you think they are doing all they can?
A: I think to answer that you'd have to understand the whole range of problems in politics, finance and economics. If I could do that, I could answer your question.

Although the question was only about Switzerland, these interviewees often spontaneously establish connections with other countries. Switzerland is compared and evaluated, not always favourably. And the negative aspects are therefore not seen as inherent merely in the present situation; they are to be found in every society, and in every epoch.

Status of foreigners in linear time discourse
There is a major difference in the status of foreigners between the two types of discourse. In linear time discourse, Switzerland is not mythicised, tension vanishes, and all the subjects, without exception, are opposed to the initiative.

The absence of tension (which is due to not idealising the Switzerland of the past), a linear representation of time and change (which is seen as irreversible, inevitable and positive), and a generalised awareness of social determinants thus define the group of subjects who display this second type of discourse.

The current social difficulties are therefore not attributed to foreigners (as scapegoats or sacrificial victims), but to the intrinsic nature of social reality itself. Remedial measures to deal with the current economic and social situation, and political and social projects at a more general level, are not defined in terms of re-establishing a mythical past, but start from the basis of the present situation and look for ways of ameliorating it. Nor is this amelioration thought of purely in voluntarist terms, but is seen as dependent on the interplay of social actors, the material reality in which they find themselves, and the international context ('The situation in the whole world').

The linear perception of time goes hand in hand with a radical non-voluntarism, a clear-cut tendency towards sociocognitive decentration and the other sociocognitive mechanisms that that implies.

A short account of some of the discoveries of the social sciences

Analysis of the subject of time thus reveals the existence of two very different ways of perceiving it, so different in fact that they rest on opposite sociocognitive structures. In other words, any sociocognitive structure does not entail a predisposition to just any perception of time.

At the more general level, our results tend, in outline at least, in the same direction as those arrived at by other researchers in the social sciences into the subject of time. These latter set out to identify the *social variations* of each phenomenon under investigation, variations according to social group, culture, ethnicity, sex, age, social position, types of activity, etc. As a result, the social sciences are forearmed against the tendency to approach any given phenomenon as a self-contained, unique, general and universal reality. For the social sciences, therefore, there is no such thing as *time*, in the singular, only *times*, which are also *social times*. There are no general theoretical or philosophical speculations about *time* in sociology. Social time cannot be identified with mathematical time, with clock time, even though in some instances we still find a fairly similar conception in the classic studies of 'budget-time'.

Even in psychology and philosophy, the idea of a single time is now increasingly regarded as illusory. Physics, too, has after more than three centuries, suddenly rediscovered the idea of the multiplicity of time, and physicists no longer try to reduce diversity and change to identity and permanence, that is to eliminate time.

> Physics today no longer denies time. It recognises the irreversible time of evolution towards equilibrium, the rhythmic time of the structures whose impulses are fed by the world that passes through them, the branching time of evolution by instability and amplification of fluctuations and even the microscopic time we introduced in the previous chapter, and which manifests the indeterminacy of microscopic physical evolution. Every complex being is constituted by a plurality of times connected to each other by means of multiple and sophisticated articulations. History, whether that of a living creature of a society, can never again be reduced to the monotonous simplicity of one single time.[16]

Let us try to synthesise into a few headings some of the discoveries of the social sciences likely to enrich our own results:

(a)   The demonstration of the *social variations* of time, the *multiplicity of social timescales*, is the most obvious discovery and, in a sense, provides the starting point.

(b)   The distinction between *clock time* and *lived time* represents a second point of reference which we need to take account of when we are dealing with the perception of time and the way in which it is

experienced from day to day by the social actors themselves. Lived time is not clock time.

(c)   Looking at it still from the viewpoint of the social actors *themselves, social rhythms* and *temporal horizons* differ markedly from one social group to another, from one type of activity to another and from one social and economic sphere to another.

(d)   Another discovery relates to the distinction between temporal *behaviour* and temporal *representations* (or social representations of time, as we would call them).

Let us now briefly illustrate these four points by means of some concrete examples.

In connection with the social variations of time and the multiplicity of social timescales, we ought first of all to recall some of the 'founding fathers' of reflection about the social determinants of time. For Halbwachs, there are as many *collective timescales as there are separate groups, or collective experiences* of time.[17] It is no longer a question of one collective memory, but of a number of collective memories.

There are numerous practical studies of the relations of dependence between conceptions of time and the traditional sociological variables.[18] It is enough to mention here some of the names connected with the work of demonstrating this plurality of time, such as Balandier, Bourdieu, Grossin, Le Goff and Mendras, among others.[19]

The factors most frequently adduced in explanation of this plurality and these variations are economic and social activity, age, family structure, financial resources, educational level and social environment.

Time can still vary among individuals from the same group, depending on whether it is linked to:

(1)   myths and legends
(2)   social activities and age groups
(3)   economic activities

Balandier's work in Africa and Bourdieu's in Algeria, for example, provide concrete illustration of this type of *intra-group variation*.

A number of studies show that attitudes and behaviour towards time in our own societies also differ considerably according to activity and occupation: a banker's time is not the same as a worker's, nor is a country-dweller's the same as that of a civil servant.[20]

The next thing to be remembered is the multiplicity of timescales any one individual comes up against in his daily life, as well as the *activity of adjustment* of these different timescales. This adjustment activity may fail and result in contradictory pressures, which reveal themselves in psychological tension

and disorganisation ('cognitive dissonance'). This is something our investigation also reveals, and we shall return to these *tension* phenomena later.

Mercure identifies an ambiguity connected with the idea of *social rhythm*.[21] Rhythm entails both continuity and discontinuity, succession and periodicity, recurrence but also change. And on top of the continuity of social rhythm there are differences in its *intensity* (strong and weak timescales), and added to discontinuity, there are differences in its *speed* and the greater or lesser rapidity with which events succeed each other.

In our societies, which are by definition 'changing', we are constantly dealing with an *acceleration* of the rhythms of life (Alvin Töffler), and of the *ephemeral* aspects of everyday life, and with a greater or lesser aptitude on the part of individuals to adapt to this acceleration; and we need to stress the difficulties many individuals have in coping with changes, such as those of place, work, environment or friends.

Sociolinguists have much to say about variable communicative competence among different social groups, and, in the area of time, one might by analogy talk about degrees of *temporal competence*. The capacity to manage temporal changes and their consequences, as well as a degree of adaptability, must be the main preconditions of any thorough temporal competence and control.

In addition to ideas of *social temporalities* and *social rhythm*, studies of time identify the importance of a third notion, that of *temporal horizon*. According to Fraisse, this means: 'the area within groups and societies that is open to the two major temporal perspectives of reconstruction of the past and anticipation of the future'.[22]

In our terms, this means that all the everyday *social practices* of individuals are a function either of plans, anticipation, expectation and hope, or else of recollections, collective memory, and past history, both real and imagined.

A fourth important idea for an understanding of time is *temporal strategy*. There are degrees to which time can be submitted to or controlled, and the variations in control and submission are once again explicable by social factors.

In the field of education, the classic work of Bernstein has shown the part played by the conception of time, temporal horizon and temporal strategies when it comes to academic achievement. People tend to reduce Bernstein's work to his identification of the relation between linguistic capability and social background. But he also shows how the two codes (elaborated and restricted) are linked to very different conceptions of time: in underprivileged backgrounds (resticted code),[23] the elaboration of long-term future plans is much less common than in privileged backgrounds. Such plans are even indeed an essential characteristic of the more privileged backgrounds, which implies a radically different general conception of time. In privileged back-

grounds, *temporal strategies* play a determining part in directing everyday social practices. Time becomes a means for obtaining certain ends, and becomes the object of long-term investments. What we find in such situations is a conscious desire to control time by taking genuine advantage of the long-term perspective. Whereas in the underprivileged social environment, it is no exaggeration to say that time is suffered rather than controlled. It might even be said that the temporal horizon of the underprivileged makes them doubly underprivileged, because we know that children from underprivileged backgrounds do less well at school and also that academic success and an extended education themselves contribute to a better consideration of plans for the future.[24]

This active, dynamic aspect of temporal horizons leads us on to the difference between *representations of time* and *temporal behaviour*. If the different ways of 'being aware of time',[25] of *representing* it, are indeed functions of types of activities, representations of time can, in turn, direct and determine conduct and behaviour. This is the aspect of social representations where they are both *structured* and *structuring*, and this is equally true of social representations of time. It is an idea that brings out the non-linear and non-mechanistic aspects of the action of social determinants, which have more to do with circularity than with unidirectional linearity. Feedback is not just an image: it corresponds to the real nature of interactions between active social phenomena.

The study of time provides practical illustration of the duality of social determinations. The two representations of time we have revealed can be explained by a range of social factors, a range of social determinations. Individuals who have a mythic–cyclical representation of time tend, generally speaking, to be older, to come from less privileged social backgrounds, and to be less socially, economically, culturally and politically engaged than those who have a linear (positive, optimistic and confident) representation of the present and the future. But while these differences in the representation of time are explicable in terms of varying social factors, the different representations of time themselves play a part in the explanation of the variation in conduct and behaviour.

Anything that can be explained can itself be an explanation. If B is explained by means of A, B can in its turn retroact on A and/or explain C. A model of this kind goes beyond the unilateral, mechanical explanation of the 'superstructure' (in this case social representations, ways of knowing) by the 'infrastructure' (the whole range of material factors). It therefore entails a new conception of social representations themselves, in which they are no longer seen as possessing less reality and determining power than material factors.

Even Marx commented that although 'beliefs' may be in contradiction with

'objective interests' this in no way excludes those beliefs from playing a determinant part in explaining collective behaviour which is 'illogical' or contrary to the notorious 'objective interests' of a given group.[26]

To sum up, then, we may say that studies concerned with time are more interested in explaining the social representations of time (by multiple economic and social factors) than with defining the explanatory power of the social representations themselves. Some studies of the determining power of social representations do exist, but there are very few of them. To say that different temporal horizons entail different kinds of behaviour, for example, is a move in this direction.

At a more general level, unilateral determinist explanation (the explanation of representational phenomena in terms of material factors) still remains the dominant paradigm not only for students of time but for the social sciences as a whole. The unidirectional explanatory approach still largely takes precedence over multidimensional and multidirectional explanations (in term of circular causality), as well as over approaches which perceive social phenomena as the result of interactions and endless processes of construction and reconstruction.

Before introducing further new dimensions into the analysis of social thought and language in use, we shall try to bring together and integrate the main results provided by the three concrete studies of centration/ decentration, causality and time.

The connections and integrations between these ought to ensure that we have a threefold empirical basis for the result we have obtained so far.

Part III

6   Integration and new perspectives

A short outline of the articulation of the results of centration, causality and time

We ran a special study on the integration of these three topics, but here we shall only be reproducing the main discoveries, without providing concrete illustrations for each point.

Whereas the first three empirical studies can be described as *horizontal*, the present approach is *vertical*; in the earlier studies we tried to define various specific aspects of time or causality by illustrating them from quotations taken from different subjects.[1] What we want to do now is identify the overall behaviour of *one individual*. We shall therefore be looking at the way in which one individual behaves in relation to centration/decentration, causality and time, and at the way these three themes connect up and lead on to each other.

In order to do this we had to analyse *whole interviews*, whence the methodological opposition between horizontal and vertical.

The perspective is still a sociological one, however, in that we are still concerned with defining *collective* ways of knowing and speaking; only in the present case we group together *significant individuals* (individuals whose ways of thinking and speaking are similar) and not quotations taken from different interviews.

We want to know the way in which different social groups behave *at the same time* in connection with centration, causality and time. It is *overall linguistic and cognitive functioning*, and its social variations, which interests us. These different types of articulations are presented in the form of logico-discursive models or ideal types.

Integration happens in two successive stages. Centration/decentration and causality are articulated first by means of the construction of two ideal or typical sociocognitive configurations (Type I and Type II); the two Ideal Types are then articulated with the topic of time to provide a diachronic dimension.

We shall only be using the most contrasting types or configurations, although of course there are in reality numerous intermediate ones.

The two ideal or typical sociocognitive configurations: Type I and Type II

Type I
This type is defined by the following components:

183

- a strongly marked social centration
- the deviancy paradigm
- indissociation between the speaker's argument and value judgements and/or his personal experience
- a discourse that appears to be a simple reflection of reality
- unidimensionality and causal supersaturation

We will recognise the link between a strong social centration and the deviancy paradigm in this first general type, as it is one that emerged in the construction of an earlier model. However, detailed (vertical) analysis of whole interviews shows that there are actually two sides to the deviancy paradigm. On the one hand there is the vehement condemnation of everything regarded as deviant in relation with the speaker's norms, yet in some cases the vehemence is reserved for an emphasis on conformity and the positive essentialisation of everything that corresponds to these norms. The difference is an important one, but we are still, of course, dealing with two different manifestations of the same sociocognitive disposition, namely an incapacity for social decentration and an exclusive and absolute commitment to his own point of view (values, norms, beliefs, etc.). A single basic sociocognitive structure may thus find expression at the experiential level either as a condemnation or accusation (of everything that is Other), or as a glorification (of the speaker's own point of view). We may therefore speak of a sociocognitive system of condemnation and glorification. These two manifestations of a very marked sociocognitive centration are expressed at the level of discourse by two formally distinct logico-discursive models.

(1) The logico-discursive model which corresponds to the social centration based on *glorification* can be expressed schematically as follows:

> *IT IS AS IT SHOULD BE*
> because of *Conformity of social actors*
>
> to the *NORM*
> because of
> *POSITIVE ESSENTIALISATION*

(2) The model of social centration based on *condemnation* belongs in an extension of the model outlined above in the analysis of the deviancy paradigm.

> *IT OUGHT TO BE LIKE THAT*
> (affirmation of the *NORM*)
>
> *IT ISN'T LIKE THAT* (deviance, abnormal situation)
> because

DEVIANCE of social actors from the *NORM*
because

NEGATIVE ESSENTIALISATION

IMITATION of another *DEVIANCE*

ALL THE SAME IT OUGHT TO BE LIKE THAT
(postulate of *voluntarism*, which implies the *transition from DEVIANCE to the NORM* and the elimination of the social actors who cannot or will not make this transition, such as foreigners).

Type II

The second type groups together the individuals who are defined by diametrically opposite sociocognitive structure. The main characteristics are as follows:

- cognitive decentration
- social decentration
- multiple causality
- materialist paradigm

The peculiarity of this type lies in the simultaneous presence of cognitive decentration (which all adults are potentially capable of) and social decentration (which is present as a constitutive, structural characteristic solely in this second type). If we had to represent its logico-discursive form, we might do so with the help of the following basic sentence:

IT IS (ISN'T) because of material factors (including the behaviour of the social actors, behaviour which is understood and more or less accepted).

It is now possible to give these models a diachronic dimension by integrating them with what we know about the theme of time.

The diachronic dimension

Remembering what we have discovered about time, we can immediately see that mythic–cyclical time fits in with the constitutive elements of Type I, and linear time with those of Type II. In fact the idealised image entailed in a mythic representation of time can only be constructed on the basis of the mechanisms of essentialism and false identification. Essentialism defines Switzerland's situation in the past as radically different from that of today, and characterised by a specific 'nature'. The false identification mechanism erases all aspects of the description of this ideal past which the speaker thinks might

be construed negatively. The same mechanisms can be seen, inverted, in the discursive construction of the representation of the present, which is seen as deviance, as alterity, which does not conform to the norm advocated by the speaker and in the name of which he wants a return to the past (voluntarism).

Linear time, on the other hand, excludes essentialism and the conception of an abnormal alterity, implying instead that different social situations (along with the human actions and behaviour bound up with them) are no more than moments in a process of historical evolution, and not natures or essences from which a system of norms can be derived which is equally valid for past, present and future. Behaviour and mental outlook are understood (even though they are not always accepted) as moments in historical development, where each moment is determined by others.

Summing up the results of all the vertical analyses, we can say that the characteristics of mythic time and linear time duplicate, at the *diachronic level*, the relations we defined earlier. In the conception of *mythic time*, the interplay of essentialisations and the perception of abnormal alterity, linked with an explanatory principle based on the deviancy paradigm, is projected on to the past/present semantic dimension. The transformation of the Type I logico-discursive model by the introduction of time thus gives the following result:

(1)   *Non-diachronic model*
    IT OUGHT TO BE LIKE THAT
    IT IS NOT LIKE THAT
    NONETHELESS IT OUGHT TO BE

(2)   *Diachronic model*
    IT OUGHT TO BE LIKE THAT
    IT ISN'T LIKE THAT ANY MORE
    IT OUGHT TO BE LIKE THAT AGAIN

The transition from the first model to the second might seem to be easier for older speakers. Yet, while (2) implies (1), the reverse is not the case, or rather it is only true of the logic of mythic thought. Utopian thought, which we did not encounter in our empirical material, would probably have the following structure:

    IT OUGHT TO BE LIKE THAT
    IT HAS NEVER BEEN LIKE THAT, ANYWHERE
    NONETHELESS IT OUGHT TO BE LIKE THAT[2]

In the conception of *linear time* it is the materialist paradigm and the forms of decentration which are projected on to the diachronic dimension. Ideologically, this projection seems less 'necessary' than the preceding one. It is in fact relatively easy to provide a causal explanation for certain kinds of present attitudes and behaviour by means of material elements, without referring

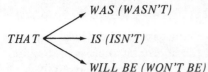

| | | | material factors |
| *THA T* | $\longleftarrow$ *IS (ISN'T)* | because of | (and taking into account behaviour of the social actors, behaviour which is understood and more or less accepted) |

Figure 6.1

either to the past or to the future. It seems to be more difficult to invoke a norm, and the non-congruence of behaviour with that norm, without projecting it either into a mythical past or into a utopian and timeless beyond. But at any rate our empirical research has clearly shown that representations of time play a more important role for people who reason in terms of the deviancy paradigm than for those speakers who take up a position within the materialist paradigm.

If, nevertheless, we had to introduce the diachronic dimension into Type II, we would probably obtain the model shown in Figure 6.1.

Regularities and anomalies

Besides the integration of the results of the three indicator areas of our study of the overall functioning of the different ways of knowing and speaking, the vertical analysis of whole interviews also has another purpose. It provides us with a concrete way of approaching the problem of the *relations between the individual and the collective*, between sociocognitive structures (which are a collective phenomenon) and the different individuals who give them reality. We need to be able to determine what is constant to any given way of knowing and what varies from one individual to another, and this involves defining the degree of rigidity or flexibility of different sociocognitive structures, and the extent to which they are determinative.

In practical terms, looking at the interviews as a whole, it was observable that the subjects interviewed conformed more or less either to Type I or Type II. We were able to distinguish three sorts of interview:

(1) first there are the *most typical interviews*, which corresponded most closely to the constructed models,

(2) then there are those which only demonstrate *some* of the characteristics of the ideal types,

(3) and finally, there are the '*anomalies*' (but bearing in mind Thomas Kuhn's dictum that it is by means of the anomalies that knowledge progresses).

Let us now briefly examine how the three categories of interview are distributed in Types I and II.

Type I interviews

The great majority of interviews grouped under Type I are typical, in that the interviews very fully demonstrate the characteristics of the Ideal Type.

Thus, of the interviews included in the horizontal analysis of the three indicator subjects, numbers 07, 54 and 45 fall into this category. In them we find the co-existence of the following traits:

- a strong sociognitive centration
- omnipresence of explanation by deviance (particularly causal supersaturation)
- reference to an ideal Switzerland in a mythical past (mythic time)
- norms identified with the past
- voluntarism forcefully asserted

The other mechanisms which go along with these primary structural characteristics are also present: the projection of a private frame of reference, the negative essentialisation of alterity, a generalised negative universe, one-dimensional criteria of perception and judgement, the contamination principle, intoxication and the naturalisation of the social.

It would be enough to say that we can often find, in a single paragraph, the main mechanisms of this whole sociocognitive structure, which illustrates the structural nature of the interdependence and connectedness of the various sociocognitive mechanisms of centration, causality and time perception. Nonetheless, it is worth quoting a concrete example:

450064

Q: What do you think of the government, in general?

A: Well, I could say a lot, though I'd rather not. First of all, as I said to you before, they do too much for foreigners, and I don't agree with that. You have to put Switzerland first. There's still plenty to be done at home before they start playing the rich benefactor, giving away taxpayers' money left and right. There's been a lot of bad management in the government; the government has managed things very badly. The previous government. The one we've got now isn't much better, but they're doing what they can. They ought to be more careful about who they let into the country. They give naturalisation to anyone. There's that Russian who walked straight into a flat in Zürich, it wasn't as easy as that for me to find an apartment.

This paragraph demonstrates simultaneously:

(1)   *the deviancy paradigm* ('they do too much for foreigners')
(2)   *resolute social centration* ('You have to put Switzerland first. There's still plenty to be done at home')

(3) *voluntarism*, in expressions like 'You have to' and 'They ought to': 'They ought to be more careful about who they let into the country.' This voluntarism goes hand in hand with the deviancy paradigm and the reference to an ideal Switzerland.

Despite the contagion and propagation of Deviance, the speaker still reasserts the primacy of the Norm and the possibility of conforming to it.

> We're lucky enough to still be a small, almost neutral, country. I say almost because they do meddle too much in matters that don't concern us, in other countries' affairs. We need to keep ourselves to ourselves, and not take too much notice of other countries' politics.

This reduction of politics to the psycho-familial (the household), which occurs frequently in this person's thought, enables the speaker to *project* his own norms of household management on to the government:

> Yes, there are always difficulties. There's been bad management in some governments, and there's been some of it in ours, and now we're a bit in debt. I've never been in debt in my housekeeping; so how come our Federal Council allowed us to run up a whole pile of debts? I think it's disgraceful. I'd be ashamed to be in debt.

Special cases and anomalies

Interviews 03 and 24 also exhaustively embody Type 1, thereby confirming the structural nature of the relations of interdependence between the three indicator subjects.

In certain cases, however, not only are all the mechanisms present but some of them take extreme forms. This happens, for instance, in interview 24, when change, seen as deviant, takes on the aspect of a plague sweeping the country, leaving in its wake a contamination which develops by the same inevitable laws as a serious illness.

Generally, though, anomalies are rare in Type 1, if not non-existent. There is only one interview (number 46) where a significant trait is absent: there is very little reference to the past, and there is no valorised idealisation of some mythical other time. The present is severely condemned, but without any reference being made to the past. It would seem that the person concerned is so repelled by the current situation that all his energy and affectivity is concentrated solely on condemnation of the present.

'Anomaly' is therefore much too strong a term to designate a case like this. The far more striking thing about Type 1, on the contrary, is the degree of similarity between the individuals in it, or in other words the highly constricting and determinant nature of the sociocognitive structure. Here we have an empirical demonstration of the *cognitive rigidity* of this central way of knowing

or, to put it another way, of the closeness of the relationship between sociocognitive structure and particular individuals, or again the weakness of interindividual variation.

Let us now see whether the Type II individuals reveal a greater cognitive flexibility when we look at the three indicators simultaneously and at whole interviews.

The Type II interviews

The great majority of the individuals in Type II also correspond to the interview types, fully embodying the basic characteristics of this way of knowing. For them, sociocognitive decentration is a general rule and becomes the 'norm'; the materialist explanation is generalised and applied to all subjects of discourse. And mythic time and an unconditionally valorised and idealised view of the past are replaced by a progressive, meliorist, linear perception of time, to the point where the term 'social change' frequently has positive connotations in itself.

Interviews 18 and 19 are especially significant, and the way they function has therefore been analysed in greater detail.

Sociocognitive decentration, which is a basic Type II characteristic, is explicitly called for by the marked desire to get through to the Other and achieve a co-ordination of viewpoints. Reciprocity is actively promulgated; the other becomes a source of enrichment. The constant effort and important cognitive work implied in this decentration is visible at every level. The speakers understand and accept attitudes opposed to their own, and they try to explain them by means of a range of social and material factors (the materialist paradigm), and show no particular fear of contrary opinions and practices.

In interview 19, for example, essentialisation and false identification are explicitly rejected; at several points the person in question insists on the need to co-ordinate different and opposing conceptions, and in the course of her explanation, having run through the elements where some comment might be appropriate, she often indicates that she does not know enough to intervene. This is a further mark of decentration.

Two different paradigms, however, are called upon to provide an explanation of the phenomenon of immigration, the materialist and deviancy paradigms. At first, the speaker assigns responsibility for immigration to the authorities. Here again are some brief extracts:

–   'All the same, the government was wrong.'
–   'They ought to have restricted entry much earlier.'

These explanations belong in the deviancy paradigm. But later on the speaker returns to *causes of the materialist type*:

– 'in a lot of sectors it was a way for employers to get cheaper labour'.

It is all as if the status of the two social actors (the employers and the government) was different;

– For *industry* the most important thing is the search for profit; this logic is neither good nor bad in itself; the employers do what it is logical for them to do; attribution of right or wrong is irrelevant.

– *The authorities*, on the other hand, have a duty to restrain this logic of profit. In this instance, having failed to do so, they are wrong and the speaker attributes responsibility for the situation to them. They are in a sense invested with a moral duty *vis-à-vis* the nation. It is therefore possible to judge them in terms of *deviancy* and *conformity*.

Of course this is no more than a hypothesis for explaining a *dissymmetry of logico-discursive treatment*. Nonetheless, it corresponds fairly well to the very widely held conception of the Welfare State as the nation's corrective to the logic of the private economy.

This is, however, a highly specific use of the deviancy paradigm and has nothing in common with its systematic and exclusive use. Social thought in use may bring together different explanatory registers, depending, perhaps, on the issue requiring explanation. A complex explanation may necessitate such diversification, at least within the framework of this second sociocognitive configuration. This in itself would indicate a greater flexibility in this way of thinking, and one which goes hand in hand with a more thorough and complex linguistic and cognitive process. From the unarguable judgements commonly passed in Type I, we have moved to an important process of logico-discursive consideration.

There is thus less of a difference than may at first appear between interviews 18 and 19, despite the specific use of the deviancy paradigm. Its intrusion here does not imply any common ground with the sociocognitive structure typical of Type I subjects. The *general form* of the reasoning is still that of Type II.

An 'anomaly'?

Interview 23, on the other hand, presents larger and more numerous divergences than the preceding case. At the start of the interview the subject conforms completely to Type II, in that he manifests extreme sociocognitive decentration by means of a number of instances of understanding and acceptance. As in the preceding cases, decentration is accompanied by a materialist explanation and a generally positive acceptance of change. Yet more than once the subject of change draws out a degree of nostalgia for a more peaceful past.

In addition to this, the explanatory system sometimes bears some similarity

to the indeterminacy paradigm. The subject sometimes presents himself as powerless, as a victim passively submitting to a somewhat undetermined social reality. He understands and explains conscientious objection from both political and religious motives, while nonetheless insisting that objectors must be genuinely sincere. He does not want any 'dishonesty'. And when he goes on to talk about the authorities' responsibility for immigration, we are closer to the moralism and voluntarism of the deviancy paradigm. But the passage which is most significant in terms of any 'anomaly' is the one where the subject talks about Action Nationale. After declaring himself resolutely non-xenophobic, he gives the following reply to this question:

Q: But what do you think about the Initiative itself?
A: What, the Action Nationale one? Hmmm . . . I didn't approve of it. But it's odd, as time goes on I've come to think they weren't completely wrong. And I can tell you that's what a lot of the Swiss population think. They weren't completely wrong.

How is this answer to be interpreted? Is he a closet 'xenophobe'? Probably not, on balance, since he says clearly that he did not approve of the Initiative. He simply realises, with hindsight, that the initiators 'were not completely wrong'. Saying this still does not mean that he would vote 'yes', even if there were to be another Initiative of the same sort. Is recognising that one's opponents are not always completely wrong not just another form of decentration? At all events, there is certainly no diabolisation or absolute condemnation of the opponent – the Other – as there would be in the deviancy paradigm.

The general form of reasoning remains, in fact, very different from that of Type I, indeed it fits in perfectly with Type II, despite these 'divergences'. And even though the speaker reveals a degree of nostalgia to begin with, there is repeated evidence later in the interview that the positive changes carry greater weight with him. There also remains the fundamental fact that this individual reveals all the essential elements of the form of reasoning characteristic of Type II: a conscious decentration, a capacity for complex materialist explanation, and a rejection of any belief that it could be possible to return to an idealised past.

Vertical analysis of the Type II interviews reveals an additional kind of cognitive and discursive decentration, which takes the form of a more marked dissociation between argument and personal experience and/or value judgements. Personal history intrudes far less often into the discourse, and when it does it tends to be *argumentative* rather than normative.

Of the conception of time, we can say that as well as the two conceptions being totally opposed to each other on a comparative basis, linear time is not merely a symmetrical reversal of the mythic and voluntaristic conception, but

generally speaking occupies a much less important place than does mythic time. The whole subject of time thus plays a much smaller part in Type II sociocognitive functioning.

The last interview we were analysing, number 23, revealed a basic difference between the two types. What may at first have appeared to be anomalies are in fact only empirical proof of the greater linguistic and cognitive complexity of Type II. Speakers of this type are never bound by any one factor in explaining social reality. Their grasp is more heterogeneous, more diversified and more differentiated: closer, in fact, to the actual nature of everyday social life.

We can therefore conclude this brief synthetic account of the vertical study of the interviews and of the integration of the results of the three indicator themes with some general statements based on concrete data:

–   It can be empirically shown that very different ways of thinking and speaking exist in everyday reality.
–   The various types of articulation between the three indicator themes show that each way of thinking and speaking possesses a form and coherence of its own. Thus the various degrees of decentration, the different forms of explanation and the differing conceptions of time do not combine randomly but in accordance with precise and clearly identifiable requirements and logics. Even though the type of object, the moment and the aim in view may involve a degree of overlap, they do not make simultaneous and undifferentiated use of the three explanatory paradigms and the two conceptions of time.
–   It has been possible to demonstrate concretely that sociocognitive structures are characteristic of whole groups.
–   It has been clearly established that these sociocognitive structures, or ways of knowing, are not commensurable. The 'overlaps' between Type I and Type II characteristics are purely specific to the occasion.
–   In each way of knowing, typical subjects represent the vast majority of cases. The divergences and 'anomalies' do not constitute genuine exceptions as the fundamental elements of each type are still present.
–   With regard to the problem of the relationship between the collective and the individual, there turns out to be no general and universal rule here either. Vertical analysis shows the relationships to be very different in Types I and II. The cognitive inflexibility characteristic of Type I explains why individuals of this type are often more *dependent* on their way of knowing than those in Type II. They are also more heteronomous and more predictable, whereas Type II individuals are defined precisely by their autonomy and their greater freedom of linguistic and cognitive manoeuvre. The more important cognitive

and linguistic work that they carry out makes them, by definition, more independent, even though this autonomy and independence represents one of the traits they have in common.

The relationships between the individual and the collective, between a sociocognitive structure and the manner in which each individual brings it into being, are thus much narrower and much less flexible in Type I than in Type II. This also explains why individuation is clearly more evident and more frequent among Type II individuals. Intense, diversified and complex, cognitive and linguistic activity, by its very nature, encourages uninterrupted development of these cognitive and linguistic abilities.

In connection with this we may note a significant fact. It has been shown that Type I subjects were characterised in particular by an absence of sociocognitive decentration. And we know that, in terms of probability, a sociocentric structure occurs more frequently in unprivileged backgrounds where education is not taken very far. By contrast, in privileged environments, especially with the benefit of extended education, the way of knowing is more decentred, the cognitive and linguistic work more elaborated and the dissociation between judgement and personal experience more frequent. But these statements will be no more than misleading generalisations if we do not qualify them further, for at least two reasons:

(1) because every individual's way of knowing is centred in one way or another. Thus we all use the paradigms of causal explanations our study has revealed. Only the proportions vary. To take an extreme example: a logician may very well have a totally decentred thought structure in his professional activity and yet make decidedly sociocentric judgements in the social, political or cultural realm. The form of thought depends on its type of subject.[3]

Scientific activity, as we know, necessarily entails a form of analytic thought, that is a highly eleborate and therefore decentred logico-discursive activity, an explanatory paradigm similar to what we have called the materialist paradigm. But this does not exclude any scientist from using the deviancy paradigm in some circumstances, as, for example, in talking about rivals in his field. There has as yet been no logico-discursive analysis of this sort of speech, but its general structure will doubtless be closer to the deviancy paradigm than to the materialist paradigm.

(2) Conversely, a subject from an *unprivileged social background*, with none of the advantages of an extended education, may nevertheless be characterised by a decentred sociocognitive structure. Similar subjects have been analysed in this study. In such cases, the extended linguistic and sociocognitive elaboration displayed by these subjects can be explained by their wide social, cultural and political activities and involvement.

This example demonstrates the importance of concepts like cognitive and linguistic *elaboration* and *development*. All individuals are capable of enriching

and developing their linguistic and cognitive competence in the course of their lives, even of changing their way of knowing, despite the fact that this theoretical possibility is in practice fulfilled very unequally between social groups and ways of knowing. The concept of *individuation* is used specifically to designate these phenomena which are both individual and socially variable.

While the concept of social structure puts the emphasis on the weightier sociological aspects, the constants, continuities and regularities, no approach which only looks at the structures and mechanical reproduction can account for actual social realities, which are a product both of structures and of particular, individual instances of structures being put into practice. The attempt to deal simultaneously with both these dimensions, the individual and the collective, enables us to provide a more adequate account of the social structures and of the factors that cause them to vary. The varying uses to which social actor subjects can put these structures (cognitive and linguistic) in order to respond to the requirements of everyday practice have the benefit of making us extend our awareness of the structures themselves. A structure which cannot account for divergences, 'anomalies' and individual practice is no more than a caricature, and becomes a pure abstraction, another universalising generalisation cut off from empirical reality.

It is as necessary to criticise the social sciences whenever their theoretical and conceptual tools become caricatures of social reality as when they imperially claim to be able to provide an exhaustive understanding of man.

Even in his social activities, man is fundamentally inexhaustible and unpredictable. This, in our view, must be the starting point if we are to have any chance of apprehending some of these actual practices.

Beyond narrow rationalism: the other logics

One of the essential aspects of our approach is our use of several different disciplines and dimensions to analyse social thought and everyday language. By using the insights of sociology, anthropology, sociopsychology and sociolinguistics we have been able to avoid some of the limitations of specialisation. And by introducing the dimension of what have been called the other logics of social behaviour (the affective, symbolic and mythic aspects), we wanted to avoid leaving these aspects aside on the grounds that they were too difficult to grasp empirically. The inclusion of these aspects thus implies a richer, more complex and more complete idea of man (and one which is therefore closer to reality) than that which is often found in approaches imbued with what we see as too narrow a rationalism.[4]

And while the introduction of these elements could mean that we lose in precision what we gain in richness, we have in fact been able to include a degree of precision.

It was in connection with the subject of time and, more precisely, of its mythic–cyclical representation, that the role of these other logics appeared most clearly and most intensely. We now need to grasp these elements at the level of linguistic form by integrating them directly into the discursive model within which this representation of time operates, the Type 1 model.

There is in fact no limit to the degree to which the analysis of a social phenomenon can be enriched by endlessly new angles of approach. However, we shall close this study with the introduction of these other logics, reiterating our view that they seem particularly important for extending our understanding of the way social thought and everyday language work.

The sociolinguistic approach, that is the approach via linguistic expression and linguistic form, lends itself especially well to understanding the role these elements of other logics can play. Sociolinguistics, as we know, focuses primarily on the variations in linguistic capacity and linguistic practice in different social milieux. But by showing that *saying is doing*, by studying the problem of the efficacy or inefficacy of discourses, it also reveals the determining power of language itself. Like social representations, the language of an individual or a social group, as well, of course, as being a function of the social and economic characteristics of that individual or group, is also both structured and structuring, and thus possesses a determining power of its own.

If we add to the formula 'saying is doing' the fact that saying (language, a way of speaking) is indissociable from the way of knowing, and if we remember that social representations are nothing more than a way of representing social reality, and therefore of knowing it, we bring the role of *language* into the study of social representations. Indeed social representations can only be grasped if we start with language, the words in which they are expressed. If we bear in mind, too, that the sociolinguistics of discourse is concerned not only with the content of language, texts and discourses but also with their *form*, the angle of approach can be defined as follows: by paying attention to the linguistic forms in which the mythic–cyclical representation of time is expressed, we can uncover dimensions of this representation or way of knowing which analysing the content alone would not even enable us to glimpse. And among the most important of these dimensions are the other logics.

The most complete discursive model so far in which this representation of time operates is the Type 1 model with the added diachronic dimension. Let us now return to these two models and demonstrate the changes which follow from the integration of some elements of other logics:

(1)   Synchronic model
    IT OUGHT TO BE LIKE THAT
    IT IS NOT LIKE THAT

IT STILL OUGHT TO BE LIKE THAT

(2) Diachronic model

IT OUGHT TO BE LIKE THAT

IT IS NOT LIKE THAT ANY MORE

IT OUGHT TO BE LIKE THAT AGAIN

Although the second model does integrate the diachronic dimension, it will be noticed that it still does not take account of all the phenomena that accompany this mythic–cyclical conception of time. The following aspects, for example, are not discursively integrated:

– the powerful *idealisation* and *moral validation* of the idealised past they want to recover at any cost,
– the *affective and emotive elements* which underlie the desire to rediscover a lost paradise,
– and the *tension* created in these subjects by the gulf that exists between the present situation (which they regard as degenerate and unacceptable) and the idealised past.

This therefore leads us to the following new model:

(3) Diachronic model + other logics:

ONCE UPON A TIME IT WAS WONDERFUL

IT IS NOT LIKE THAT ANY MORE

(which is explicable by . . .) → Projection → Tension

IT OUGHT TO BE LIKE IT ONCE WAS AGAIN

(which is possible if . . .) → Voluntarism

→ Asceticism, etc.

The first basic sentence integrates the following elements of other logics:

– idealisation of the past
– its unconditional valorisation, and its exclusively positive moral validation.

This sentence thus represents the common denominator, the deep structure of all the surface statements produced by individuals who have a mythic–cyclical conception of time and who talk about the positive aspects of the past in relation to a present situation which they regard as degenerate and unacceptable: once there was harmony, consensus, people listened to each other, agreed with each other, society was like a community, warm, close and pleasant, somewhere where life was good. They were not concerned with Others. They lived among themselves. There wasn't all this agitation and overcrowding you get everywhere nowadays; people didn't try to copy foreign ways of doing things. Money and comfort and material well-being weren't the

main values and they weren't an obsession. The country was made up of 'Swiss villages' not sprawling, cold, anonymous, unsettling towns, in which people 'will soon start dropping like flies' when they're hit by pollution.

Although this first basic sentence sums up in a not very schematic way all the catastrophist attitudes to the current situation, and the ones idealising the past, it also contains another fundamental element: the fact that the past thus idealised is both *ahistorical* and *atemporal*. The past in fact is never precisely defined. There is merely a ONCE or an ELSEWHERE which is neither located nor dated. Furthermore, this indeterminate once and elsewhere was WONDERFUL. This is the world of fairy tales or myths, not the real world with its inherent constraints. In this connection it might even be correct to talk of mythic thought. In fact the role of myth seems to be so important that it becomes not just a subject but a *general form of thought*, even a *form of discourse*. We have already noted that at the discursive level these statements are not analytic; they tell stories rather than explaining anything. The language takes on the *form* of a narrative, a story, a mythical tale: once upon a time things were wonderful.

The mythic–cyclical representation of time seems also to lend itself particularly well to the most varied and profound *projections* of aspirations and desires. Where the degenerate present is not simply denied – in the borderline cases, the individuals do not even want to think about the present situation, they are so attached to (or they dream so much about?) a wonderful past – it is rejected unconditionally. When subjects do agree to attempt some degree of explanation of the current degenerate situation, it is in order that they can locate the cause and the responsibility (to explain it would be to justify it) on external elements, such as foreigners. Even where they admit that some Swiss individuals – the deviants – share the responsibility for the degeneration, there is no way they can oppose them practically, as that would mean that it would be impossible to achieve the harmony they so much desire in the in-group. Which is the reason for the PROJECTION on to foreign, outside elements, on to a scapegoat.

Affective investment

Finally there is the phenomenon of the *tension* created by the gap between an idealised past and a degenerate present, a tension which includes both *emotive* and *affective* aspects which reappear in the very form taken by thought and language. An emotive and affective form of language and thought has a totally different linguistic structure from one that is analytic and didactic, the latter being characteristic of the linear representation of time. In the former there is more expression (of emotive or affective states) than analysis or explanation. The expressive function of language is superadded and can

overflow and even swamp the primary instrumental function of simple communication and analysis.

So far we have looked at the last discursive model sentence by sentence, but to identify these tension phenomena we must turn our attention to the *relations* between the model's three basic sentences. A model of this sort, which reflects the form of thought and discourse which it is supposed to represent, is in fact a totality, a structure possessing characteristics which the component elements of the structure, taken separately, do not have; the *relations* between the component elements are as important as the elements themselves.

The desire to regain this wonderful past is not simply an intellectual one: it is strongly charged with emotive and affective elements. The following extract from one of the interviews – 'Things won't be easy if we expel the immigrants, but I'm prepared to suffer and make sacrifices if it means we'll get the old Switzerland back again' – illustrates this tension and shows the powerful *affective investment* of this desire and the discourse which expresses it.

This brings us to an important problem. The myth of a lost paradise or of a Golden Age (whether set in the past or in the future) undoubtedly constitutes one of the most fundamental mythemes in any society. Yet it seems to be the case that analyses of myths only deal with images, even when what is involved is mythic thought. The emotive and affective aspects which all myth includes, at least for the individuals who experience them concretely, are almost never taken into account when they are analysed.

Jung and his school, however, are somewhat more sensitive to this dimension.[5] Without wanting to become involved in arguments over the notion of archetype, it does seem possible to treat the myth of the lost paradise or a Golden Age as a kind of archetype, simply insofar as it is omnipresent and transcultural. Jung regards archetypes as 'patterns of behaviour' that possess a considerable dynamic power, and it is the affective and emotional elements that give them their particular dynamic in power in the psychic life. In addition, archetypes have an instinctual dimension which further augments their determining power.

Whether these aspects are called irrational, emotive, affective, instinctual, archetypical or elements of other logics, other ways of thinking, there can be no doubt that they play an important part in the orientation of the behaviour of some individuals, social groups and even whole societies.

Eliade, too, tells us that in all societies, even industrialised ones, there is an *affective and symbolic capacity* within every individual,[6] and that even where this capacity has atrophied and withered away over decades or centuries, it is always susceptible of being regenerated and reinvested.

Jung further demonstrates that an archetype is not merely an image, or

even an abstract representation, with no material, concrete substratum. Individuals or groups who are guided in their behaviour and their imaginative worlds by archetypes do not act according to purely figurative or abstract representations. All archetypes, myths and symbols are founded simultaneously on an *image* and an *emotion*. Jung speaks in this context of numinosity or *psychic energy*, i.e. in the terminology we have been using, of emotions and affects. The word 'energy' has the advantage of foregrounding the concrete and active nature necessarily entailed in the realities to which notions of affectivity and emotion refer. But emotion and affectivity are not inferior, 'secondary' realities, even though they may be more difficult to grasp using traditional analytic processes. Like social representations, they have fully as much reality as bricks and mortar.

The staying power of myths or symbols, and the fact that they can be sources of representations and actions, comes as much from the investment of these energy forces (emotive or affective) as it does from their purely imagistic and figurative aspects, if not more. But narrowly rationalistic approaches – which are even to be found in the study of myths and symbols – disregard this dimension, despite the fact that it is fundamental to psychic energy, to the emotive and affective aspects of behaviour.

We therefore do not believe that a discourse like that of the mythic–cyclical representation of time can be adequately understood without the added dimension of the affectivity and emotion of psychic energy. There is no other way to take account of the intense *investment* that characterises the discourse, and which is not solely derived from representations and images of time. This is why we have suggested using the terms 'affective economy' and 'affective semantics': affective economy to designate this psychic energy, emotion and affectivity, as an organising presence or potentiality (or competence) in the structure and general operational rules of the discourse; and affective semantics to refer to content, the concrete objects invested within the framework of this organisation by any given concrete social actor subject. This last detail is important as a reminder of the need to maintain the *variationist* perspective whatever the phenomenon under consideration. Even the capacity for myth and symbol, psychic – emotive and affective – energy, varies in form and extent between different cultures, social groups and ways of knowing. In practical everyday reality, similarly, there is no ONE general form of affective, symbolic and mythic capacity, but a variety of them.

The analysis of time alone has already demonstrated that this capacity plays a visibly greater part in the mythic–cyclical representation than in the linear. And the same differences are to be seen again at the level of the form as well as of the content of the discourse.

The specifically linguistic characteristics of this affective and emotive discourse require extensive empirical investigation.[7] But it is possible even so

to identify some of them at this stage. Certainly we seem to be dealing with a specific discursive style. The narrative form of the mythic tale has in addition a genuine *style which is powerfully invested and rather strained*. This strained tension is also visible in the speaking subject's investment of his own utterances. The speaker is personally implicated in any condemnation of the multiple evils of the present. And so these emotive and affective drives, intruding into the discourse, break the 'correct', fluent grammatical sequence and give the discourse a brusque, jerky form.[8]

In linear time discourse, on the other hand, these different discursive characteristics are more or less completely absent. The discursive functioning is closer to that of the materialist paradigm: the style is didactic, analytical, argumentative and linear. In fact the discourse seems to progress by means of a logic very similar to that of traditional grammatical sequence. The linear development of the discourse is not constantly interrupted by sudden and (from the point of view of traditional, 'correct', grammatical logic) 'illogical' disconnected emotive and affective terms.

An individual social actor subject does not represent and invest just any type of time, in any way (in any discursive form) . . .

In conclusion, we can also say that taking other logics into consideration throws new light on another central problem, that of the efficacy of political discourses.

It has been established that subjects who adopt an ideological discourse like that of the supporters of 'xenophobic movements' conform essentially to Type I; that is, they have, among other things, a mythic–cyclical representation of time, and particularly marked elements of other logics – affective, mythic and symbolic capacities. The sixteen important points set out in the introduction to the subject of time demonstrated that this capacity can never be perceived as a conglomeration of 'reactionary' elements, because it has a basic reality of its own, without any a priori ideological 'coloration'. It represents a potentiality present in all of us, even though its position and intensity may vary considerably from one individual or social group to another.

As far as the problem of the efficacy of discourses is concerned, it seems to be the case that conservative political forces are more aware of this affective and symbolic capacity and invest it more easily and on a larger scale. The leaders of the 'xenophobic movements' indeed acted accordingly. There is a noticeable similarity between the subjects of their discourse and some of the statements by our (Type I) interviewees. In reality, things are even more complicated. In their discourses, these movements have only appealed to part of this affective, mythic and symbolic capacity. They have reactivated and invested the symbols and myths (those for example of an idealised and mythical Swiss past) which were ready to be emptied and used parasitically as means to their own political ends. This reintroduces the distinction between

social thought and ideology, in which social thought designates the funda-mental categories, schemes and processes which underlie the way of knowing of any given social group, whereas ideology is the secondary reality that retains some, but only some, of the elements of social thought (of one or more ways of knowing), these being precisely the ones which can be used parasiti-cally to further the ends of an ideology.

We hope that we have demonstrated that the efficacy of an ideological discourse cannot be measured solely by its capacity to spread ideas but also by its ability to create a belief in certain symbols and myths and to invest them affectively, and thus in its capacity to *inspire love or hatred* of certain objects and social categories (by providing given subjects with an opportunity to love themselves and hate 'Others' or 'deviants'). These dimensions can play a role which is as important as, if not more important than, the political, social and economic circumstances of any given period, in explaining the efficacy of certain discourses.

Our contention is that it is no longer possible to ignore these elements of other logics by consigning them to the realm of the 'irrational' or the 'illogical'. We need, on the contrary, to try to define more precisely the nature and role of the particular logics of the 'illogical' and 'irrational',[9] as the realities these terms conceal have their own logics, even though they are more difficult to define in empirical terms.

For although man is fundamentally inexhaustible and unpredictable, it is still the duty of the disciplines concerned with the study of man to try to push back the frontiers of the unknown.

Notes

1 General introduction

1 See *Pensée sociale, langage en usage et logiques autres*, Lausanne, Editions l'Age d'Homme, 1982.

2 By 'base' we mean the working classes and middle classes, following a social typology which is concise but determinant as far as the aims of this work are concerned.

3 This tendency to privilege the statements of those in command or authority is also to be found in content analysis.

4 In our analysis of these linguistic practices, we have drawn on the work of sociolinguists such as Bernstein, Labov, Halliday and Bourdieu.

5 In Switzerland, the term 'Neinsager' is applied to those who more or less systematically reject the proposals of central government. It would be hard to find a better example of the ethnocentrism of the dominant way of thinking, which is regarded as self-evidently the only right and legitimate one. 'Neinsager' are defined entirely negatively, on the basis of, and in terms of, the legitimated way of thinking, which does not – and cannot – recognise the specificity, the alterity, the nature or the logic which characterise ways of thinking different from its own. They are granted no positive value or consistency, but are simply regarded as not being what they ought to be.

6 If 100,000 signatures are collected from Swiss citizens, it is possible to propose amendments to the federal constitution. Central government then has to put the proposal to the whole of the Swiss electorate by referendum.

7 Launching a 'popular initiative' of this sort entails considerable expenditure, which restricts the theoretical possibilities of this institutional method.

8 For a study of xenophobia, see Windisch, *Xénophobie? Logique de la pensée populaire*, Lausanne, Editions l'Age d'Homme, 1978.

9 On this point, however, we need to dissociate ourselves very clearly from the 'critique of science' approach, many of whose advocates have never done any actual concrete work in any scientific discipline and tend to treat science as if it were no different, in the end, from ideology, religion or myth.

10 It is more usual to regard the Other as different from oneself than to regard oneself as different from the Other.

11 This approach always chooses particular, isolated examples, taken out of context, because they can be used to confirm a theoretical proposition formulated independently of the concrete reality which the example is meant to represent. Hence the term *'ad hoc* examples'.

2 Theoretical and methodological foundations

1 About 100 topics, in addition to that of immigrant workers, were tackled in these interviews, so that we could discover the deep structure of a way of knowing.
2 The concepts of assimilation and accommodation are taken from Piaget's genetic epistemology.
3 See Mounin, 'Les Langues et les mentalités', *ARC* (72) 57–61.
4 The classic problem, posed by Whorf, of the correlation between linguistic structure and mental attitude underlies these investigations. We are trying, in fact, to provide empirically based, linguistic (or, as we would say, discursive) proof of different ways of thinking. Or, rather than trying to prove one by means of the other, we are trying to identify their mutual articulation, the way the nature of their interactions varies depending on social group.
5 See *Language and Learning*.
6 See Chomsky, *Reflections on Language*, New York, Random House, 1975.
7 For a fuller account of this idea see Windisch *et al. Pensée sociale*, Chapter 3, pp. 43–62.
8 These two images could be compared with Weber's ideal types, as they are not found in such an extreme form in the social sciences.
9 The analysis of polemical discourse is also especially useful in illustrating the typically conflictual forms of linguistic interactions.
10 The reader will be aware that our approach is designed to be a reminder of the conflictual dimension. This choice is also explicable because interest in conflict is much less frequent in the realm of thought and language.
11 Such an approach seeks, therefore, to transcend the traditional dichotomies such as linguistic/extralinguistic, language/thought, thought/action, language/action, etc.

3 Cognitive centration

1 When a form of egocentrism is collective, we talk of collective egocentrism or sociocentrism.
2 Remember that xenophobia is not an attitude in itself, but stems from an exacerbated nationalism, i.e. precisely from a powerful sociocognitive centration.
3 Ethnocentrism, which is a very fashionable term in the social sciences used to designate particularly the West's historic attitude to other civilisations, is also a form of sociocentrism.
4 The quotations Windisch uses to illustrate egocentrism are listed in Battro's *Dictionnaire d'épistémologie génétique*, Paris, PUF, 1966. The English translation of this work, however, contains extracts which are often confused or confusing, and occasionally quite wrong. I have therefore used the existing English translations of the works cited, wherever I could find them. *Trans.*
5 The concept of reversibility is used in two rather different senses, in Piaget's system and in Gabel's theory of ideology, for example. Where Piaget takes reversibility to be the criterion and the condition of operational and scientific thought, Gabel uses the concept to indicate spatialising, non-dialectical thought. In Gabel's work, however, reversibility is a function applied to historical or social phenomena, and not to mental operations.

6 It was sometimes impossible to avoid the intrusion of a third person into an interview that was planned to be with one person only.

7 In the analysis of discourse – in this case political discourse – we know that direct reported discourse is frequently assumed, whereas indirect reported discourse is generally not assumed. The latter is used precisely to invalidate the discourse of the other in the course of discussion.

8 For example: one 'deviant' foreigner becomes proof of the tendency of all foreigners towards deviancy.

9 Moralism, or moral reification, is a sociocognitive mechanism which consists of explaining a given phenomenon not by reference to a series of material and immaterial factors, but solely in terms of moral factors, so that the different social phenomena produced by a given society, for instance social change, are explained in terms of the selfishness, culpability, betrayal or unwillingness of some individual or group, preferably foreigners or other 'deviants'. Change itself is usually regarded as an abnormal, or deviant, phenomenon, which means in turn that it can only be explained by the behaviour of deviant groups or individuals.

10 'Man has a passion for identity, which is the fundamental idea of Meyerson's epistemology, but one which extends far outside the epistemological realm. It finds expression in such varied phenomena as sexual fetishism, morbid rationalism (and generally schizophrenia), a fondness for uniforms (mental and sartorial), monarchism and that whole area which Bouthoul calls heterophobia' (J. Gabel, 'Conscience utopique et fausse conscience' in Le Discours utopique, Colloque de Cerisy, 1975.

11 A movement for independence which led to the creation of the new Canton of Jura.

4 Social causality

1 See Windisch et al., Pensée sociale.

2 By using the terms logico-discursive activity, or logico-discursive form, we want to bring out the indissociability between cognitive activity and discursive activity.

3 This sociocognitive mechanism goes hand in hand with other mechanisms such as homogenisation, identification, essentialisation and sociocentrism.

4 In fact, we know that these capital exports have an inverse effect.

5 Certainly an exaggeration.

6 The Action Nationale (AN) is therefore one of the movements fighting 'foreign overpopulation'.

7 Agreement between the employers and the unions designed to settle differences by negotiation.

8 See Windisch et al. Xénophobie?, pp 115–40.

9 He would probably have used the dominant explanatory paradigm 'in normal times'.

10 It is quite clear that this form of egocentrism is not purely cognitive.

11 The term 'enunciating subject' derives from the area of linguistics that deals with 'utterance' (énonciation). But here it is a subject of the utterance caught in action, in its actual practices.

12 Lévy-Bruhl, Notebook, trans. P. Rivière, (Oxford, Blackwells), 1975; cited in L. Poliakov, La Causalité diabolique, Paris, Calmann-Lévy, 1980, p. 16.

13 J. Piaget, *The Moral Judgement of the Child*, trans. Marjorie Gabain, London, Routledge and Kegan Paul, 1932 [Paris, 1932, p. 13].

14 Poliakov, L. (1980), p. 24.

15 Cf. Albert Einstein: 'Demons are everywhere: it is probable that, in a general way, belief in the action of demons lies at the root of our concept of causality.' Cited in L. Poliakov, *La Causalité diabolique*, p. 7.

16 Although we have restricted ourselves to a very empirical definition of the most immediate functioning of the ordinary person's causal explanation, we have nonetheless indicated that the subject of causality generally has preoccupied, and continues to preoccupy, numerous philosophers and researchers. This is not the place to offer even a brief résumé of this work, but we can provide a succinct reminder of some of the general orientations of some of these concerns. From a sociological perspective, a classic study was carried out in 1942, R. M. McIver's *Social Causation*, New York, Harper and Row, 1964 (1942), followed a little later by S. Toulmin, *The Uses of Argument*, Cambridge University Press, 1958. In social psychology, the subject of causation has been tackled particularly by S. Moscovici, *La Psychanalyse, son image et son public*, Paris, PUF, 1961, and more recently in 'The phenomenon of social representations' in R. M. Farr and S. Moscovici (eds.), *Social Representations*, Cambridge University Press, 1984. But it is primarily philosophers and epistemologists who have been concerned with the problem. Meyerson published his *De l'explication dans les sciences* in 1921 (Paris, Payot, 1927). And in the field of epistemology, the question of explanation was elaborated in response to the problem raised by Dilthey at the end of the nineteenth century, according to which it should be possible to distinguish between explanation and understanding (*Erklären* and *Verstehen*), a distinction which confirmed that separating the sciences of nature and the sciences of mind. But the neo-positivists rejected that explanation and only allowed *Verstehen* a place in discovery, not in explanation itself. The prevailing model in their epistemology was the one developed by Hempel and Oppenheimer, referred to as the D–N model, i.e. deductive-nomological (see C. G. Hempel, *Aspects of Scientific Explanation*, New York, Free Press, 1965). The situation changed little under the influence of post-Wittgenstein philosophy of language. A new discussion was initiated with the publication of Henrik von Wright's *Explanation and Understanding*, London, Routledge and Kegan Paul, 1971, in which as Apel puts it, 'the motives and positions of the German theoreticians of *Verstehen* were given a new lease of life by the presuppositions of a theory of action linked to an analysis of language' (*Neue Versuche über Erklären und Verstehen*, (ed.) Apel *et al.*, Frankfurt, Suhrkamp, 1978.) Von Wright's arguments are also discussed in the book.

Whereas these theories of explanation are often confined to the scientific domain, the same cannot be said of Piaget's genetic epistemology. The aim of this has always been to study the sciences on the basis of their origin in natural thought. He defines causal explanation in terms of the presence of three elements. Laws, or regularities between facts, the deduction of laws, or the necessary connections between them, and the existence of a real substrate, the construction of a model 'adapted to the facts themselves, and such as is able to make deductive transformations correspond to real transformations'. The essence of Piaget's theory of causal explanation is to be found in P. Fraisse and J. Piaget (eds.)

Experimental Psychology: Its Scope and Method, London, Routledge and Kegan Paul, 1968; M. Bunge, F. Halbwachs, T. S. Kuhn, J. Piaget and L. Rosenfeld (eds.), *Les Théories de la causalité*, Paris, PUF, 1971; R. García and J. Piaget, *Les Explications causales*, vol. 26, 'Etudes d'épistémologie génétique', Paris, PUF, 1971; and *L'Explication dans les sciences*, 'Introduction: Le problème de l'explication', Paris, Flammarion, 1973. For an extension of this approach from a more discursive perspective, see the work of J.-B. Grize and his team at the Centre de Recherches Sémiologiques (CdRS) at Neuchâtel, who attempt an explanation from the point of view of 'natural logic'. See particularly the following publications: *Quelques réflexions sur l'explication*, Travaux du CdRS, No. 36, 1980; *Le Discours explicatif*, parts 1 and 2, Travaux du CdRS, Nos. 38 & 39, 1981; 'L'Explication: approche sémiologique' in *Revue Européenne des Sciences Sociales*, 19 (1981), no.56, These contain work by Grize, M.-J. Borel, J. Chesny, M. Ebel, A. Morf, A. Lecomte and D. Miéville. In the same perspective there is also the study by C. Wülser, *Actes de langage explicatifs*, Travaux du CdRS, no. 40, 1982. Taking their theory of discursive operations as a starting-point, they see explanation as a transformation which works on an original schematisation (O_1), to make a problematised schematisation (O_2) and finally a resolution of this problematisation by means of explanation (O_3). Grize distinguishes his team's approach to explanation from that of von Wright, which he describes as logical, from Perelman's, which he describes as philosophic, from Fodor's, which he describes as epistemological and from Piaget's, which he describes as psychological (*Quelques réflexions*, p. 1). He describes his own approach as semiological insofar as it occupies the area between grammar and meaning. His concern is 'not to study the form of the text for itself, nor to identify what it means, but to find out by what operations the author of the text creates meaning' (*ibid.*, p. 2).

Another contribution from CdRS, mainly from Borel and Lecomte, is the distinction between Justification and Explanation. In fact, a semiological approach to explanation is bound to come up against the linguistic marker 'because'. This sometimes introduces a Justification, when it is at the level of Being. From this they deduce that the speaker can either be situated as a witness, which constitutes explanation, or as an agent, which constitutes justification. This leads Lecomte to distinguish between a justificatory 'I say', a sub-modality of an informative 'I say', and an explanatory 'I say', which is a sub-modality of a performative 'I say'. This distinction between Justification and Explanation also lies at the heart of the Theory of Argumentation elaborated by Kopperschmidt from a perspective similar to that of Habermas (see *Argumentation, Sprache und Vernunft*, part 2, Urban-Taschenbücher, 1980). But he regards informative discourse as the discourse concerned with facts and justificatory discourse as concerned with *Geltansprüche*, or claims of validity (which can be concerned with truth, justice, sincerity, understanding). Kopperschmidt also distinguishes between events endowed with meaning (action) and others which are events in the external world. The latter relate to explanation from Causes, while the former relate to explanation from Motives. This returns us to the distinction between *Erklären* and *Verstehen*. To the two types of answers to *Informationsfragen*, there are two corresponding types of justificatory discourses, theoretical discourse which is concerned with claims to validity such as truth, and practical discourse which is concerned with claims to

validity to do with the *Richtigkeit* or correctness of action. The qualification 'informative' seems to be less adequate for talking about justification than for talking about explanation. As far as the current state of theoretical discussion about the problem of causality proper is concerned, we should also mention the collection of texts in *Kausalität. Neue Texte*, Stuttgart, Reclam, 1981, which brings together contributions mainly from British and German authors, and includes a useful bibliography.

At a more empirical level, we should mention in conclusion that our three paradigms of explanation are similar to the explanatory types which Paul Veyne arrives at in his reflections on explanation in history. For him, though, historical explanation 'is hardly any different from the kind of explanation we use every day' (*Comment on écrit l'histoire*, Paris, Seuil, Collection Points, 1978, p. 69). He concludes that there are three explanatory factors in history: 'One is chance, by which we mean superficial causes, incident, character and opportunity. Another is causes or conditions or objective data, which we shall call material causes. And the third is freedom and decision-making, which we call final causes', (p. 72). It can be seen that there are some analogies here with the indeterminacy paradigm, the materialist paradigm and the deviancy paradigm.

These similarities also demonstrate the interest there is in achieving a better understanding of the most ordinary and everyday forms of explanation alongside the more theoretical speculations on the subject.

5 The perception of time

1 This argument links up with some linguistic and semiological theories which argue that it is not words which refer, but we who refer by means of words: it is not the sign which is the subject of linguistics and semiology, but signifying activity by means of signs.

2 Narcissistic completeness can also be seen as a form of centration. For further detail on narcissism, see S. Ferenczi, *Thalassa*, Paris, Payot, most recent French edition, 1977; B. Grunenberger, *Le Narcissisme*, Paris, Payot, 1971; J. Chasseguet-Smirgel, 'Essai sur L'Idéal du Moi', *Revue française de psychanalyse*, nos. 5–6 (1973).

3 By using a semiotic analysis (paradigmatic plan) it can be shown that ideological discourses can be defined in terms of a number of clearly determined oppositions. So, in a conservative ideology, one necessarily finds the oppositions past/present and town/country. This past/present opposition may itself be reduced to the combination of two semantic categories, the oppositions between: SIMPLE AND COMPLEX and ORDER AND DISORDER.

The past is simple and ordered, the present complex and disordered. Other oppositions such as Discipline/Laxness, Healthy/Unhealthy, Work/Idleness, Honesty/Dishonesty, etc. can be seen either as synonymous categories or as in hyponymic or hypotaxic relation with the two preceding oppositions.

4 Patriotic centration is a sociocognitive centration which is based on patriotism.

5 J. J. Wunenburger, *L'Utopie et la crise de l'imaginaire*, Paris, Delarge, 1979.

6 *Ibid*. p. 36.

7 *Ibid*. p. 31.

8 J. Gabel, *La Fausse Conscience*, Paris, Minuit, 1962. Trans. as *False Consciousness* by Margaret A. Thompson and Kenneth A. Thompson, Oxford, Blackwell, 1975.

9 R. Ruyer, *L'Utopie et les utopies*, Paris, PUF, 1950.

10 By using psychoanalytic language we are emphasising the importance of the affective dimension as well as the cognitive one. But finally it is necessary to show that there is no abstract, general or universal affectivity, only affectivity which is socially determined by social variations, i.e. only *socio*affective structures, paralleling the sociocognitive structures.

11 R. Girard, *La Violence et le sacré*, Paris, Grasset, 1972.

12 *Ibid.* p. 146.

13 Our thanks to Verena Holstenson, who collaborated on the research into linear time discourse.

14 See J. Dubois, 'Enoncé et énonciation', *Langages*, 13 (1969), 100–10, who proposes four concepts for an approach to the phenomena of utterance in discourse: (1) distance; (2) tension; (3) modalisation; (4) transparency/opacity. Sociocognitive decentration necessarily implies such a distance.

15 S. Freud, *The Future of an Illusion*, Complete Works, Hogarth Press, 1961, vol. 21, p. 31.

16 I. Prigogine and I. Stengers, *La Nouvelle Alliance*, Paris, Gallimard, 1979, p. 275.

17 M. Halbwachs, *La Mémoire collective*, Paris, PUF, 1968; trans. as *Collective Memory* by F. J. Ditter and V. Y. Ditter, New York and London, 1980.

18 On this, see the useful critical survey by D. Mercure, 'L'Etude des temporalités sociales', *Cahiers internationales de sociologie*, 67 (1979), 263–76.

19 G. Balandier, *Le Temps et la montre en Afrique noire*, Bienne, Fédération horlogère Suisse, 1963; P. Ricoeur *et al.*, *Les Cultures et le temps*, Paris, Payot, 1975; P. Bourdieu, 'La Société traditionelle', *Sociologie du travail*, January–March 1963, 25–44.; J. Le Goff, 'Temps de l'Eglise et temps marchand', *Annales*, 3, 1960, 417–33; H. Mendras, 'La Fin des paysans', *Futuribles*, Paris, 1967, pp. 97–100.

20 See for example W. Grossin's study, *Les Temps de la vie quotidienne*, Paris and The Hague, Mouton, 1974.

21 See E. Durkheim in *Les Formes élémentaires de la vie religieuse*, Paris, Alcan, translated as *The Elementary Forms of the Religious Life*, by J. W. Swain, London [1915], 'It is the rhythm of social life which is at the basis of the category of time', cited in Mercure, 'L'Etude des temporalités sociales'.

22 P. Fraisse, *Psychologie du temps*, Paris, PUF, 1967.

23 B. Bernstein, *Class, Codes and Control*, London, Routledge and Kegan Paul, 1971–5.

24 Fraisse, *Psychologie du temps*, pp. 182ff.

25 G. Gurvitch, 'La Multiplicité des temps sociaux' in *La Vocation actuelle de la sociologie*, Paris, PUF, 1963, vol. 2, pp. 325–430.

26 See for example Marx's analysis in *The Eighteenth Brumaire of Louis Bonaparte*, 1852.

6 Integration and new perspectives

1 In fact to define a particular sociocognitive mechanism, or a particular form of explanation, we had precisely to demonstrate that they were present in a group of individuals.

2 This sort of logico-discursive model would certainly enable us to account for a number of political utopias.

3 Our ideas here are very close to those of E. E. Evans-Pritchard in *Primitive Religion*, Oxford, Clarendon Press, 1965. This work is a noteworthy critical and historical synthesis of a long-running debate about primitive (pre-logical) thought and logical thought. This Manichean dichotomy is categorically refuted, and it is demonstrated that logical, rational and objective thought exist equally in primitive societies. Whatever the society, the type of thought is linked to the type of object it is applied to. A 'primitive' may well address a fetish on one occasion and call upon objective thought on another.

The reason for mentioning this one writer, when there are many others who have done similar work, is because he presents an extensive critique of the many errors which mark the history of this problem: evolutionism, psychologism, sociologism, sociocentrism. 'Armchair theoreticians' also come in for heavy criticism.

4 Our approach might, for example, be situated midway between the recent, interesting theory of communication put forward by Habermas in his *Theory of Communicative Action* (trans. by T. McCarthy, London 1984 and Cambridge 1987) which we nevertheless regard as 'idealist and optimistic rationalism', and a more pessimistic, Lacanian concept, which starts from the impossibility of communication, given that it must necessarily be 'travestied', 'skewed', compounded of 'failures', or even 'raving'. Habermas on the other hand acknowledges the (theoretical) possibility of transparent and 'sincere' interpersonal communication. In the tradition of 'enlightened rationalism', he believes in the possibility of changing everyday communication and 'freeing' it from the factors that make it mutually incomprehensible.

We do not think it is possible to conceive everyday communication as 'falsified' or 'impure' or 'in need of liberation'. Everyday communication is simply richer and more complex than some theoretical models imply, although this does not mean that ordinary people speaking to each other use bad faith or try to trick each other deliberately.

This is why we try to show that everyday communication is not (or should not be) either 'rational' or 'irrational', but that it is simply a function of a large number of factors – social, cognitive, political, affective, symbolic, or mythic – and that these multiple determinations can be approached empirically.

5 See works by Jung listed in Bibliography.

6 M. Eliade, *Images et symboles*, Paris, Gallimard, 1952 (trans. as *Images and Symbols: Studies in Religious Symbolism* by P. Mairet, London, 1961).

7 This is, in fact, the subject of another research programme. Apart from the problem of defining the specifically linguistic and discursive indicators of affectivity, it will also be looking at the following kinds of problem: relations between social representations and language, social conflicts and language (the linguistic functioning of polemical discourse), as well as the contributions of some logicians and sociologists who have worked on the problem of the 'rationality' of everyday thought.

8 These brusque intrusions of affectivity suggest that models of the sort used in 'catastrophe theory' may perhaps be more useful for formalising these

destructuring irruptions than some more mechanical and reproductive models of society.

9 Our criticisms of excessively narrow rationalism do not, however, have anything at all to do with the recent anti-rationalist trend, advocated particularly by thinkers who were, not so long ago, embattled defenders of another extreme trend of thought, out-and-out structuralism.

Bibliography

Adorno, T. W., Frenkel-Brunswick, E., Lewinson, D. J. and Sanford, N. R. *The Authoritarian Personality*, New York, Harper & Brothers, 1950.

Ansart, P. *Les Idéologies politiques*, Paris, PUF, 1974.

'Science politique et psychologie: la passion politique', *Europa, Revue d'études interdisciplinaires*, vol. 2, no. 2, Spring 1979, 129–37.

Anzieu, D. 'L'Illusion groupale', *Nouvelle revue de psychanalyse*, no. 4, Autumn 1971. *Le Groupe et l'inconscient*, Paris, Dunod, 1978.

Apel, K. O., Mannine, J. and Tuomela, R. *Neue Versuche über Erklären und Verstehen*, Frankfurt, Suhrkamp, 1978.

Austin, J. L. *How to Do Things with Words*, Oxford University Press, 1962.

Bachmann, C., Lindenfield, J. and Simonin, J. *Langage et communications sociales*, Paris, Hatier-Credif, 1981.

Bakhtine, M. *La Marxisme et la philosophie du langage, Essai d'application de la méthode sociologique en linguistique*, Paris, Minuit, 1977 (1929). Published in English as *Marxism and the Philosophy of Language* by V. N. Vološinov, trans. L. Matejka and I. R. Titunik, New York and London Seminar Press, 1973.

Balandier, G. *Anthropo-logiques*, Paris, PUF, 1974.

Bally, Ch. *Le Langage et la vie*, Geneva, Droz, 1965 (1925). *Traité de stylistique française*, 2 vols., Berne, Francke, 1965 (1944).

Bardin, L. *L'Analyse de contenu*, Paris, PUF, 1980.

Bateson, G. *Steps Towards an Ecology of Mind*, London, Intertext, 1972.

Battro, A.M. *Dictionnaire d'épistémologie génétique*, Paris, PUF, 1966. Translated as *Piaget: Dictionary of Terms* by Elizabeth Rütschi-Herrmann and Sarah F. Campbell, Oxford, Pergamon Press, 1973.

Bauche, H. *Le Langage populaire*, Paris, Payot, 1920.

Beauvois, J.-L. and Ghiglione, R. *L'Homme et son langage. Attitudes et enjeux sociaux*, Paris, PUF, 1981.

Benjamin, W. *L'Homme, le langage et la culture*, Paris, Denoël-Gonthier, 1971.

Benveniste, E. *Problèmes de linguistique générale*, Paris, Gallimard, 1966. Translated as *Problems in General Linguistics* by M. E. Meek, Coral Gables, Miami, Florida, 1971.

Bernstein, B. *Class, Codes and Control*, 2 vols., London, Routledge and Kegan Paul, 1971, 1973.

Besançon, A. 'Cronos et chronos' in *Histoire et expérience du moi*, Paris, Flammarion, 1971.

Bisseret, N. 'Langages et identité de classe: les classes sociales "se parlent"', *L'Année sociologique*, 25 (1974), 237–64.

'Classes sociales et langage: au-delà de la problématique privilège/handicap',

L'Homme et la société, no. 27–8 (1975), 247–70.

Borel, M. J. *Discours de la logique et logique du discours*, Lausanne, Editions l'Age d'Homme, 1978.

Bourdieu, P. 'L'Economie des échanges linguistiques', *Langue française*, no. 34 (May 1977).

    La Distinction, Paris, Minuit, 1979.

    'Le Nord et le Midi, contribution à une analyse de l'éffet Montesquieu' in *Actes de la recherche*, no. 35 (1980).

    Le Sens pratique, Paris, Minuit, 1980.

Bourdieu, P. and Boltanski, L. 'Le Fétichisme de la langue', *Actes de la recherche en sciences sociales*, no. 4 (July 1975), 2–32.

Bright, W. *Sociolinguistics*, The Hague, Mouton, 1966.

Bunge, M., Halbwachs F., Kuhn, Th. S. and Rosenfeld, L. *Les Théories de la causalité*, Etudes d'épistémologie génétique, 25, Paris, PUF, 1971.

    L'Explication dans les sciences. Introduction: le problème de l'explication, Paris, Flammarion, 1973.

Cahiers de linguistique française, Faculté de Lettres, Université de Genève: no. 1 'Actes de langage et structure de la conversation', 1980; no. 2, 'Les Différents Types de marqueurs et la détermination des fonctions des actes de langage en contexte', 1981.

Calvet, L. J. *Linguistique et colonialisme: petit traité de glottophagie*, Paris, Payot, 1974.

    La Production révolutionnaire: slogans, affiches, chansons, Paris, Payot, 1976.

Centre de Recherches Linguistiques et Sémiologiques de Lyon. *Le Discours polémique*, Presses universitaires de Lyon, 1980.

Certeau, M. de. *La Culture au pluriel*, Paris, UGE, 10/18, 1974.

Certeau, M. de *et al.* *Une Politique de la langue*, Paris, Gallimard, 1975.

    L'Invention du quotidien, 2 vols., Paris, UGE, 10/18, 1980.

Certeau, M. de. and Giard, L. *L'Ordinaire de la communication*, Paris, Dalloz, 1983.

Chasseguet-Smirgel, J. 'Essai sur l'Idéal du Moi', *Revue française de psychanalyse*, 5–6 (1973).

    'Quelques réflexions d'un psychanalyste sur l'idéologie', *Pouvoir*, no. 11 (1979).

Chauveau, G. 'Analyse linguistique du discours jaurésien', *Langages*, no. 52 (1978), 5–108.

Chomsky, N. *Language and Mind*, New York, Harcourt, Brace and World, 1968.

    Reflections on Language, New York, Random House, 1975.

Cicourel, A. V. *Sociologie cognitive*, Paris, PUF, 1979 (1973).

Cohen, J. J. 'Some remarks on Grice's views about the logical practices of natural language' in Y. Bar-Hillel, *Pragmatics of Natural Language*, Dordrecht, Reidel, 1971, pp. 50–68.

Cohen, M. *Matériaux pour une sociologie du langage*, 2 vols., Paris, Maspéro, 1971 (1956).

Collin-Platini, M. 'Une analyse d'un discours politique' (De Gaulle), *La linguistique*, vol. 14, fasc. 1 (1978).

Communications, no. 20 (1973), 'Le Sociologique et le linguistique'.

    no. 30 (1979), 'La Conversation'.

    no. 32 (1980), 'Les Actes de discours'.

Cotteret, M. and Moreau, R. *Le Vocabulaire de Général De Gaulle*, Paris, A. Colin, 1969.

Coulthard, M. *An Introduction to Discourse Analysis*, London, Longman Group, 1977.

Courdesses, L. 'Blum et Thorez en mai 1936: analyses d'énoncés', *La Langue française*, no. 9 (1971), 22–33.

Courtial, J.-P. *La Communication piégée*, Paris, Robert Jauze, 1979.

Courtine, J.-J. 'Analyse du discours politique', *Langages*, no. 62 (June 1981), 9–128.

Dauzat, A. *Les Argots*, Paris, Delagrave, 1929.

Dieckmann, W. *Sprache in der Politik: Einführung in die Pragmatik und Semantik der politischen Sprache*, Heidelberg, C. Winter, 1975.

Dijk, T. A. van. 'Cognitive and conversational studies in the expression of ethnic prejudice', *Text*, vols. 3–4 (1983).

Dittmar, N. *Soziolinguistik, exemplarische und kritische Darstellung ihrer Theorie, Empirie und Anwendung*, Frankfurt, Athenäum Fischer Taschenbuch, 1973.

Doise, W. and Mugny, G. *Le Développement social de l'intelligence*, Paris, Inter-Editions, 1981.

Douglas, J. D. *Understanding Everyday Life*, London, Routledge and Kegan Paul, 1971.

Douglas, J. D. and Johnson, J. M. *Existential Sociology*, Cambridge University Press, 1977.

Duala-M'bedy, M. *Xenologie. Die Wissenschaft vom Fremden und die Verdrängung der Humanität in der Anthropologie*, Freiburg/Munich, Karl Alber, 1977.

Dubois, P. *Le Vocabulaire politique et social en France de 1869 à 1872*, Paris, Larousse, 1962.

'Enoncé et énonciation', *Langages*, no. 13 (1969), 100–10.

Ducrot, O. 'Logique et linguistique', *Langages*, no. 2 (1966).

Dire et ne pas dire, Paris, Hermann, 1972.

Durkheim, E. *The Elementary Forms of the Religious Life*, trans. J. W. Swain, London, George Allen and Unwin, 1915.

Ebel, M. and Fiala, P. *Sous le consensus, la xénophobie, Paroles, arguments, contextes, 1961–81*, Lausanne, Institut de Science Politique, Mémoires et Documents no. 16 (1983).

Eliade, M. *Images et symboles*, Paris, Gallimard, 1952. Translated as *Images and Symbols: Studies in Religious Symbolism* by P. Mairet, London, Harvill Press, 1961.

Elster, J. *Logic and Society*, London, Wiley and Sons, 1978.

Ulysses and the Sirens. Studies in Rationality and Irrationality, Cambridge University Press, 1979.

'L'Irrationalité: explication et compréhension', *MSH Informations*, Paris, no. 33 (1980), 17–19.

Ervin-Tripp, S. M. *Language Acquisition and Communicative Choice*, Stanford University Press, 1973.

Escarpit, R. *Théorie générale de l'information et de la communication*, Paris, Hachette, 1976.

Evans-Pritchard, E. E. *Theories of Primitive Religion*, Oxford, Clarendon.

Farr, R. *On the Varieties of Social Psychology*, Paris, 1977 (roneo).

The Nature of Human Nature and the Science of Behaviour, London, 1978 (roneo).

Farr, R. and Moscovici, S. (eds.) *Social Representations*, Cambridge University Press, 1984.

Faye, J.-P. *Langages totalitaires*, Paris, Hermann, 1972.

Théorie du récit, Paris, Hermann, 1972.

Fenner, M. *Partei und Parteisprache im politischen Konflikt*, Berne, Benteli, 1981.

Ferenczi, S. *Thalassa*, Paris, Payot, 1977.

Fillmore, Ch.-J. 'Pragmatik und die Beschreibung der Rede' in Anwäter, Kirsch and Schröter, *Kommunikazion, Interaktion, Identität*, Frankfurt, Suhrkamp, 1976.

Fishmann, J.-A. *Readings in the Sociology of Language*, The Hague, Mouton, 1968.
Sociolinguistique (Preface by A. Verdoodt), Brussels/Paris, Labor/Nathan, 1971.
Advances in the Sociology of Language, The Hague, Mouton, vol. 1, 1971; vol. 2, 1973.

Flahault, F. *La Parole intermédiaire*, Paris, Seuil, 1978.

Fontanier, P. *Les Figures du discours*, Paris, Flammarion, 1968

Foucault, M. *Les Mots et les choses. Une archéologie des sciences humaines*, Paris, Gallimard, 1966. Translated as *The Order of Things* by A. Sheridan, London, Tavistock, 1970.
L'Ordre du discours, Paris, Gallimard, 1971. Translated as *The Discourse on Language* by Rupert Swyer, included as Appendix to US edn of *The Archeology of Knowledge*, New York, Pantheon, 1972.

Fraisse, P. *Psychologie du temps*, Paris, PUF, 1967.

Fraisse, P. and Piaget, J. (eds.) *Experimental Psychology: Its Scope and Method*, London, Routledge and Kegan Paul, 1968.

Franz, M.-L. von. *Le Temps, le fleuve et la roue*, Paris, Chêne, 1979.

Frege, G. *Ecrits logiques et philosophiques*, Paris, Seuil, 1971.

Frie, H. *La Grammaire des fautes*, Paris, Gueuthner, 1929.

Freud, S. *Civilization and its Discontents, Complete Works*, vol. 21, London, Hogarth Press, 1961.
The Future of an Illusion, Complete Works, vol. 21, London, Hogarth Press, 1961.

Fromm. E. *Le Langage oublié*, Paris, Payot, 1980.

Gabel, J. *La Fausse Conscience*, Paris, Minuit, 1962. Translated as *False Consciousness* by Margaret A. Thompson and Kenneth A. Thompson, Oxford, Blackwell, 1975.
Sociologie de l'áliénation, Paris, PUF, 1971.
Idéologies, Paris, Anthropos, vol. 1, 1974; vol. 2, 1978.

García, R. and Piaget, J. *Les Explications causales*, Etudes d'Épistémologie Génétique', vol. 26, Paris, PUF, 1971.

Gardin, B. 'Discours patronal et discours syndical', *Langages*, no. 41 (1976), 13–46.

Gardin, B. and Marcellesi, B. *Sociolinguistique, approches, théories et pratiques*, 2 vols., Paris, PUF, 1980.

Garfinkel, H. *Studies in Ethnomethodology*, New York, Prentice Hall, 1967.

Garmadi, J. *La Sociolinguistique*, Paris, PUF, 1981.

Giglioli, P. *Language and Social Context*, Harmondsworth, 1972.

Girard, R. *La Violence et le sacré*, Paris, Grasset, 1972.

Goffman, E. *Asylums*, New York, Doubleday, 1961.
Rituals: Essays on Face-to-Face Behavior, Garden City, New York, Anchor Books, 1967.
Strategic Interaction, Oxford, Blackwell, 1970.

Goody, J. *Literacy in Traditional Societies*, Cambridge University Press, 1968.

Green, A. *Le Discours vivant*, Paris, PUF, 1973.

Gretler, A. *et al. Etre migrant, approches des problèmes socio-culturels et linguistiques des enfants migrants en Suisse*, Berne, Lang, 1981.

Grice, P. *Logic and Conversation*, William James Lectures at Harvard, Harvard University Press, 1968.

Grize, J.-B. 'Logique et discours pratique', *Communications*, 20 (1973), 92–100.

'Argumentation, schématisation et logique naturelle', *Revue européenne des sciences sociales*, 12, 32 (1974), 183–91.

'Pour aborder l'étude des structures du discours quotidien', *Langue française*, 50 (May 1981), 7–19.

De la logique à l'argumentation, Geneva-Paris, Droz, 1982.

Grize, J.-B. *et al*. Travaux du Centre de Recherches Sémiologiques de Neuchâtel:
'Quelques réflexions sur l'explication', 36 (1980)
'Le Discours explicatif', 38 and 39 (1981)
'Actes de langage explicatifs', 40 (1982)

Grize, J.-B., Borel, M.-J., Chesny, J., Ebel, M., Morf, A., Lecomte, A. and Miéville, D. 'L'Explication: approche sémiologique', *Revue européenne des sciences sociales*, vol. 19, 56 (1981).

Grunenberger, B. *Le Narcissisme*, Paris, Payot, 1971.

Guilhaumou, J., Maldidier, P., Prost, A. and Robin, R. *Langage et idéologies*, Paris, Ed. Ouvrières, 1974.

Guillaume, G. *Principes de linguistique théorique*, Quebec-Paris, Klincksieck, 1973.

Guillaumin, C. *L'Idéologie raciste*, Paris, Mouton, 1972.

Guiraud, P. *L'Argot*, Paris, PUF, 1956.

Les Gros Mots, Paris, PUF, Que sais-je? no. 1597, 1976.

Gumperz, J.-J. *Language in Social Groups*, Stanford University Press, 1971.

Gumperz, J.-J. and Hymes, D. *Directions in Sociolinguistics. The Ethnography of Communication*, New York, Holt, Rinehart and Winston, 1972.

Gurvitch, G. 'La Multiplicité des temps sociaux' in *La Vocation actuelle de la sociologie*, Paris, PUF, 1963.

Habermas, J. *L'Espace public*, Paris, Payot, 1978.

Theorie des kommunikativen Handelns, 2 vols., Frankfurt, Suhrkamp, 1981. Translated as *The Theory of Communicative Action* by T. McCarthy, London, Heinemann, 1984 and Cambridge, Polity Press, 1987.

Hagege, Cl. 'Place de la "Grammaire des fautes" d'Henri Frei dans la linguistique au XXe siècle', Poitiers, *Annales de la section de linguistique*, 1974, 1–36.

Halbwachs, M. *La Mémoire collective*, Paris, PUF, 1968. Translated as *Collective Memory* by F. J. Ditter and V. Y. Ditter, New York and London, Harper and Row, 1980.

Hall, E. T. *La Dimension cachée*, Paris, Seuil, 1971.

Le Langage silencieux, Tours, Mame, 1973.

Halliday, M. A. K. *Language as Social Semiotic*, London, Arnold, 1978.

Harris, P. and Heelas, P. 'Cognitive processes and collective representation', *Archives européennes de sociologie*, March 1980.

Harris, Z. S. 'Discourse analysis', *Language*, 28 (1952), 18–23 and 474–94.

Heath, S. B. *Ways with Words. Language, Life and Work in Communities and Classrooms*, Cambridge University Press, 1983.

Helmick-Beavin, J. and Jackson, D. D. *Une logique de la communication*, Paris, Seuil, 1972 (1967).

Hempel, C. G. *Aspects of Scientific Explanation and Other Essays in the Philosophy of Science*, New York, Free Press, 1965.

Herzlich, Cl. 'La Représentation sociale' in S. Moscovici (ed.) *Introduction à la psychologie sociale*, 1972, vol. 1, pp. 303–35.

Hudson, R. A. *Sociolinguistics*, Cambridge University Press, 1980.

Huet, S. and Langenieux-Villard, Ph. *La Communication politique*, Paris, PUF, 1982.
Huston, N. *Dire et interdire, éléments de jurologie*, Paris, Payot, 1980.
Hymes, D. *Language in Culture and Society*, New York, Harper and Row, 1964.
  'On communicative competence' in J. Pride and J. Holmes (eds.) *Sociolinguistics*, Harmondsworth, 1972.
  Foundations in Sociolinguistics: An Ethnographic Approach, Philadelphia, University of Pennsylvania Press, 1974.
  'Modèles pour l'interaction du langage et de la vie sociale', *Etudes de linguistique appliquée* (trans. G. Quillard), no. 37 (January–March 1980), 127–53.
Jakobson, R. *Essais de linguistique générale*. Translation from the English by Nicholas Ruwet, Paris, Minuit, 1963.
Jodelet, D. 'Réflexions sur le traitement de la notion de représentation sociale en psychologie sociale' in *Communication-Information*, vol. 6, no. 2–3, Quebec, 1984.
Jung, C. G. *L'Energie psychique*, Geneva, Librairie de L'Université, Georg & Cie, 1969 (1956).
  Aspects du drame contemporain, Geneva, Librairie de L'Université, Georg & Cie, 1971 (1948).
Jung, C. G., Franz, M.-L. von, Henderson, Joseph L., Jacobi, Jolande and Jaffé, Aniela. *L'Homme et ses symboles*, Paris, Laffont, 1982 (1964). Published in English as *Man and his Symbols*, London, Aldus Books, 1964.
Kaufmann, S. *L'Inconscient politique*, Paris, PUF, 1979.
Kerbrat-Orecchioni, C. *L'Enonciation, de la subjectivité dans le langage*, Paris, A. Colin, 1981.
Klaus, G. *Sprache der Politik*, Berlin, VEB Deutscher Verlag der Wissenschaften, 1971.
Kopperschmidt, J. *Argumentation, Sprache und Vernunft*, part 2, Urban-Taschenbücher, 1980.
Kress, G. and Hodge, R. *Language as Ideology*, London, Routledge and Kegan Paul, 1979.
Kuhn, T. S. *The Structure of Scientific Revolutions*, University of Chicago Press, 1962.
Labbe, D. *Le Discours communiste*, Paris, Presses de la Fondation Nationale de Science politique, 1977.
Labov, W. *Language in the Inner City*, University of Pennsylvania Press, 1972.
  Sociolinguistique, Paris, Minuit, 1976.
  Le Parler ordinaire, Paris, Minuit, 1978.
Labov, W. and Fanshel, D. *Therapeutic Discourse*, New York, Academic Press, 1977.
Laffont, R. *et al. Introduction à l'analyse textuelle*, Paris, Larousse, 1976.
Lakoff, S. *Linguistique et logique naturelle*, Paris, Klincksieck, 1976.
Laks, B. 'Langage et pratiques sociales, étude sociolinguistique d'un groupe d'adolescents', *Actes de la recherche en sciences sociales*, no. 46 (1983). *Langages*.
  no. 11 (1968), 'Sociolinguistique', ed. J. Sumpf.
  no. 13 (1969), 'Analyse du discours', eds. J. Dubois and J. Sumpf.
  no. 17 (1970), 'L'Enonciation', ed. T. Todorov.
  no. 18 (1970), 'L'Ethnolinguistique', ed. B. Pottier.
  no. 23 (1971), 'Le Discours politique', ed. L. Guespin and J.-B. Marcellesi.
  no. 24 (1971), 'Epistémologie de la linguistique', ed. J. Kristeva.
  no. 32 (1974). 'Le Changement linguistique', eds. S. Lecointre and J. Le Galliot.
  no. 41 (1976), 'Typologie du discours politique', ed. L. Guespin.
  no. 46 (1977), 'Langages et classes sociales, le marrisme', ed. J.-B. Marcellesi.

Langue française. no. 4 (1969), 'La Sémantique', ed. A. Rey.

no. 9 (1971), 'Linguistique et société', ed. J.-B. Marcellesi.

no. 15 (1972), 'Langage et histoire', eds. J.-C. Chevalier and P. Kuentz.

no. 34 (1977), 'Linguistique et sociolinguistique', ed. P. Encrevé.

Lasswell, H., Nathan, L. *et al. Language of Politics. Studies in Quantitative Semantics,* Cambridge, MA, MIT Paperback, 1968 (1949).

Latour, B. and Fabbri, P. 'La Rhétorique de la science. Pouvoir et devoir dans un article de science exacte', *Actes de la recherche en sciences sociales,* no. 13 (1977).

Lecomte, A. and Miéville, D. 'L'Explication: approche sémiologique', *Revue européenne des sciences sociales,* vol. 19, 56 (1981).

Leroi-Gourhan, A. *Le Geste et la parole,* 2 vols. Paris, A. Michel, 1964–5.

Lévi-Strauss, C. *La Pensée sauvage,* Paris, Plon, 1962. Translated as *The Savage Mind,* London, Weidenfeld and Nicolson, 1966.

Lévy-Bruhl, L. *La Mentalité primitive,* Paris, Alcan, 1922. Translated as *Primitive Mentality* by Lilian A. Clare, London, George Allen and Unwin, 1923.

Luria, A. R. *Cognitive Development, its Cultural and Social Foundations,* Cambridge, MA, Harvard University Press, 1979.

MacIver, R. M. *Social Causation,* New York, Harper and Row, 1964 (1942).

Maingueneau, D. *Genèse du discours,* Brussels, Pierre Mardaga, 1984.

Initiation aux méthodes de l'analyse du discours, Paris, Hachette, 1976.

Sémantique de la polémique, Lausanne, Editions l'Age d'Homme, 1983.

Maldidier, D. 'Lecture du discours de De Gaulle, par six journaux parisiens: 13 mai 1958', *Langue française,* no. 9 (1971).

'Le Discours politique de la guerre d'Algérie: approche synchronique et diachronique', *Langages,* no. 23 (1971).

Marin, L. *Le Récit est un piège,* Paris, Minuit, 1978.

Martinet, A. *Le Langage,* Paris, Gallimard, La Pléiade, 1968.

Matore, G. *La Méthode en lexicologie,* Paris, Didier, 1953.

Mercure, G. 'L'Etude des temporalités sociales', *Cahiers internationales de sociologie,* 67 (1979), 263–76.

Meyer, M. *Logique, langage et argumentation,* Paris, Hachette, 1981.

Meyerson, E. *De l'explication dans les sciences,* Paris, Payot, 1927 (1921).

Milgram, S. *Soumission à l'autorité,* Paris, Calmann-Lévy, 1974.

Miller, S. *Les Pousse-au-jouir du Maréchal Pétain,* Paris, Seuil, 1975.

Millet, S. *La Stratégie du verbe,* Paris, Dunod, 1980.

Milner, J.-Cl. *L'Amour de la langue,* Paris, Seuil, 1978.

Moscovici, S. *La Psychanalyse, son image et son public,* Paris, PUF, 1961.

Introduction à la psychologie sociale, 2 vols., Paris, Librairie Larousse, vol. 1, 1972, vol. 2, 1973.

Communication given to a colloquium on *Représentations sociales,* Paris, 8–10 January 1979.

Psychologie des minorités actives, Paris, PUF, 1979. Translated as *Social Influence and Social Change* by Carol Sherrard and Greta Heinz, London, Academic Press, 1976.

Ossipow, W. *La Transformation du discours politique dans l'Eglise,* Lausanne, Editions l'Age d'Homme, 1979.

Perret-Clermont, A.-N. *La Construction de l'intelligence dans l'interaction sociale,* Berne, Lang, 1981.

Peytard, J. 'Pour une typologie des messages oraux' in *La Grammaire du français parlé*, (ed.) A. Rigault, 1968, pp. 73–80.

'Lecture(s) d'une "aire scripturale": la page de journal', *Langue française*, no. 28 (December 1975), 39–59.

Piaget, J. *The Language and Thought of the Child*, trans. Marjorie Warden, London, Kegan Paul, 1926; rev. edn and trans. Marjorie Gabain, London, Routledge and Kegan Paul, 1959.

The Child's Conception of Causality, trans. Marjorie Gabain, London, Routledge and Kegan Paul, 1930.

The Moral Judgment of the Child, trans. Marjorie Gabain, London, Routledge and Kegan Paul, 1932.

Introduction à l'épistémologie génétique II, 3 vols., Paris, PUF, 1950.

The Psychology of Intelligence, trans. Malcolm Piercy and D. E. Berlyne, London, Routledge and Kegan Paul, 1950.

The Origin of Intelligence in the Child, trans. Margaret Cook, London, Routledge and Kegan Paul, 1953.

The Child's Construction of Reality, trans. Margaret Cook, London, Routledge and Kegan Paul, 1955.

Play, Dreams and Imitation in Childhood, trans. Gattegno and Hodgson, New York, Norton, 1962.

The Child's Conception of Time, trans. A. J. Pomerans, London, Routledge and Kegan Paul, 1969.

The Child's Conception of Movement and Speed, trans. G. E. T. Holloway and M. J. Mackenzie, London, Routledge and Kegan Paul, 1970.

Essai de logique opératoire, Paris, Dunod, 1972 (1949).

Piaget, J. and Inhelder, B. *The Child's Construction of Quantities*, London, Routledge and Kegan Paul, 1974.

Piattelli-Palmarini, Massimo (ed.) *Language and Learning: The Debate Between Jean Piaget and Noam Chomsky*, London, Routledge and Kegan Paul, 1980.

Poliakov, L. *La Causalité diabolique*, Paris, Calmann-Lévy, 1980.

'Causalité, démonologie et racisme, retour à Lévy-Bruhl?', *L'Homme et la société*, no. 55–8 (1980), 215–39.

Posch, G. (ed.) *Kausalität. Neue Texte*, Stuttgart, Reclam, 1981.

Prigogine, I. *Physique, temps et devenir*, Paris, Masson, 1980.

Prigogine, I. and Stengers, I. *La Nouvelle Alliance*, Paris, Gallimard, 1979.

Prost, A. 'Combattants et politiciens, le discours mythologique sur la politique entre les deux guerres' in *Langage et idéologies*, Paris, Ed. Ouvrières, 1974, pp. 117–49.

Provost, S. 'Approche du discours politique: "socialisme" chez Jaurès', *Langages*, no. 13 (1969).

Rastier, F. *Idéologie et théorie des signes*, The Hague-Paris, Mouton, 1972.

Reboul, O. *Langage et idéologie*, Paris, PUF, 1980.

Richaudeau, F. *Le Langage efficace*, Paris, Denoël, 1973.

Rigault, A. 'La Grammaire du français parlé', *Le Français dans le monde*, 57 (June 1968) (reprinted Paris, Hachette, 1971).

Robin, R. *Histoire et linguistique*, Paris, A. Colin, 1973.

Roche, J. *Le Style des candidats à la présidence de la République*, Toulouse, Private, 1971.

Roig, Ch. *La Grammaire politique de Lénine*, Lausanne, Editions l'Age d'Homme, 1980.

Rossi-Landi, F. *Il linguaggio come lavoro e come mercato*, Milan, Bompiani, 1968.

Ruyer, R. *L'Utopie et les utopies*, Paris, PUF, 1950.

Sacks, H. 'An initial investigation on the usability of conversational data for doing sociology' in D. Sudnow (ed.) *Studies in Social Interaction*, New York, Free Press, 1972, pp. 32–4.

Sapir, E. *Language: An Introduction to the Study of Speech*, Oxford University Press, 1921.

Saussure, F. de. *Course de linguistique générale*, Paris, Payot, 1931 (1916). Translated as *Course in General Linguistics* by W. Baskin, New York, McGraw-Hill, 1974.

Sauvageot, A. *Analyse du français parlé*, Paris, Hachette, 1972.

Schleflen, A. E. 'Systèmes de la communication humaine' in Y. Wilkin (ed.), *La Nouvelle Communication*, Paris, 1981, pp. 145–57.

Schenkein, J. *Studies in the Organization of Conversational Interaction*, New York, Academic Press, 1978.

Schnelle, H. 'Language communication with children, toward a theory of language use' in Y. Bar-Hillel (ed.), *Pragmatics of Natural Language*, Dordrecht, Reidel, 1971, pp. 173–94.

Searle, J. R. *Speech Acts*, Cambridge University Press, 1969.

Simonin-Grumbach, J. 'Pour une typologie des discours' in J. Kristeva *et al.* (eds.), *Langue, discours et société*, Paris, Seuil, 1975, pp. 85–121.

Sinclair, J. and Coulthard, M. *Towards the Analysis of Discourse. The English Used by Teachers and Pupils*, Oxford University Press, 1975.

Sociologie et sociétés, no. 2, 1973: 'Sémiologie et idéologie'.

Sperber, D. *Le Symbolisme en général*, Paris, Hermann, 1974. Translated as *Rethinking Symbolism* by A. L. Morton, Cambridge University Press, 1975.

Sudnow, D. (ed.) *Studies in Social Interaction*, New York, Free Press, 1972.

Todorov, T. 'L'Enonciation', *Langages*, no. 17 (1970).

M. *Bakhtine, le principe dialogique*, Paris, Seuil, 1981. Translated as *Mikhail Bakhtine, the Dialogical Principle* by W. Godzich, Manchester University Press, 1984.

Toulmin, S. E. *The Uses of Argument*, Cambridge University Press, 1974 (1958).

Tournier, M. 'Les Vocabulaires politiques à l'étude aujourd'hui (1962–1982)', *Raison présente*, 62 (1982), 79–101.

Trubetskoy, N. S. *Anleitung zu phonologischen Beschreibung*, Göttingen (1939). Translated as *Introduction to the Principles of Phonological Descriptions* by L. A. Murray, The Hague, Nijhoff, 1968.

Trudgill, P. *Sociolinguistics*, Harmondsworth, 1974.

Turner, R. *Ethnomethodology*, Harmondsworth, 1974.

Unrug, M.-C. d'. *Analyse de contenu et acte de parole*, Paris, Delarge, 1974.

Veron, E. 'Vers une logique naturelle des monde sociaux', *Communications*, no. 20 (1973), 246–78.

Veyne, P. *Comment on écrit l'histoire*, Paris, Seuil, 1978.

Vignaux, G. *L'Argumentation. Essai d'une logique discursive*, Geneva, Droz, 1976.

Vygotsky, L. S. *Thought and Language*, ed. and trans. Eugenia Hanfmann and Gertrude Vakar, Cambridge, MA, MIT Press, 1962; John Wiley and Sons, New York and London, 1962.

Watzlawick, P. *Le Langage du changement*, Paris, Seuil, 1980 (1978).

Weakland, I. *Sur l'interaction*, Paris, Seuil, 1981.

Wermus, H. 'Essai de représentation de certaines activités cognitives à l'aide des prédicats avec composantes contextuelles' in *Archives de psychologie*, 1976.

Le Sentier étroit, Actes du Colloque sur les Critères de Vérité, APUG, Geneva (forthcoming).

Whorf, B. L. *Language, Thought and Reality*, Cambridge, MA, 1956.

Windisch, U., Jaeggi, J.-M. and Rham. G. de. *Xénophobie? Logique de la pensée populaire*, Lausanne, Editions l'Age d'Homme, 1978.

Pensée sociale, langage en usage et logiques autres, Lausanne, Editions l'Age d'Homme, 1982.

Wittgenstein, L. *Remarques sur le Rameau d'Or de Frazer*, Lausanne, Editions l'Age d'Homme, 1982. Translated as *Remarks on Frazer's 'Golden Bough'* by A. C. Miles, ed. and revised by Rush Rhees, Retford, Brynmill, 1979.

Wright, H. von. *Explanation and Understanding*, London, Routledge and Kegan Paul, 1971.

Wunenburger, J. J. *L'Utopie et la crise de l'imaginaire*, Paris, Delarge, 1979.

Index